THE ABORTIONIST OF HOWARD STREET

THE ABORTIONIST
OF HOWARD STREET

MEDICINE AND CRIME IN
NINETEENTH-CENTURY NEW YORK

R.E. FULTON

 THREE HILLS

AN IMPRINT OF CORNELL UNIVERSITY PRESS

ITHACA AND LONDON

First published 2024 by Cornell University Press
Printed in the United States of America

Library of Congress Cataloging-in-Publication Data

Names: Fulton, R.E., 1992– author.
Title: The abortionist of Howard Street : medicine and
    crime in nineteenth-century New York / R.E. Fulton.
Description: Ithaca [New York] : Three Hills, an
    imprint of Cornell University Press, 2024. | Includes
    bibliographical references and index.
Identifiers: LCCN 2023045718 (print) | LCCN
    2023045719 (ebook) | ISBN 9781501774829
    (hardcover) | ISBN 9781501774836 (pdf) |
    ISBN 9781501774843 (epub)
Subjects: LCSH: McCarty, Josephine, 1826– |
    Abortion—United States—History—19th century. |
    Women—New York (State)—Social conditions—
    19th century.
Classification: LCC HA767.5.U5 F858 2024 (print) |
    LCC HA767.5.U5 (ebook) | DDC 364.1/85092
    [B]—dc23/eng/20231128
LC record available at https://lccn.loc.gov/2023045718
LC ebook record available at https://lccn.loc.
    gov/2023045719

For Charlie, who told me to write a book,
and for Stephen, who wanted to read one

CONTENTS

PREFACE

The story that follows is completely true—as far as I can tell.

Josephine McCarty, alias Emma Burleigh, alias Virginia Seymour, née Josephine Fagan, was a real woman who lived mainly in New York State in the mid-nineteenth century. She was at once an ordinary woman and an extraordinary one. She grew up on her mother's farm, taught school as a young woman, got married, and raised six children. She was not famous within her lifetime. But she came to my attention, as a historian, because in 1872, she shot and killed a man in a dispute over child support—and because, as news of that crime spread, so did the fact that its perpetrator was already engaged in criminal activity. Josephine McCarty was an abortionist.

In 1872, abortion at any stage of pregnancy was a felony in New York State. But that was a relatively recent development, the result of strategic lobbying campaigns by organized physicians who raised ethical, medical, and professional concerns about the routine practice of abortion in nineteenth-century homes and doctors' offices. Acting as representatives of the medical profession, these doctors also responded to broader cultural anxieties: about families, race, urbanization, immigration, gender, sex, and much more. The same cultural shifts that informed the successful campaign against abortion in nineteenth-century New York shaped Josephine's life in myriad ways, up to and including the murder trial that was the starting place for my research.

In order to tell Josephine McCarty's story, this book also follows the history of abortion in the United States between approximately 1792—the year her mother was born—and 1872, the year of Josephine's trial, and the year she largely vanished from the historical record. It's the story of American women's control over their reproductive health, and how that control went from a largely private and unexamined matter to one of the most talked about and scrutinized aspects of American political life. Josephine McCarty's lifetime saw pregnancy and its absence, once family matters, become sensationalized by the press, monetized by shrewd capitalists, and fiercely debated among male doctors and lawmakers, who spent thousands of hours discussing whether, when, how, and from whom a woman should get an abortion.

But abortion itself did not, ultimately, play a major role in Josephine's life. She spent about eight years as an abortionist—far fewer than, for instance, Ruth Barnett, the central figure in Rickie Solinger's *The Abortionist* (1994), who devoted her entire fifty-year career to the practice. Josephine was much more than an abortionist: she also worked as a bookseller, a political lobbyist, a night nurse, a sewing machine salesman, and a Confederate spy. After her trial, she abandoned her abortion practice and apparently retired completely. And, to my knowledge, she never had an abortion herself.

On paper, it seems like Josephine McCarty's life might not have that much to tell us about the history of abortion in America. But abortion is about much more than just the medical procedure: it's about motherhood and fatherhood, economic inequality, scientific knowledge and medical authority, family law, sex, rape, cultural and legal definitions of crime, intimate partner violence, race, misogyny and feminism, and, on top of all of that, love.

Josephine was a mother and she lost children. She grew up on a farm and spent her life working for upward class mobility. She studied medicine in an era where scientific understandings of not just reproduction but health in general were in rapid flux. She was divorced, she had affairs, she had a lot of sex, and she accused at least two men of sexual violence. She committed plenty of crimes other than abortion, including the murder that made her briefly famous. And she was acquitted of that murder, in the end, because her defense attorneys argued convincingly that she'd committed the crime out of love for her children. Each one of these things has a great deal to tell us about the history of abortion in nineteenth-century New York, how it became a crime in Josephine's lifetime, and what that meant for the women who lived through those decades.

This book is a nineteenth-century history inevitably shaped by the political landscape of the twenty-first. But it's also Josephine's version of her story: the basis of this book, the central source from which all my research spun out, is a series of three lengthy articles published in the *Utica Daily Observer* between May 4 and May 7, 1872. In these three articles, the *Observer* reproduced Josephine's testimony in her murder trial.[1] On the stand, she told her life's story, starting in childhood and running all the way up to the day when she shot Milton Thomson, the father of her children.

As you read this book, you'll see these three articles cropping up again and again in the endnotes. Throughout my research, Josephine's testimony gave me clues—what to look for in the historical record, and where. She said that she'd adopted her fourth child from a woman who gave birth at Philadelphia's Blockley Almshouse in 1859; I drove down to Philadelphia and hunted through the voluminous birth registers at the City Archives. She mentioned her confinement in the Old Capitol Prison during the Civil War; I went to the National Archives in Washington, D.C., to search the prison's records. She told the story of a brief affair with a man named "Thompson" in Pittsfield, Massachusetts; I stopped off in Pittsfield on my way home from Boston to scan hotel and boarding house guest books for one of her many names.

Some of these threads led me in new directions; others turned out to be dead ends. And as I started thinking about Josephine's story as a piece of abortion history, I generated my own leads, reading the work of scholars like James Mohr, John Riddle, Rickie Solinger, and Leslie Reagan, who laid the foundations of abortion history in the late twentieth century. But Josephine was always my primary research guide—which brings me to the fundamental problem of this book.

Can you imagine a more fallible primary source than a nineteenth-century newspaper transcript of trial testimony, or a more unreliable narrator than a person on trial for her life? Josephine had every reason to lie. She also had reasons, both legal and personal, to bend the truth about her criminal history, her sex life, and her health. In some places, the lies are obvious; in those cases, I've given my best guess at the truth, but it can only ever be an informed guess. In other places, the line between probable truth and probable falsehood is murkier, and in those places I've done my best to give each possibility an equal hearing. I leave it up to the reader to draw final conclusions.

I also leave it up to the reader to draw their conclusions on the central question of this book, which was also the central question of Josephine's trial: Was she a good woman or a bad one?

Of course, that's a simplistic question. But it came up again and again, not only in the historical record of Josephine's trial, but in readers' early responses to her story. To some, Josephine was an obvious hero; to others, she was a more suspicious, amoral character. It came up in my own reading, too. When I first encountered Josephine in 2015 as a young feminist, I loved the idea of an unapologetic feminist heroine defying the strictures of an increasingly misogynist society by practicing abortion.

Only that's not what I found when, at her prompting, I dug into the sources. Instead, I found a woman apparently motivated by profit far more than feminist ideals, and a society that cared a lot more about Jewish immigrant abortionists than a white Protestant single mother who helped women "in trouble" end their pregnancies. I found a woman who seemed to love her children intensely but who also abandoned them more than once. I found a woman who, in the few scraps of published writing purported to have come directly from her pen, voiced impassioned feminist arguments with glaringly obvious ulterior motives.

After all this work, I'm still not sure who Josephine McCarty was. But I know that her story—the one we wrote together, more or less—is a good one.

ACKNOWLEDGMENTS

Writing a book can feel like a solitary pursuit—even more so in the long pandemic year during which I ended up doing most of my writing. But this book couldn't exist without the intellectual, material, emotional, and financial support of so many people.

The group of people to whom I owe the greatest debt are the many librarians and archivists who helped to find and access materials, understand their context, and connect them to the bigger picture of Josephine's life. In particular, I want to thank Matt Herbison, archivist at the Legacy Center, who reached out about Mary Edward Walker, helped me research Josephine's days in medical school, and gave me a fantastic archival experience; the staff of the Albany County Hall of Records, especially Jill Hughes, who helped me find Maggie Campbell's inquest file and the deed to 62 Howard Street; the staff of the Philadelphia City Archives, New York State Archives, Albany Rural Cemetery, Utica Public Library, Oneida County Historical Society, National Archives, Syracuse University Libraries Special Collections, Greene County Historical Society, Surratt House Museum, and others, who answered my questions and opened their archives to me; and Christopher Hoolihan of the Edward G. Miner Library at the University of Rochester Medical Center, who helped me do the research in the Edward C. Atwater Collection of American Popular Medicine that began my interest in abortion history.

I also want to thank Marcie ver Ploeg, an invaluable patron and champion of this book. Marcie, who has done her own extensive research on Josephine's life and crimes, reached out to me while I was living in Rochester and helped to fund and collaborate on research trips to Utica and Albany. She also provided me with my copy of the *Woman's Truth Teller*. Without Marcie, this book could never have been completed.

I also need to thank the people who made me a historian: namely, the faculty of the Department of Humanities and Social Sciences at Clarkson University and the Department of History at the University of Rochester. I especially want to thank Laura Smoller, whose class on disease and history allowed me to do the research that began my obsession with the history of abortion. Dr. Smoller's enthusiastic support made my brief time in graduate school more than worth it. I'm grateful to Laura Ettinger, whose class on the history of the American family I have returned to over and over in the process of writing this book. Without Dr. Ettinger's enthusiastic example, I might have taken a lot longer to drop my stubborn resistance to studying "women's subjects" in history. I owe an enormous debt to Karen Buckle, in whose class on "Gender and Crime in Early Modern Europe" I realized for the first time that abortion is a human right, and to Joseph Duemer, the first person who told me that I could write. Finally, my deepest thanks go to Stephen Casper, who taught me to be unapologetically ambitious and to love history obsessively, and whose unfailing and outrageous generosity has supported my career at every turn. Without Stephen, I would not be a historian.

I started this book in 2015, the same year I dropped out of graduate school. Writing a book outside of the academy is hard for many reasons (number one: spotty database access; number two: lack of funding). But two groups of people supported me throughout the seven-year process. I want to thank the educators at the Lower East Side Tenement Museum, where I worked from the summer of 2017 to the summer of 2020, for teaching me how to tell a story, for modeling good public history work every day, for being my union comrades, and for knowing the value of ordinary, tiny histories.

These acknowledgements could not be complete without an enormous thanks to the women of the *Nursing Clio* blog. When I discovered *Nursing Clio* in 2015, I had no idea how much I would come to owe to this collective of writers and scholars. They have become my academic family, my cheerleaders, and my friends. It would take pages to enumerate all the ways they've made this book a reality, but I want to give special thanks to Laura Ansley and Lizzie Reis, who read drafts of my book proposal and provided invaluable feedback.

I spent a long time trying to find a home for this book. Michael McGandy believed in the book and in me from our first conversation through an exhaustive revision process. To him and to the whole editorial staff of Three Hills and Cornell University Press, I owe my deepest thanks.

Finally, my family: especially Julia, who spent something like five hours on a Zoom call helping me unpack every single word of every abortion law passed in New York State in the nineteenth century; Tulip, Dusty, and Honey, who are the best editorial assistants a writer could ask for; and Charlie, my best friend. In 2015, when I came back from a long and boring day at work and told her about this crazy story I'd read about an abortionist who shot a guy in 1872, Charlie told me to write a book. Since then, she has read every draft, listened to my rants, driven with me to archives, supplied me with chocolate and tea, told me when I was wrong, told me when I was right, and kept me going in every possible way. I have never met anyone who loves women like my wife does. This book is a reflection of that love.

One last acknowledgement has to go to American folk musician Jay Ungar for composing "Ashokan Farewell," without which I could not have written this book.

HISTORICAL FIGURES

Lewis Babcock
(1838–1905)

Lead attorney for the defense at the trial of Josephine McCarty. "A first class lawyer when sober," according to officials at the Oneida County Poorhouse.

Phebe Burleigh
(c. 1792–1864)

Josephine's mother. An anxious woman twice widowed.

Margaret Campbell
(c. 1849–71)

A patient of Josephine under her alias of Dr. Emma Burleigh. Died in her office under suspicious circumstances. Official cause of death: peritonitis.

Charles H. Doolittle
(1816–74)

The judge presiding over the trial of Josephine McCarty in May 1872.

John Perdue Gray
(1825–86)

Head of the New York State Lunatic Asylum in Utica, NY. A believer in biological psychiatric theory, and the star witness for the prosecution.

Henry H. Hall
(1837–72)

A coal merchant from Ogdensburg, NY, and nephew to Milton Thomson. Shot on a Utica streetcar on January 17, 1872, by Josephine McCarty.

Robert O. Jones
(1841–1901)

Josephine's lawyer. A competent attorney with no expertise in murder trials.

Daniel Magone
(1829–1904)

Member of the prosecution. A celebrated attorney from Ogdensburg, NY, and a skilled speech-maker.

Josephine McCarty, née Josephine Fagan, alias Emma Burleigh, M.D., alias Virginia Seymour (1826–98)

An abortionist, a mother, a spy, a doctor, a blackmailer, Milton Thomson's mistress of eighteen years. On trial for her life for the murder of Henry H. Hall in 1872. A bad woman?

Robert McCarty (c. 1805–70)

An inventor from parts unknown, obsessed with selling a new kind of steam-powered gun to anyone who would buy it. Josephine's first (and only) husband.

Eugene, Ella, Terrence, Louis, Ernest (Juddie), and **Josephine**

Josephine's children.

David J. Mitchell (1828–74)

Josephine's defense attorney. Examined the bulk of the witnesses. Previously defended General George W. Cole on similar charges.

Daniel C. Pomeroy (1813–78)

Josephine's defense attorney. A spectacular orator.

Madame Restell, née Ann Trow, alias Ann Lohman (1812–78)

The most infamous abortionist of the nineteenth century.

Charles B. Sedgwick (1815–83)

Examined most of the witnesses for the prosecution. Previously prosecuted General George W. Cole for murder.

David C. Stoddard (1831–1905)

Oneida County District Attorney and head of the prosecution. An old political rival of Lewis Babcock.

Horatio Robinson Storer (1830–1922)

The young Boston physician who took up his father David Humphrey Storer's call to crusade against abortion in the mid-1800s.

Milton Thomson (1824–93)

An insurance agent from Utica, NY, and a friend from Josephine's school days. Allegedly the father of Juddie and Josie, her two youngest children.

William P. Wood (1821–1903)

The superintendent of the Union's Old Capitol Prison in 1862, and later head of the Secret Service. Josephine's prison warden, and possibly her later employer.

Chapter 1

Mother and Daughter

On the morning of January 17, 1872, the city of Utica, New York, sat under a cold winter sun. Along the central artery of Genesee Street, streetcars led by steaming horses ferried commuters across dry snow. By mid-morning, as eighteen-year-old John Dodd, driver for the Utica and New Hartford Line, piloted his streetcar up Genesee Street, the horses' hooves had churned the fresh powder into brown mud.

It was nearly 10 a.m. when the car reached Oneida Square, heading for its final destination at the downtown terminal. As they passed through the intersection, John Dodd noticed a tall woman in a heavy veil and a warm muff on the east side of the street. He got ready to slow the horses, but the woman made no signal for the car to stop, so John passed on.

A few hundred yards past the square was John's next stop: 321 Genesee Street. It was the home of Milton Thomson, a respected insurance agent and a regular passenger of the Utica and New Hartford line. As the car approached the house, John heard a shout from the other side of the street. It was the woman from Oneida Square; evidently, she'd changed her mind about waiting out in the cold. He slowed the horses, let her on, and carried on again to stop outside the Thomson house.

When Mr. Thomson emerged from the house, he wasn't alone. He boarded the streetcar with another man, both settling themselves comfortably near the central wood stove that kept the car warm through the bitter cold of an upstate January. The strange woman sat across from them. While the conductor took their fares, John got the horses moving again, and they proceeded along Genesee Street.

A few minutes later, a gunshot shook the streetcar.

While John brought the horses to a halt, chaos broke out in the car behind him. A minute later, the woman with the veil jumped off the back of the streetcar and started walking along Genesee Street in the direction the car had been headed. The conductor followed, clutching the woman's muff and calling after her. Accompanied by one of the passengers, he chased the stranger down the street.

Turning back toward the passenger compartment, John saw what had happened. Mr. Thomson was still seated on the bench, blood pouring from his face. But his friend was on the floor, dragging himself through the straw that covered the bottom of the car, leaving a messy trail of gore behind him. Horrified, John turned back to the horses and spurred the car faster down the street, toward the Butterfield Hotel. There were doctors there who could help the injured passengers. But by the time the car pulled up outside the hotel just minutes later, Milton Thomson's friend was dead.

By that evening, the papers had the story. The deceased was Henry H. Hall, an Ogdensburg coal merchant and Milton Thomson's nephew. He'd been in town visiting his uncle for a few days and was meant to return to his family soon. Nobody believed that Henry Hall, a stranger in Utica, had been the target of the shooting. Just moments after pulling away from 321 Genesee Street, the other passengers on the streetcar had seen the strange woman in the veil aim a pistol at Milton Thomson's face and pull the trigger. It was Henry Hall's bad luck that the bullet went directly through Thomson's face and into his nephew's chest.

The accidental victim wasn't the only unusual thing about the incident; so was the gender of the shooter. "For a parallel to the crime now chronicled," the press proclaimed, "there is no record in local annals. A woman was at the bottom of it all. A woman's brain devised the murderous plan, and a woman's nerve coolly executed it."[1]

That woman's name was Josephine McCarty—at least, that was her legal name. As the newspapers quickly reported, she'd gone by many over the course of her life. McCarty was her married name, but she'd been divorced for years. She was born Josephine Fagan, but in Albany, where she'd come from, she lived under the name Virginia Seymour. To most, though, she was Emma Burleigh, M.D., a private physician well known to the women of the Albany region. "The Murderess," the headlines said, was "Said To Be an Abortionist."[2]

She was said to be quite a lot of things. Within days of Henry Hall's death, newspapers throughout the state were circulating rumors about the mysterious—and now briefly infamous—Josephine McCarty. She'd been a kept mistress of Albany politicians, the papers said; she'd been a Confederate spy during the Civil War. One thing was certain: for many years, she'd been Milton Thomson's mistress, and two of her three children were allegedly his. She'd come to Utica to beg for child support after they were thrown out of their Albany home, and when Thomson refused, she fired the deadly shot.

Arrested just minutes after disembarking from the streetcar, Josephine McCarty was charged with first-degree murder. On May 1, 1872, her trial began. From the beginning, it was an odd case. Multiple people had seen her fire the shot that killed Henry Hall, but everyone agreed that she had no motive to kill *him*—only Milton Thomson, whom she'd failed to kill. But rather than push for a reduced charge—manslaughter or attempted murder, for instance—Josephine McCarty's lawyers launched a full defense of their client, arguing that she should not be held responsible for Henry Hall's death and should go free.

Whether or not she'd killed Henry Hall wasn't the issue; everyone knew that she had. The question was whether or not she should be punished for it. In practice, this meant that the trial focused heavily on Josephine McCarty's character—on the question, in other words, of whether she was a good or a bad woman.

In order to sway the jury's sympathies, Josephine McCarty's lawyers would have to put before them the whole story of Josephine's life—not just the days leading up to the killing or even her relationship with Milton Thomson. The testimony covered everything from her tumultuous first marriage to alleged threats of violence by Milton Thomson to evidence from medical experts who insisted that Josephine had been temporarily insane at the time of the shooting. In turn, the prosecution called witnesses to testify to Josephine's sanity, her shady sexual history, and—last but not least—her career as an abortionist.

But the one thing that both prosecution and defense seemed to agree on was that, good or bad, Josephine McCarty was not *unusual*. For the defense, she was an ordinary mother who loved her children and was pushed by that very love over the brink of sanity and into violence. For the prosecution, she was ordinary in all the wrong ways: promiscuous, manipulative, and unscrupulous both in her business and her personal life.

When Josephine took the stand in her own defense, she began her testimony by talking about her childhood. And so that is where this book begins: with Josephine's childhood and early life, not far from the city where she was arrested for murder in 1872. But unlike the testimony for the defense, this story isn't an attempt to vindicate Josephine McCarty. Instead, it's an attempt to unravel the unanswered question of her trial: If Josephine *was* ordinary, what do her life and crime say about ordinary women in nineteenth-century America? Josephine's story offers a window into women's ambitions, their freedoms, and the limits placed on them by a complex legal net of state and federal laws, constantly changing throughout the century in response to the shifting anxieties of a white male professional class: doctors, lawmakers, and journalists. It's the story of how single mothers got by in an era where marriage was key to women's survival; it's the story of how women endured, and sometimes resisted, a range of abusive treatment from men they loved, or needed, or both; and it's the story of how, within Josephine McCarty's lifetime, abortion went from a rarely discussed part of the medical mundane to a flashpoint for middle-class Americans' anxieties about sex.

To tell Josephine's story, we have to start where she did: with her childhood. In fact, we're going a little farther back than that. The story of Josephine McCarty's life starts with the woman whose name she took when she began her medical practice: Mrs. Phebe Burleigh Fagan, her mother.

In the center of New York State there is a valley. It's a pocket of farmland and minor cities between the Adirondacks and the Catskills, and the only formally recognized region of New York that doesn't border another state or country. To the south, New York City dominates the salty Atlantic edge of the "Empire State"; to the west, Rochester and Buffalo bleed into Ohio's Rust Belt. But in between, a river rises out of north-central Oneida County and travels through low green hills and open fields to Cohoes, where it flows into the mighty Hudson and from there into the Atlantic Ocean. This river, and the often-overlooked region named after it, takes its name from Kanien'kehá'ka people, the Keepers of the Eastern Door: *Mohawk*.

Utica sits in the western portion of the valley. South of Utica, at the valley's southernmost edge, lies a farm situated between two villages whose combined population has never exceeded four thousand people. It's not a big parcel of land; the fields sit in the angle between two county roads, giving the farm the shape of an abbreviated triangle. It's changed hands many times over the years, but it was once the property of Terrence and Phebe Fagan, the parents of Josephine Augusta Fagan—the woman who would become the Mohawk Valley's most notorious abortionist and murderer in 1872.

The Fagan family were newcomers to New York when they settled on the farm in the village of Augusta in 1833.[3] Phebe Burleigh was born in New England; her husband Terrence in Ireland; and Josephine was born about five hundred miles south of Augusta in the city of Richmond, Virginia. In a time when so many people could expect to live and die within a twenty-mile radius of the place of their birth, the Fagan family's path to the Mohawk Valley was unusual. When Josephine was seven, the family made the long journey north from Richmond to settle on the farm. When they arrived, Phebe changed her daughter's middle name from *Augusta* to *Virginia*: a reminder of where she'd come from.[4]

Phebe and Terrence spent five years in their new lives as landowners before tragedy intervened. The *Annals of Oneida County* describes the incident succinctly: "Terence [sic] Fagan was killed July 12, 1838, by falling from his wagon, and the horses stopping with one of the wheels resting upon his neck."[5] Within a year, Phebe had remarried, but her second husband, Camp Williams, was dead by 1841. She buried him next to Terrence, on a little hill overlooking a field, and carried on alone, hiring workers to help her run the farm.

By 1841, Phebe Burleigh Fagan Williams was a single mother, and her daughter an only child. It was an unusual family structure for the 1840s, made even more unusual by the difference in their ages. Census records indicate that Phebe Burleigh was born within a year or two of 1792, making her nearly fifty when her second husband died. Josephine, on the other hand, was probably born in October of 1826, when Phebe was thirty-four years old.

While having just one child at age thirty-four wasn't impossible in the early 1800s, it was a long way from the norm. Of course, it's possible that Phebe had trouble conceiving, or that she had repeated miscarriages during the twelve years of her marriage to Terrence, neither of which would be likely to show up in public records. But there's one other obvious explanation for the fact that Josephine Fagan was an only child: Phebe might have used some form of birth control to limit the size of her family and the timing of her pregnancies.

According to the historian Rickie Solinger, women like Phebe born between 1760 and 1799 had, on average, 8.33 pregnancies, most of which could be expected to come to term. By 1800, the average married white woman in the United States had seven children over the course of her adult life.[6] Of course, those numbers are averages—many women could, and did, have fewer than seven children, and many of those women who did give birth to seven or more children saw some die in infancy or childhood. The cycle of reproduction typically started early, too. In her study of reproductive practices in the late eighteenth and early nineteenth centuries, the historian Susan Klepp writes that women in the pre-Revolutionary period

> bore nearly as many children as possible under the marriage and breast-feeding conventions of the time, typically marrying in their late teens or early twenties and nursing each child for a year or two before becoming pregnant again. If all was well, married women gave birth roughly every eighteen months or two years until menopause.[7]

Women of Phebe's mother's and grandmother's generations, in other words, "were physical beings whose lives conformed to biological rhythms."[8]

It wasn't ignorance about birth control that kept women engaged in endless cycles of pregnancy, childbirth, breastfeeding, and childrearing. In fact, as the historian John Riddle has shown, cultures throughout the Western world had understood, and used, various means of birth control since ancient times.[9] It wasn't just misogyny, either, though there was plenty of that in the late eighteenth century. But in the context of a growing colony—one engaged in a revolution against the world's largest empire and waging a long-term war with Indigenous nations—reproduction had enormous power as a political weapon. It's no accident that birth rates in the American colonies exceeded those of Europe in this period. As white settlers fought to gain control over the land and resources of North America, Susan Klepp explains, "women's bodies had created abundance and a symbolic, if not always actual, form of wealth" that helped colonists establish a foothold in places like the Mohawk Valley.[10]

In other words, it simply made political and economic sense for colonists to embrace the idea that "the normative condition of women, the center of housewifery, was procreation." But Phebe was born in or around 1792, about fifteen years after the revolution ended America's status as a colony and ushered in the new Republic. By the time she reached childbearing age—1808 or 1809—things had started to change. From cities like Richmond to rural settlements like Augusta, the American empire was solidly planted in eastern soil. The Enlightenment ideals of liberty and self-determination that spurred so many male colonists to revolt in the late eighteenth century translated to new values of "bodily independence and self-control" for their wives.[11]

In the decades leading up to and following the American Revolution, Susan Klepp discovered, "many American women rejected a lifetime of childbearing and began limiting births" for the first time. Pregnancy, once treated as a celebrated biological imperative, now became a social duty that "women undertook voluntarily for rational, sentimental, and instrumental purposes."[12] Large families became a "luxury," rather than an expectation, and political rhetoric increasingly celebrated married women not for their biological reproductive capacity but for the imagined moral superiority that made them the ideal leaders of the households in which a new generation of citizens would grow up.[13]

Of course, the fact that birth control became a more important and more routine part of life for women of Phebe's generation doesn't mean it's the only explanation for Phebe's small family. Like most women of her day, Phebe didn't leave behind a diary to fill in the gaps between lines on the federal census. But it's just as likely—if not more so—that Phebe chose, for one reason or another, to avoid pregnancy and childbirth. Josephine always described her mother as an anxious woman; maybe, like many nineteenth-century women, she was afraid of the looming threat of death that accompanied any pregnancy.[14] Or maybe, as the wife of an immigrant farmer, she recognized practical limits to her and Terrence's ability to raise a large family.

We'll never know for sure why Josephine had no siblings, but if Phebe did use birth control, we know quite a lot about the methods she might have employed. Historians like Janet Farrell Brodie, John Riddle, and others have uncovered the wide variety of approaches nineteenth-century Americans used to control their reproduction. Some, such as coitus interruptus (pulling out), aimed to prevent pregnancy from happening in the first place. Some women who were happy to stop at one or two children—or who simply wanted a longer break in between pregnancies—used prolonged breastfeeding to prevent or delay a second (or third, or fourth) pregnancy. Then there was the rhythm method, a natural family planning strategy in which women tracked their menstrual cycles and tried to time intercourse for the times when they were least likely to conceive. But another important approach to reproductive control in this early period was the use of emmenagogues—herbs and medications that stimulated menstruation, thus restoring a woman's flow and preventing a potential pregnancy or terminating one already in effect. One of the most important modes of birth control in early America, in other words, was abortion.

Applying that word—so emotionally fraught, so politically charged in the twenty-first century—to the practice of restoring menstrual flow in early nineteenth-century America is cheating, so to speak. It's an anachronism. The word "abortion"—from the Latin *aboriri*, which means "to disappear" or to "miscarry"—refers, and has always referred, to the premature end of a pregnancy (that is, to its termination prior to childbirth).[15] But its contemporary meaning—the *intentional* removal of pregnancy—is a surprisingly new invention. In the early nineteenth century, the distinction between abortion, miscarriage, and birth control was a lot foggier. The presence of the phrases "*spontaneous* abortion" and "*forced* abortion" in medical texts from the period indicates that neither was taken for granted from the word itself.

The modern concept of abortion depends on a modern understanding of pregnancy itself—one that was out of reach in the early nineteenth century. Today, the stages of pregnancy are familiar, rigidly defined, and easily visualized through the lens of medicine. Microscopic images tell us what an embryo looks like, what a pregnancy materially *is* in the first weeks after conception. Later on, ultrasound technology gives us a literal window into the mythical journey of the fetus. Someone who becomes pregnant in 2023 can, thanks to an abundance of apps, books, and websites, envision each week of gestation through visual metaphors: *your baby is the size of the tip of your eyeliner brush; your baby is the size of a cute vintage wallet; your baby is the size of a large movie popcorn.*[16]

In Phebe's day, nobody was sharing sonogram pictures with their coworkers or holding up an avocado to their belly to imagine the fetus inside. No one talked about trimesters; instead, the major milestone that defined pregnancy was *quickening*. To be "quick with child," in the language of the day, was to be far enough along in pregnancy to feel the movement of the fetus. Before that point, there was no definite way to be sure that you were actually pregnant—not even a doctor could be sure without that vital sign of life. But quickening is a fundamentally inexact, non-scientific concept. In most viable pregnancies, it happens between the sixteenth and twenty-fourth weeks. That's a wide window! What's more, some people don't feel the movement of the fetus at all until labor is imminent—or if they do, they assume it's something else.[17] The result: in a legal and medical context where quickening marked the official beginning of pregnancy, any action a woman might take before that point to prevent conception or end a pregnancy could not really be considered abortion.

Absent a clear understanding of just what was taking place in the womb, nineteenth-century understandings of pregnancy focused on the woman, not the fetus—and then, as now, no two women's pregnancies were the same. Women who treated their pregnancies through the use of emmenagogues in the early nineteenth century did not, as far as we can tell, envision that as a feminist political practice or even a means of long-term family planning. Rather, Susan Klepp argues, "women focused on their present circumstances, especially their current physical and emotional health, as apparent in the regularity of their menstrual cycles."[18] Every woman's "present circumstances" were different, and so was every woman's potential pregnancy and its possible solutions. For many women, pregnancy was the expected and welcomed outcome of sex with their husbands. But for women without the means to provide for another child, a potential pregnancy was an economic problem. For unmarried women, a potential pregnancy was a social problem with two solutions: marriage, or medication to restore the menstrual cycle. For a woman whose previous pregnancies had been physically or emotionally traumatic, a potential pregnancy was a medical problem, and a psychological one, too. In other words, pregnancy carried all the many weighty meanings in the early 1800s that it does today.

But women in the early nineteenth century lacked the well-oiled language of reproductive rights that operates today. Klepp explains that "definitions of disease," rather than ideas of *autonomy* and *choice*, "provided women with a vehicle for dealing with unwelcome pregnancies." *Amenorrhea*—a medical term referring to an abnormal absence of menstrual periods—was more than a sleight of hand allowing women to terminate unwanted pregnancies; it was, and remains, a legitimate medical diagnosis with a variety of potential causes, only one of which is pregnancy. Klepp points out that "the physical signs thought to be specific to the disease of hysteria—an inflated belly, perceived motion, vomiting, and colic—mirror some of the early symptoms of pregnancy."[19] Without hormonal tests that could scientifically prove (or disprove) pregnancy, doctors and women alike relied on women's self-report to decide how to treat a menstrual stoppage. And because the all-important moment of quickening also relied on a woman's self-report, many women in the early 1800s had more practical control than we might imagine over when and how they became pregnant and stopped being pregnant.

When Phebe Burleigh started to feel sick or put on weight in early 1826, she probably knew what was happening. If she and Terrence had tried and failed to conceive in the past, or if she'd had previous miscarriages, she might have been excited when she felt Josephine moving in her belly and knew for sure that this was really happening. But, again, she didn't leave a diary. If she wrote letters about her pregnancy to family or friends, they're lost to time. Maybe she was afraid. Maybe she agreed to carry Josephine to term out of a sense of duty—to Terrence, to her family, to her religious beliefs, or to that grand idea of "republican motherhood" Linda Kerber writes about. Maybe, like couples today, Terrence and Phebe thought that a baby might breathe new life into a failing relationship. Maybe they were lonely.

Or maybe what still happens to people today all the time happened to Phebe: the condom broke (read: her calendar was wrong), the morning-after pill (read: herbal mixture) failed, and she found herself too far along for birth control. Even today, more than 90 percent of abortions take place in the first trimester of pregnancy, when medication—the new-and-improved answer to nineteenth-century emmenagogues—is all that's needed to terminate.[20] Past twelve weeks, things get more complicated. Between sixteen and twenty-four weeks, the same period when the moment of quickening usually takes place, a surgical abortion becomes the only feasible option. In the twenty-first century, surgical abortion is extremely safe. But in the early 1800s, long before the advent of antiseptic surgery, very few surgeries of any kind were safe. Given the choice between carrying a pregnancy to term and risking a surgical abortion after quickening, a majority of women would choose the former.

A surgical abortion after quickening would also have been a crime, but that was probably not a major factor in Phebe's decision. In the early years of the republic, the United States followed the common law tradition of England where abortion was concerned. Common law, as the historian James C. Mohr explains, "did not formally recognize the existence of a fetus in criminal cases until it had quickened," a determination which could only be made by the pregnant woman.[21] Following that logic, abortion was considered a crime under common law only *after quickening*, when "the fetus itself had manifested some semblance

of a separate existence."²² Only the physician who performed the procedure would have been guilty of a crime under common law if Phebe
had sought a surgical abortion in 1826, and even that crime was loosely
defined and rarely prosecuted.

But three years after Josephine's birth—and four years before the
Fagans moved to New York State—the Empire State took a major first
step away from the common law precedent. In Title 2, Article 1, Section 9 of the 1829 version of the Revised Statutes of the state of New
York, legislators passed a law that dictated,

> Every person who shall administer to *any woman pregnant with a
> quick child,* any medicine, drug or substance whatever, or shall use
> or employ any instrument or other means, with intent thereby to
> destroy such child, *unless the same shall have been necessary to preserve
> the life of such mother,* or shall have been advised by two physicians
> to be necessary for such purpose, shall be deemed guilty of man-
> slaughter in the second degree. [emphasis mine]

Under this new law, abortion after quickening became a felony in
the state of New York, punishable by confinement in the state prison
for no less than four and no more than seven years. Any doctor who
performed a medical or surgical abortion on a patient quick with child
was guilty of second-degree manslaughter, unless they could demonstrate that the procedure had been necessary to save the mother's life.
This law marked the first use of what would come to be known as the
"therapeutic exception" of abortion laws: the loophole that permitted
abortion only in life-or-death situations.

But that wasn't the only change introduced by the 1829 New York
statutes. In addition to the felony charges opened up in Title 2, Title 6
of the Revised Statutes introduced a misdemeanor charge for abortion,
stating,

> Every person who shall wilfully administer to *any pregnant woman,*
> any medicine, drug, substance or thing whatever, or shall use or
> employ any instrument or other means whatever, *with intent thereby
> to procure the miscarriage of any such woman,* unless the same shall
> have been necessary to preserve the life of such woman, or shall have
> been advised by two physicians to be necessary for that purpose;
> shall, upon conviction, be punished by imprisonment in a county
> jail not more than one year, or by a fine not exceeding five hundred
> dollars, or by both such fine and imprisonment. [emphasis mine]

In other words, abortion prior to quickening became a crime for the first time in New York State just four years before Phebe and her family moved there.[23] Born in Virginia in 1826, Josephine Fagan had come into a world where Americans, as the historian James Mohr puts it, "could and did look the other way when they encountered abortion," because "nothing in their medical knowledge or in the rulings of their courts compelled them to do otherwise."[24] Now, growing up as a young woman in the first state to ban abortion at all stages of pregnancy, she would encounter a reproductive landscape dramatically altered from her mother's.

Why did New York State outlaw abortion in 1829—and why did it matter for Josephine, who was only seven when she moved to New York? It's a big question, one that the next few chapters will work to unpack. Abortion law rarely if ever represents an explicit or uncomplicated attempt to, in the language of twenty-first-century third-wave feminism, "control women's bodies." And, indeed, the 1829 statutes themselves included no penalties whatsoever for women who sought out abortions. Every abortion law, rather, is an expression of much broader concerns: about reproduction; about sex; about families and who should have them, and when, and how; about the safety of the most vulnerable—a category subject to change and to varying points of view.

In the 1820s, male legislators viewed women as one such a vulnerable category—*some* women, anyway. If there was one identifiable concern most obviously responsible for how the New York legislature revised the state law in 1829, it was a pervasive fear for the safety and morality of young, unmarried white Protestant women. That was, after all, the primary demographic that Americans associated abortion with: not with married women or people who already had children, but with nice single girls in trouble. As Solinger puts it, "abortion was defined as a problem because of its association with the promiscuity (the separation of sex and reproduction) of unmarried females."[25] By restricting the practice of post-quickening abortion, the manslaughter charges made available by the Revised Statutes targeted untrained medical practitioners whose treatments too often killed the desperate young women who approached them in a delicate situation. The misdemeanor charge, on the other hand, functioned as a more general discouragement of *all* abortions, including those that were less dangerous but just as scandalous.

Neither law was consistently enforced or regularly prosecuted; the mere fact that they existed on the books in New York State gave legal form to lawmakers' anxiety about the women of their class. Girls like Josephine—white Protestants within or adjacent to the growing middle class—grew up under those laws in New York in the 1830s and 1840s. Some of them got pregnant out of wedlock; some got abortions; some died, and their lives and deaths were absorbed into the great morality tale about the dangers of illicit sex and failed womanhood. Others followed the straight and narrow path: they married nice men, had children, and devoted themselves to bringing up strong moral citizens.

But those weren't the only two paths available for women in the 1840s, when Josephine came of age. As cities grew and the household economy lost its grip on American life, more and more young women sought purpose, experience, and profit outside of the home.[26] Josephine was one of them. In 1842, at sixteen, Josephine Fagan enrolled in classes at the Oneida Conference Seminary, a coeducational secondary school twenty miles west of Augusta in Cazenovia, New York.

One of the primary reasons that women pursued seminary or academy training in the 1840s, apart from a love of learning or a desire for independence, was to find work and earn a place in the middle class. Women who graduated from such schools often became writers, joined literary societies and other voluntary associations, or engaged in the non-voting political activism of abolition and temperance movements. In doing all these things and more, educated women helped to shape public opinion and claim membership in an elite class, despite their limited legal status. But above all, the historian Mary Kelley writes, "an advanced education opened the door to economic self-support." Teaching provided a far steadier income for educated women than writing or activism, and by the early nineteenth century, a majority of teachers in American primary schools were women. In fact, women whose parents were not wealthy might begin teaching before they even finished their own education in order to pay tuition.[27]

Josephine's education at the Cazenovia seminary, which took her out of her mother's household for the first time, placed her in the very small percentage of women—as few as 1 percent, by some scholars' estimates—pursuing secondary education in the United States in the years between the American Revolution and the Civil War. That small percentage, however, actually reflected an increase in equality visible in women's education in the early nineteenth century.[28] In the first fifty years of the Oneida Conference Seminary's existence, approximately one quarter of its students were women; the year before Josephine enrolled there, women made up the entire graduating class.[29] Moved by the same Enlightenment ideals of reason and equality that shaped patterns of reproduction in the post-Revolutionary period, young women from middle- and working-class families began pursuing the higher education that had previously been available only to the daughters of elite families. Approximately 10 percent of women seeking such education went to the 182 female-only academies established between 1790 and 1830, but the remainder, like Josephine, attended co-educational institutions where they received education in the same subjects as men, though often in separate classrooms.[30]

The curriculum at the Oneida Conference Seminary reflected those new standards: the five main departments of study included courses not only in reading, penmanship, and grammar but also in geography, US history, chemistry, geology, algebra, natural philosophy, civil engineering, rhetoric, and logic. Josephine might have taken courses in elocution, the science of government, and bookkeeping.[31] If she took any courses in embroidery or dancing—the core curriculum at many earlier ladies' seminaries—they were electives.

Students at female academies in the antebellum period stressed in letters to friends and relatives how busy they were, and the Oneida Conference Seminary was no different. Josephine was expected to get up at 5 a.m. every morning, clean her room at 5:30 a.m., and study in blocks from 5:30 a.m. to 7 a.m., from 9 a.m. to noon, from 1 p.m. to 4 p.m., and finally from 7 p.m. to 9 p.m. In the midst of that packed schedule, though, she found room for social life: during her two years at the seminary, she struck up a friendship with a clerk at the general store run by a Mr. Robert Norris, who had stepped into the role of guardian for Josephine after the deaths of her father and stepfather. Mr. Norris's clerk, a young man named Milton Thomson, was about her age and, like her, he had grown up near Utica. The two became close while Josephine worked through her education, and in 1844, when Josephine left Cazenovia to take her first full-time teaching job at a female academy in the Hudson Valley, Milton Thomson sent her a letter asking for her hand in marriage.[32]

She turned him down. Instead, after a few months downstate, she left New York altogether and traveled south to Washington, DC, accompanied by the academy's principal, Mrs. Crocker. Their plan was to open a school for girls in the nation's capital. For four or five weeks, the two stayed in a boarding house on Pennsylvania Avenue, hoping to gather information and make connections that would allow them to establish the new school. But here, just as in New York, Josephine found time for pleasure alongside business. At the boarding house, she made the acquaintance of a man named Robert McCarty. He was also from New York; maybe that coincidence was the conversation starter that got them talking. But they had more in common. Robert, like Josephine, was ambitious: he was an inventor, bent on selling his patented steam gun to the US military. He was in his mid-forties, over twice Josephine's age, but he took a special interest in her—and she in him.

The school in Washington never got off the ground. Mrs. Crocker became sick; Josephine ran out of money. About a month after arriving in Washington, they took separate paths. In the winter of 1844, Josephine traveled over the Potomac to the small plantation town of Port Tobacco, where she worked as a live-in governess for the family of Richard Barnes, a judge of the Orphans' Court and the maternal uncle of the famous Maryland congressman Barnes Compton.[33] On her way to Port Tobacco, Josephine received a letter from Robert McCarty asking for her hand in marriage. This time, Josephine said yes. While she taught Judge Barnes's children over the winter of 1844–45, Robert wrote to Robert J. Norris, asking for his approval as Josephine's guardian. He apparently received it, because when summer rolled around, Josephine made the trip back across the Potomac to Georgetown where, in July 1845, she married Robert McCarty. That autumn, the newlywed couple moved to New York City to start a new life together.

Describing the paths of the thousands of women who attended academies and seminaries between the American Revolution and Civil War, Kelley writes, "Women came to these schools from cities and villages and from towns large and small. In their subsequent lives, some would earn their livelihood as teachers. Others would take their place in elite planter or wealthy merchant families."[34] By 1844, Josephine had done both and achieved some measure of financial self-sufficiency. But wealthy husbands and good jobs weren't the only reasons women sought education in the mid-nineteenth century. In an address to the New York State legislature in 1819, the educational reformer Emma Willard argued that a high-quality education would make women "good wives, good mothers, or good mistresses of families: and if they are none of these," Willard cautioned, "they must be bad members of society."[35]

In New York, as Robert McCarty's wife, Josephine would begin her second career: not as a teacher, but as a mother. In doing so, she would have a chance to prove who and what she was: a good wife, a good mother, or a bad member of society.

Chapter 2

A Cigar Girl and a Wicked Woman

Josephine's new husband, Robert McCarty, was unlike any of the men she'd grown up with. He wasn't a farmer or a shop clerk; he was an inventor.

Maybe this was what drew Josephine to him, despite the difference in their ages. Robert's invention—the focus of his career—was a steam-powered gun that would, he believed, "provide an entire revolution in the science of modern warfare" by eliminating the need for a steady supply of gunpowder.[1] When Josephine met him in Washington in 1845, though, the revolution hadn't yet arrived. Robert had held a US patent for his gun since 1838, but he lacked the thing that matters most for any inventor: buyers. He'd come to Washington no doubt hoping to catch the attention of the secretary of war or other military officials, but the only person he impressed, evidently, was Josephine.

So Robert left Washington at the end of the summer and took his new wife to live in the place where ambition goes to sink or swim: New York City. When Josephine and Robert McCarty arrived in 1845, New York was in the midst of a population explosion. It was already the largest city in the nation by a pretty significant margin, but between the 1840 census and the 1850 census, New York's population would go from 391,114 to 696,115, a dizzying increase almost unmatched in the history of the metropolis.[2] Throughout the decade, new New Yorkers came from all over: they poured off ships from Ireland and the Germanic states at Castle Garden; they were born in tenements and townhouses and, occasionally, lying-in hospitals; and they came from the surrounding countryside in huge numbers, drawn in by the promise of jobs as the country's largest port nursed steadily on the stream of revenue from the Erie Canal.

New York City was—and is—a wholly different place from the state with which it shares a name. Although distinct "upstate" and "downstate" New York identities wouldn't coalesce until the twentieth century, the early nineteenth century already saw lines being drawn between the state's urban center and the rural communities feeding it. The city, in the minds of many New Yorkers, represented danger, particularly to the most vulnerable. While rural places like Augusta stood for safety, morality, and the security of the household economy, the city was their opposite: violent, corrupt, and precarious.

Of particular concern to moralists, lawmakers, and mothers—to authorities both official and unofficial, that is—was the fate of the thousands of young single women who moved to New York City from rural towns and family farms in the 1840s. For a young woman who left her mother's home for a job in the city, working outside the home opened up new opportunities for independence, but with those came a loss of social ties. In the city, a woman's workplace was separate both geographically and socially from where she ate and slept. For most young working women, the rapidly-rotating, mixed-gender population of an urban boarding house replaced a stable local community. People worried about young men, too—at least, their mothers did. But the general fears of violence that still cling to rural perceptions of city life took a distinct form when it came to young women. The threat of sexual assault—at once very real and inflated in the collective imagination—hung around accounts of young women's urban moves.

Of course, it wasn't just the possibility of rape that worried people; it was the potential for young women, removed from the watchful eye of neighbors who'd known them and their parents all their life, to engage in consensual sex outside of marriage. Rattling around in the vast anonymous danger zone of New York City, a good country girl could become loose in every sense: untethered from a familiar social circle capable of regulating her sexuality, but also detached from the resources that would have protected her from both scandal and physical harm at home.

Through both consensual and nonconsensual sexual encounters, these unattended women could become pregnant with illegitimate children—which put them in a doubly dangerous position. Being a single mother in the 1840s didn't just come with social stigma; giving birth to a child out of wedlock also meant feeding, clothing, and raising that child without the support of a wage-earning husband. While urbanization brought new economic opportunities for women, life without a husband was still expensive and dangerous, especially in a city of strangers.

But the alternative was just as dangerous, if not more so. In a small town, a woman who didn't want to be pregnant could turn to her mother, her neighbor, or her local midwife for birth control or abortifacients. An unwed expectant mother in the city had fewer options. You could buy the right medications at local shops, but you might not know or trust the person you bought them from. You could order "female pills" from an address you found in the newspaper, or you could ask around at work or among your roommates to find a doctor—if you knew them well enough and trusted them.[3] But could you really trust a city doctor operating outside the law and away from the watchful eye of a community who would notice your loss? The twin ordeals of childbirth and abortion, already weighed down with the high stakes of parenthood and the possibility of death, became even more terrifying in the city.

But the city was where Josephine Fagan—now Josephine McCarty—became a mother. Within three months of her marriage to Robert, she was pregnant with their first child, conceived around the time of her nineteenth birthday. The pregnancy was almost certainly both wanted and expected as the natural next step after marriage—but even if it wasn't, Josephine would have had a more difficult time than her mother getting out of it.

In May of 1845, just two months before Josephine married Robert, New York State revised its abortion statutes. The Laws of 1845, which took effect during Josephine's first pregnancy, made several crucial changes to the state's position on abortion, the most important of which was a new clause in Section 3: "Every woman who shall solicit of any person any medicine, drug, or substance or thing whatever, and shall take the same, or shall submit to any operation, or other means whatever, with intent thereby to procure a miscarriage, shall be deemed guilty of a misdemeanor." Until 1845, the only anti-abortion statutes in the country punished doctors who performed abortions—not their patients. Now, for the first time in US history, New York State had made it illegal to get an abortion.

The passage of that law just before Josephine moved to the city wasn't a coincidence. In fact, the fears bound up in the legislature's 1845 "Act to punish the procurement of Abortion" related directly to women like her—two women, in particular. The first was a young rural transplant just like Josephine: young, pretty, and ready to settle into a respectable life as a wife and mother. Her name was Mary Rogers. The other was everything Josephine would become: a married woman carving out a place among the city's upper middle class as a professional abortionist. Her name—and it was not even her real name—was Madame Restell. Just before Josephine arrived in New York City, Mary Rogers's death and Madame Restell's role in it reshaped the landscape of reproductive politics in New York State.

Mary Cecilia Rogers, born around 1820, was the fifth child of Phebe Rogers. Like Phebe Burleigh, Mrs. Rogers had been married twice, first to Ezra Mather, a distant relative of Cotton and Increase; and then, shortly before Mary's birth, to Daniel Rogers. Like Phebe Burleigh, Phebe Rogers buried both her husbands before her youngest daughter reached adulthood. Left a single widowed mother, Phebe Rogers responded differently than Phebe Williams. Instead of resigning herself to a solitary life on her farm, she looked outward. "Most likely," historian Amy Gilman Srebnick writes, "the family losses of the 1830s propelled Phebe to leave what she had always known and move with her putative child, Mary Rogers, in the late 1830s to New York City."[4]

New York, by all accounts, agreed with Mary Rogers. Arriving at just seventeen years old, she quickly found both work and love—the things, that is, that most young New York transplants are still looking for today. At John Anderson's Broadway tobacco emporium, customers knew her as "the beautiful cigar girl." And as co-proprietress of the boarding house Phebe opened on Nassau Street in 1840, Mary met a lot of men. A lot of them liked her; she liked them. Within Mary's first four years in New York, Srebnick recounts, she was romantically involved with "a corkcutter, a clerk, a sailor, a prosperous shopkeeper and future real estate tycoon, a naval officer, and a politician's son."[5]

One of Mary's most serious connections was with the corkcutter, a man named Daniel Payne. Like Robert and Josephine, they had met in a boarding house, the one that Mary ran with her mother at 126 Nassau Street. Within six months of their first meeting, Daniel and Mary were engaged. Then, on the morning of July 25, 1841, something happened.

At first, nobody was sure what had happened. Mary had left that morning to visit her aunt Jane uptown, strolling off alone through the quiet Sunday streets. Daniel kissed her goodbye; they made plans to meet later that evening. Then evening came and went, and Mary didn't return. She left no note, no clues as to where she could have gone; she was simply gone.

By morning, Daniel was alarmed. He began searching for her, going to lengths that few New Yorkers today would brave, even with the benefit of 24-hour train service: in a single day, he visited Harlem, Williamsburg, Hoboken, and even Staten Island. But he didn't find Mary on that Monday—in fact, he didn't find Mary at all. Search parties were organized to locate the missing cigar girl, and on Wednesday, July 28, a couple of men searching the area of parkland in Hoboken, New Jersey, known as the Elysian Fields stumbled on a body floating in the waters of the Hudson River.[6] A former boarder (and former lover) named Arthur Crommelin identified the body as Mary Rogers. An initial autopsy conducted by Dr. Richard Cook of Hoboken found that Mary had been beaten, sexually assaulted, and strangled with a piece of lace.[7]

The murder was, officially, never solved. Police investigated numerous suspects, including her fiancé, Daniel Payne, who died by suicide on October 8 near the spot where Mary's body had been found, apparently consumed with grief and tormented by the lack of closure in Mary's case. None of her other ex-boyfriends turned up any promising leads, and it soon became clear to the public that the police had no idea how Mary Rogers had come to be floating in the Hudson, battered and abused.

Nobody knows who first speculated that Mary had died after a botched abortion. Maybe the police put the theory forth when they couldn't find any conclusive evidence. Maybe people who knew her from the boarding house drew the line from her active romantic history to the possibility of an illicit operation. Wherever it came from, the speculation became a rumor and then, as rumors often do, an accepted truth. Within a year after Mary's death, Srebnick writes, "it became an unspoken conclusion that her death was the result of an abortion gone awry. She had gone to Hoboken that fateful Sunday not to enjoy the pleasure of the Elysian Fields, but to end an unwanted pregnancy."[8]

The idea of abortion didn't come out of nowhere. In 1842, the Hoboken innkeeper Frederika Loss confessed on her deathbed to having admitted Mary Rogers to her inn on July 25th in the company of a young doctor who attempted to induce a "premature delivery."[9] When the operation went wrong, Loss's son dumped Mary's body in the Hudson. The confession was deemed legally inadmissible, and authorities made no attempt to locate or prosecute the mysterious young physician, but the story stuck, and as public discourse transmuted it from rumor into something that carried the weight of truth, a name got stuck to it as well—a name already familiar to many New Yorkers. By the time Robert and Josephine moved to the city, people had been whispering, writing, and shouting this name with increasing fury for four years. The name was Madame Restell.

Madame Restell was a business sobriquet; the legal name of the person who eventually became the popular culprit for Mary Rogers's death was Ann Lohman, originally Ann Trow. She was an English immigrant, once widowed and now married to a printer with whom she raised a daughter from her previous marriage named Caroline. Ann Lohman arrived in New York in 1831, six years before Mary and Phebe, and opened a business selling abortifacients out of an office at 148 Greenwich Street. This business eventually expanded to include surgical abortions and a private lying-in clinic where women could give birth in secrecy and give their children up for an adoption that "Madame Restell" would arrange.

Technically, all of this was illegal. The 1829 statutes prohibited abortion at all stages of pregnancy, with penalties of up to seven years in state prison for an operation undertaken after quickening. But the presence of a law on the books doesn't always mean an end to the crime—not while there are police willing to take a bribe, participants willing to keep their mouths shut, and grand juries willing to dismiss charges. Abortion might be illegal, but for most people it was still part of everyday life. Madame Restell was not the only abortionist operating in New York City at that time—her biographer Clifford Browder notes competition from a Mrs. Bird and a Madame Costello—she was simply the most visible. Throughout the 1840s, a reader opening the pages of nearly any New York daily newspaper was likely to see an ad for Madame Restell's services.

She was also the most inflammatory—something she encouraged, probably consciously, by riding around the city in a carriage drawn by four horses. This made her critics extremely angry. Bad enough that a woman was performing illegal abortions and profiting off of them; worse still to see her flaunt that wealth in public.

Unfortunately for Madame Restell, she entered the public eye in time to become infamous just weeks before the death of Mary Rogers. In March 1841, a few months before Mary's disappearance, Mrs. Ann Maria Purdy's husband called the police to take a deathbed statement from her concerning Mrs. Restell. Mrs. Purdy said that she'd been to the Greenwich Street office after falling pregnant in the summer of 1839, and Madame Restell had given her some medicine to take. Mrs. Purdy had taken that medicine to a doctor, who advised her that it was oil of tansy and turpentine and "extremely dangerous," and so she had stopped taking it.[10] This put her back in her original position—pregnant against her will—and so in July she returned to Madame Restell's office, where a man performed an operation on her. Before she left the office, Madame Restell warned her not to breathe a word of what had happened there: both of them could go to state prison, she explained, and Mrs. Purdy was at an even greater risk than Restell herself. The following week she miscarried as promised, but Mrs. Purdy's health had never been the same since; tuberculosis took hold of her within the year. Now her doctor told her that she was dying, and before that happened, she wanted to clear her conscience and warn others against the fate she'd suffered.

Madame Restell had lied, of course. Under the 1829 statute, only the abortionist could be considered legally responsible for a terminated pregnancy—in this case, Madame Restell. Arrested in late March, she was indicted on four counts, two for administering poison with intent to procure a miscarriage and two for employing instruments for the same purpose. On April 28, Mrs. Purdy died, and on July 14, less than two weeks before Mary Rogers disappeared, the trial of Madame Restell began.

It was, Browder observes, "one of the first—if not *the* first—highly publicized abortion trials in the country."[11] And, if the verdict can be taken as an indication of the public's feelings about abortion, it was clear which way the wind was blowing. It took a jury of Madame Restell's male peers about ten minutes to find her guilty. Her defense team immediately appealed the decision, and the State Supreme Court overturned the verdict in 1842 on the grounds that Mrs. Purdy's death-bed confession was inadmissible. Before a new trial could be called, the district attorney dropped the charges against Madame Restell.

It didn't matter. The unfortunate timing of the Purdy trial meant that Madame Restell was at the peak of notoriety at just the right moment to become the villain in Mary Rogers's story. Never mind that she'd been in police custody when she was supposed to have been performing Mary's ill-fated abortion; she was a bad woman profiting off of a bad job, and she formed a satisfying answer to the unanswerable tragedy of Mary's death.

Mary Rogers and Madame Restell—two women separated by class, age, and nationality but in 1841 separated only by a few city blocks—represented two distinct facets of middle-class Americans' cultural anxieties in the mid-nineteenth century. Mary was the quintessential victim of the moral and physical perils of the city: young, single, and sexually active, she had lived out the nightmares of moral reformers by dying violently only a few years after moving to the city from the rural New England home of her Puritan ancestors. "Removed from the interiority of the home" by her job at the tobacco emporium, Srebnick writes, "Rogers became the public woman who inspired a constant discussion about nonprocreative sex, the female body, abortion, and some notion of the dangers of sexuality."[12]

Madame Restell represented a different kind of danger. She was a foreigner, an immigrant woman with no formal medical training whose coach-and-four announced loudly to New Yorkers that her clients were not Mary Rogerses but rather well-off, presumably married women. Theoretically, her lack of training posed a threat to her patients' physical safety, but the fact that her business remained so profitable even after her arrest and conviction suggests that the vast majority of her patients had a far better experience than Mrs. Purdy. The most pressing threat of Madame Restell's business was not to the safety of women but to the social order. A skilled and discreet abortionist could help women conceal illicit affairs, seek out premarital sex, and generally maintain control over their reproduction without input or oversight from husbands or other men.

As the 1840s progressed, Madame Restell became the public target of a burgeoning anti-abortion movement. In 1845, Enoch E. Camp and George Wilkes founded a true crime newspaper called the *National Police Gazette*, which frequently published sensational pieces on the evils of abortion and the "three hags of misery" (Restell, Bird, and Costello) who had made the crime a thriving trade in New York City. Long on drama, short on facts, the *Gazette* harnessed middle-class men's anxieties about the health, safety, and sexual activities of their wives and daughters and made good money off of it. "An immediate success," Clifford Browder reports, "the *Gazette* claimed a circulation of 8,600 by its fifth week, when it enlarged its format, and 15,000 by the ninth, with distribution throughout the country."[13] In the pages of the *Gazette*, Madame Restell appeared before the eyes of the city as a "wholesale female strangler," a "modern Thug of civilized society," and a literal witch, depicted in an illustration printed on March 13, 1847, cradling a demon with bat wings that was munching on a baby.[14] The threat she posed to the sanctity of the "civilized" family could not have been much clearer.

But in the same year that the *Gazette* published its first issue, Madame Restell's profession drew further attention from the government. Four years on from the death of Mary Rogers and the first trial of Madame Restell, the New York State legislature passed "An Act to punish the procurement of Abortion, and for other purposes."[15] The first two sections of the act were largely a restatement of the 1829 statutes: Section 1 stated that abortion after quickening was still second-degree manslaughter, while Section 2 laid out penalties for misdemeanor abortion prior to quickening. The only significant difference was that prescribing and advising were now criminal acts: a doctor or midwife didn't have to actually perform the operation to be criminally liable. And for any abortion, jail time was now mandatory—at least three months before quickening and four years after.[16]

But Section 3 introduced a new crime: getting an abortion. Soliciting medicine and taking it to produce a miscarriage, or submitting to an operation for the same purpose, was now a misdemeanor in New York, punishable by three to twelve months in the county jail, a thousand-dollar fine, or both. Sections 4 and 5 went further, stating that "any woman who shall endeavor privately . . . to conceal the death of any issue of her body, which if born alive would by law be a bastard, whether it was born dead or alive, or whether it was murdered or not, shall be deemed guilty of a misdemeanor." For a first offense, she could be imprisoned in the county jail for up to a year; for a second, she could be sent to state prison for two to five years.

It's an outrageous law with upsetting implications. Taken together, Sections 3 through 5 of the 1845 act speak to a shared fear of lawmakers that women were abdicating motherhood for the sake of sex. Abortion and infanticide could both serve to cover up the results of extramarital sex—and the mention of "bastard" children in Section 4 makes it clear that it was extramarital sex specifically that was at issue. Under the 1845 law, a married woman who concealed a stillbirth wasn't committing a crime; an unmarried woman was.

Luckily for Josephine, her first child was born without event in July of 1846. She named him Eugene. Within a few months, she was pregnant again; Eugene's sister Ella was born in September 1847.[17] The same month, Madame Restell was arrested and arraigned on five counts under the new abortion statute: procuring an abortion on the person of one Maria Bodine by medicine, an unknown instrument, her hand, her finger, and "violent means unknown." The jury found her guilty. Dressed for the sentencing in "a rich black silk gown, a handsomely trimmed black velvet mantilla, and a white satin bonnet with a lace veil," Madame Restell received the maximum sentence permitted by law: one year in the city penitentiary on Blackwell's Island.[18]

While Madame Restell served out her sentence on Blackwell's Island, Josephine gave birth to her and Robert's third child in November of 1848. She named him after her father, Terrence. Terrence, like his siblings, was likely born in a boarding house somewhere in Lower Manhattan. Josephine and Robert spent the first three years of their marriage in a semi-itinerant fashion, hopping between New York boarding houses and traveling up the Hudson intermittently to spend summers in Augusta with Josephine's mother.[19]

Anyone who has spent time in New York City during the summer can probably imagine why the McCartys preferred to spend the hottest months of the year outside of Manhattan. When you crowd hundreds of thousands of people onto a tiny island, the garbage and biological waste they produce has nowhere to go. While the city was smaller in the 1840s than it is now, it also lacked a sanitation department. Waste management, in fact, was largely managed by wild pigs roaming the streets.

But there was another reason for the family to avoid the city in summer: cholera.

In December of 1848, just a month after Terrence was born, cholera broke out in the working-class immigrant neighborhood of Five Points, said to be carried into the city by escaped passengers from a ship quarantined offshore.[20] For a few months, the winter cold kept the disease more or less in check, but as spring approached and the island began to thaw out, cholera spread through the city, killing hundreds and then thousands. In the spring of 1849, with the city groaning and dying around him, Robert McCarty booked passage on a ship for England, leaving Josephine with the children and fourteen dollars in cash.[21]

Josephine, Eugene, Ella, and Terrence McCarty spent the summer of 1849 at Phebe Williams's farm in Augusta some 275 miles from the epidemic, which reached its peak in June, killing 5,000 New Yorkers. According to the 1850 federal census, in October of that year Josephine and her three children were living on Phebe Williams's farm, staying past the poisonous summer season into the Mohawk Valley's rich autumn. As autumn deepened into winter, Josephine split her time between Augusta and New York, boarding in the winter of 1849–50 at the Howard Hotel close to what is now the World Trade Center, and later at a private boarding house on Water Street near the present site of the Brooklyn Bridge.[22] What she was doing in New York isn't clear, but it's most likely that she was looking for work, which was easier to find in the city than in Augusta.

Then, in the spring of 1851, Josephine received a letter from Robert, who had been writing intermittently from England since his departure two years earlier. Now he wanted Josephine to cross the ocean and join him, and to bring the children with her. He had been selected as a judge at the Great Exhibition of the Works of Industry of All Nations, a world's fair held in London in a massive hall known as the Crystal Palace. It was the opportunity of a lifetime. The passage would have been expensive, but Robert presumably provided the funds, because that spring Josephine, Eugene, Ella, and Terrence boarded the packet ship *Margaret Evans*, captained by one Isaiah Pratt, and embarked for England.[23] The journey across the Atlantic from New York to Gravesend in Kent, where Robert met the family in the spring of 1851, would have taken close to a month. Even if Robert had been willing or able to spring for a stateroom, those three weeks on the ocean with three small children would probably not have been the happiest of Josephine's life—but at the end of the journey stood the Crystal Palace of Hyde Park, 1,851 feet long and 128 feet tall and glimmering with the promise of a new industrial age.

Much has been written of the Crystal Palace. Historians have tried to sum up the entirety of the nineteenth-century imagination in its 990,000 square feet of glass and light, folding politics, industry, science, and the fundamentals of existence together into a kaleidoscope of interpretations. The cultural theorist Tony Bennett argues that the Crystal Palace was "a counter-revolutionary measure," an extension of the state's work of surveillance and discipline: Bentham's Panopticon masquerading as a glorified agricultural fair.[24] The social historian

Wolfgang Schivelbusch, in his study of the cultural impact of railroad travel on nineteenth-century people's experiences of time and space, discusses the "perceptual shocks" the Crystal Palace created in its visitors by abstracting time and space in "the culmination and termination of ferro-vitreous architectural functionalism."[25]

Historians will probably continue to argue for years about what the Crystal Palace meant; what it was, in the most basic terms, was an enormous glass-and-iron greenhouse erected in the middle of Hyde Park, designed by a gardener named Joseph Paxton, made possible by new sheet-glass construction techniques, and filled to bursting with exhibits from twenty-five countries around the globe. From May 1, 1851, through to October of the same year, some fourteen thousand exhibits went on display, including such wonders as the recently plundered Koh-i-Noor diamond, Samuel Colt's pistol, and Frederick Bakewell's early predecessor to the fax machine. Alongside these marvels, visitors might stop by the United States's corner of the palace to observe a specimen of "Burrow's mustard" contributed by S. D. McCulloch of Lexington, Kentucky; "autumnal leaves" from Providence, Rhode Island; and, from Josephine's own Oneida County, a "sample of oatmeal manufactured at Clark's Mills" near Utica.[26] The exhibition had something for everyone.

Among all the claims historians have made for the exhibition's impact on the long nineteenth century, one seems unshakable: the Crystal Palace at Hyde Park saw the first installment of public toilets in recorded history, invented by George Jennings and available to all visitors for the reasonable price of a penny. Over the five months of the fair's operation, some 827,000 people used the toilets at the Crystal Palace, amassing a healthy revenue for the organizers.[27]

For the first twenty-five days of its operation, the exhibition was the exclusive province of the powerful and the wealthy; Queen Victoria and Prince Albert, instrumental in the vision and funding for the fair, strolled through the exhibition halls. But on May 26, 1851, the remarkable happened: the price of admission dropped to a shilling a head on weekdays, Monday through Thursday. The weekends would remain limited to those with means, but during the week, nearly any person in all of Britain who could get the day off and make the journey to Hyde Park would be able to walk among the exhibits, spend pennies at the toilets, and take in exhibits of industry and imagination from around the entire world. As laborers from the countryside poured into London for their glimpse of the palace, Robert McCarty jumped at the chance to show off to his wife and children the monumental enterprise in which he was to play a minor part. After traveling from Gravesend back to Robert's lodgings in London, it is likely that one of the family's first stops was in Hyde Park.

The exhibition would have occupied most of Robert's time in the spring and summer of 1851. Serving on the jury of experts judging Category V ("Machines for Direct Use, Including Carriages and Railway and Navy Mechanism") along with the mathematician Reverend Henry Moseley, engineer Robert Napier, and Wilhelm Engerth, the Austrian inventor of the world's first mountain locomotive, Robert was responsible for judging a total of 537 exhibits, 16 of which represented the efforts of his home country.[28] The first jury meeting was on May 12, followed by eighteen subsequent sessions and daily meetings of sub-juries throughout the month of June.[29] With the Crystal Palace stuffed to the seams, being a judge was a busy job. During this time, Josephine and the children were left to their own devices in a city of unthinkable size and unfamiliar geography.

The excitement was short-lived. Shortly after arriving in England, Josephine discovered two things: first, that Robert was carrying on an affair with another woman, and second, that he had become "diseased," exposing her to what was almost certainly a sexually transmitted infection. The fight that those revelations started came to a head approximately six months later. While the family was living at Knighton on the Isle of Wight, Robert took all three children and disappeared, leaving Josephine alone.[30]

Bereft of her children in a strange country, Josephine spent weeks searching fruitlessly for Eugene, Ella, and Terrence, eventually discovering them sometime around the summer of 1852. When she found them, Terrence was sick, as was his father, and Robert's disease, which had split them up in the first place, temporarily proved a source of reconciliation. Josephine, out of pity or wifely duty or a determination to remain with her children, agreed to nurse her husband through his illness. Her kindness or resignation, whatever it was, was not repaid: when he recovered, the pair separated once more. Again, Robert proved content to relinquish his wife but not his children. When Josephine made it clear that she wanted to return to New York with her children, Robert took them again and, as she explained at her trial years later, "went off on the Continent."[31] A certificate of arrival at the Port of London on September 20, 1852, confirms that Robert McCarty, "gentleman," had returned from Antwerp on that day following a fourteen-day absence from the country.[32]

Why was Robert so intent on retaining custody of the couple's children, and why would he resort to abduction to keep them away from
Josephine? Why not simply divorce her, petition in court for custody, and
be done with it? The answer lies in the rapidly shifting state of paren-
tal custody rights on both sides of the Atlantic in the mid-nineteenth
century. Although this family drama played out in England, Robert and
Josephine were still citizens of New York State, which wouldn't establish
legal provisions for joint custody in cases of divorce until 1860. English
common law established through cases like Rex v. DeManneville that
the "natural right" of custody lay with the father.[33] But in this, as in the
case of abortion, American authorities were starting to move away from
the common law precedent. As the ideology of republican motherhood
instilled in Americans a deep belief in the unique powers and responsibilities of mothers, judges began to award custody of children to mothers rather than fathers. Though a growing women's rights movement
encouraged this change, with custody rights included as a key issue at
the 1848 Seneca Falls Convention, the argument for maternal custody
for most judges rested not on the logic of feminism but on the principle
of the child's best interests. In other words, the goal was not to extend
women's legal rights but to follow the pseudoscientific principle that
women were best suited to healthy child-rearing.

In New York State, the landmark 1842 case Mercein v. People created
a precedent for overriding common law tradition, stating that "by the
law of nature, the father has no paramount right to the custody of his
child."[34] The question of fitness could now be weighed equally between
both parents—and the mother, held by current scientific knowledge to
be the natural caretaker of young children, held a clear advantage in
many cases, particularly those where the child in question was under
five years, physically weak, or (what amounted for many to the same)
a girl.[35]

In the McCarty case, Robert would have had a weak argument for
custody. In the first place, all three children were young: Eugene, the
oldest, was only six in 1852, and Terrence was only three, still well
within the age range at which an American judge might be inclined to
award his custody to his mother on the grounds of "the law of nature."
Moreover, one of the children was a girl; American courts often leaned
toward the mother in custody cases involving girls. Probably more
important than the children's gender and age was the fact that Robert,
despite his prestigious position on the board of jurors at the Great Exhibition, didn't have steady employment capable of providing a stable

income for three young children. Throughout his time as a father, Robert had moved constantly, never settling into a single occupation, and his departure for a foreign country just a year after his youngest son's birth would hardly have deepened a judge's faith in his ability to give Terrence and his siblings a stable home. By contrast, Josephine, despite having fewer employment opportunities, could point to her mother's farm back in New York as an ideal place to raise three children, and her experience as a teacher as proof of her ability to nurture young minds as well as bodies—and to bring in a steady paycheck. And, while Robert's alleged infidelity might not count against him in this era, Josephine's continued faithfulness to her husband would have represented, to any nineteenth-century judge, a strong argument for her moral character.

Unable to depend on a judge to award him custody of his children, Robert resorted to the brutally practical route of abduction and physical separation. He took the children away from Josephine, and when she hunted them down, he took them again. After that second separation, she recalled, she tried one more time "to get one of the children" and briefly succeeded. As she explained at her trial,

> The child and I were taken to the depot by the police; we remained protected by the police till afternoon, when they put me on the train in the care of a gentleman; when we got to London, Mr. McCARTY's two mechanics tried to wrench the child away; the gentleman interfered and there was a general fight; the police asked me to go to a justice; we went to the London Police Bureau; the police said they wanted nothing to do with it; when I stepped out Mr. McCARTY knocked me down and took the child.[36]

This would be the last time that Josephine McCarty saw any of her and Robert's children. She attempted, apparently, to obtain a divorce from him while in England, but divorce in England prior to the 1857 Matrimonial Causes Act was notoriously rare: it required a private Act of Parliament and was granted only for adultery. According to Sybil Wolfram's exhaustive study, Parliament granted only 193 divorces between 1800 and 1857—and of those, only four were granted to women, who in addition to adultery had to prove incest or bigamy as compounding offenses.[37] On top of all this, the process was staggeringly expensive, making divorce effectively the province of the aristocracy until the 1857 Act created a separate divorce court and added cruelty and desertion to the grounds women could use to procure divorces. However, prior to 1857, anyone without the grounds or funds for a full legal divorce could apply to the ecclesiastical courts for a divorce *a mensa et thoro*—a divorce "from table and bed," or what we would call a legal separation. This option would not allow the partners to remarry, but nonetheless Josephine paid a visit to the ecclesiastical court before she left England.[38] But she "was stopped, as [she] had no marriage certificate." What had become of her marriage certificate? Robert had taken it, maybe in anticipation of Josephine's next move.

By 1854, stranded without a home, a family, or even her marriage certificate in a strange country whose police force and judiciary system had made it clear they wouldn't help her, Josephine gave up any hope of reclaiming her children. That spring, she boarded the steamer *Hermann* bound for New York. The state census confirms that by the next year she had taken up residence on her mother's farm, childless and listed only as the child of Phebe Williams, the head of her own meager household.

In April of 1854, Josephine stepped off the *Hermann* into a New York that had changed markedly from the one she had left three years ago. In her absence, the city had gained some hundreds of thousands of new residents, mainly from Ireland and the Germanic states of central Europe; the *New-York Daily Times* (soon to be renamed the *New York Times*) had published its first of many thousands of issues; and Isaac Merritt Singer had opened a shop selling the sewing machines that had dazzled visitors to the Hyde Park Crystal Palace across the ocean. New York had even held its own Exhibition of the Industry of All Nations while Josephine was away; the New York Crystal Palace was still standing in Bryant Park when she got off the boat at the tip of Manhattan.

Between May 16 and June 3, three ships would arrive in New York's port carrying cholera from Liverpool.[39] The *North America*, the *Progress*, and the *Charles Crocker*, bearing between them some 1,897 immigrants, each waited in quarantine at Staten Island while a total of one hundred and fifty passengers died of cholera. In spite of city officials' efforts to contain the disease on the ships, the *New York Daily Times* reported that the "fearful malady ha[d] made its appearance" next door in Brooklyn, where two had already died and two more were not expected to recover. By June 6, the *Times* reported sixteen more deaths. New Yorkers could no longer ignore the facts: cholera had come to the city for the summer. By the time cases finally fizzled out in mid-November, cholera had claimed 2,447 lives.[40]

Josephine escaped the epidemic by a matter of weeks. Returning to the city as a single woman, without children and without a way to make a living on her own, she bought a ticket north to her mother's farm in the Mohawk River Valley. Traveling up the Hudson River to Albany and then west to Augusta, Josephine could not have predicted that her solitary journey home would lead her to rekindle an old relationship. Waiting back in Utica was Milton Thomson, the store clerk who had once asked Josephine to marry him.

CHAPTER 3

"Bent on Making Quick Money"

Josephine Fagan McCarty and Milton Thomson had very little in common. Born just a few years apart, they were both in their late teens when they met, while Thomson was a clerk at Robert Norris's store and Josephine was a seminary student. Both had grown up in the Utica area. But beyond that, Josephine and "Tom," as she called him, came from different classes and different places and were headed in two very different directions in life.[1]

Josephine and her family were outsiders in the Mohawk River Valley: Southerners and, in her father Terrence's case, immigrants. With her mother widowed at a young age and no prospects in town, Josephine did what many small-town kids do when they grow up: she left. On the heels of Tom's failed marriage proposal in 1845, Josephine had fled fast and far from Oneida County—to Washington, to New York City, and all the way to England.

Tom, meanwhile, stayed put. Unlike the Fagans, the Thomsons had been in the Mohawk Valley for generations. Tom's great-grandfather William Babbitt had served heroically during the American revolution and helped to found the town of Paris, southeast of Utica.[2] Three generations later, Tom was one of six children born to Jesse and Irene Thomson, leading members of Oneida County's ascendant middle class.[3]

Disappointed as he was by Josephine's rejection, Tom moved on. Eight years later, on June 7, 1852, he married Helen Welton, the youngest daughter of a local businessman whose family had been in the region nearly as long as the Thomsons.[4] Around the same time, Tom opened an insurance agency along with his brothers Mortimer and LaMott. From their office at 193 Genesee Street, they wrote policies with the Aetna Insurance Company of Hartford, Connecticut, the Hartford Fire Insurance Company, and the Home Insurance Company of New York City and boasted clients from places as far flung as Toronto, San Francisco, and Liverpool, England.[5] Tom's life progressed steadily in Josephine's absence, and before long it had been over a decade since they'd spoken face to face.

Then in 1854, the summer after Messrs. M. H. & M. G. Thomson opened officially for business on Genesee Street, Tom happened to take an afternoon ride along the country lanes stretching south of Utica toward Oriskany Falls.[6] The route took him well outside the path between the offices of the insurance agency and his and Helen's house in Utica. Passing through Augusta's town center, his carriage approached a stream near Newell's Corners. There was a woman sitting near the bank of the creek, watching the water. Tom thought he knew her. He slowed the carriage, and the woman looked up. It was Josephine Fagan, sitting by the side of the road in old Oneida County, just as if she had never left her mother's farm.

Tom brought his carriage to a stop and leaned out to talk to Josephine. "Do you know the way to Mr. Hunter's house?" he asked, hoping she would recognize him.

It didn't work. "I know nobody," she said.

Dropping the pretense of asking for directions, Tom said, "My father fed his flocks on these hills. Don't you know me?"[7]

She didn't, or she said that she didn't—it had been ten years, after all, since she last saw him, and they'd both changed in that time. It wasn't until he told her his name that Josephine finally recognized him. Desperate to extend the conversation, Tom invited himself to dinner at her mother's house, to which Josephine agreed. He knew the way, and she preferred to walk, so Tom rode ahead alone to Phebe Williams's farm, and when Josephine turned up some time later, she found her mother and her old friend deep in conversation.

Tom stayed for dinner that night. A few weeks later, he found a reason to drop by again. Seven or eight times over the summer of 1855, Milton Thomson visited Phebe Williams and her daughter at the farm by Newell's Corners, sometimes eating a meal with both of them and sometimes riding out alone with Josephine.[8] Over the course of these visits, he heard the whole tragic story of Josephine's life since their last communication: the unhappy marriage, the trip to Europe, the loss of the children and Josephine's desperate, impossible fight to reclaim them. During one of their one-on-one rides, maybe emboldened by the privacy of the countryside, Tom confessed that he wished he'd waited to get married.[9] If he had known she would return from Europe without a husband just three years later, he would never have married Helen Welton. He would have waited for Josephine; he could have helped her pick up the broken pieces of her life and made her the wife of one of Utica's up-and-coming businessmen.

The fact that the paths of their lives had once again crossed at all was unexpected. Only tragedy had brought Josephine back to Oneida for an extended period of time, and Tom's solo ride through Augusta could only be a coincidence, as far as it was from his usual city circuits. But for all that seemed to keep the two of them apart, there was something between them: attraction, fascination, and maybe even genuine care, mutual or otherwise. No longer an available bachelor, Tom didn't propose to Josephine in the summer of 1855, but he did the next best thing: he offered her financial support.

In the 1850s, an American woman separated from her husband occupied a fairly limited social position. Without a legal divorce, she couldn't remarry, but without a husband's income, she had to find ways of supporting herself financially. In talking with Josephine over the course of the summer, Tom no doubt saw the precarity of her situation. She was, if nothing else, an old friend, and as an established businessman, he was in a position to help.

But Josephine's financial situation wasn't as hopeless as we—or Tom—might imagine. When we think of women's work in the mid-1800s, we tend to picture a relatively restricted set of available roles: the seamstress, the laundress, the maid, the teacher. The assumption is that women, particularly single women, could take on jobs that were essentially extensions of gendered household labor, or they could do service work, or they could become teachers—which was, and is still, partly a form of childcare—but they couldn't hold management positions, own their own businesses, or make money in any but a few traditionally "feminine" fields. From this perspective, it's hard to imagine that Josephine had very many job prospects as a single woman approaching middle age in the 1850s.

In fact, though, she had plenty. The business historian Susan Ingalls Lewis calls the persistent belief in women's inability to participate in business a "zombie theory"; it's hard to kill, staggering along long after it ought to have died.[10] And yet, as Lewis demonstrates, it isn't really true: women could and *did* own and run businesses in the mid-1800s, occasionally with the assistance of husbands or male family members, but often independently. In her study of female business owners in nineteenth-century Albany, Lewis reveals that tens of thousands of women in this era operated groceries, saloons, bookshops, millineries, and other small businesses, and that these "unexceptional women" supported themselves and their families through these enterprises for years or even decades.[11]

There was just one problem. "Most women who succeeded in 'big' business" in the mid-nineteenth century, Susan Ingalls Lewis writes, "required capital from men—generally fathers, husbands, or lovers—to launch their ventures."[12] After her separation from Robert, Josephine didn't have the capital to open a business; her family's only enterprise was the farm, and there's no indication that it brought in any money beyond what Phebe needed for subsistence. Instead, Josephine sought out a job that required no overhead investment.

Today, lots of women without the time, marketable skills, credentials, or inclination to pursue a formal career turn to multi-level marketing schemes or other casual sales positions to bring in money. It's an easy line of work to get into without too big an investment of capital, and it promises huge returns—which rarely materialize. In much the same way, plenty of women in Josephine's era made their living as saleswomen, a position that offered flexibility along with opportunities for exploitation.

Adolphus Ranney, a New York publisher originally from the Utica area, gave Josephine her first sales job. Adolphus was the same age as Josephine and Tom and had grown up in the same area, but in adulthood he, like Josephine, left the area, starting a small publishing business in Manhattan.[13] In the fall of 1855, Ranney hired Josephine to sell his most recent publication, a home medical manual written by Harmon Knox Root, another Oneida County contemporary who'd left for bigger, if not better, things.[14]

Josephine's income as an agent for Ranney might have been enough to support her as a single woman, but it probably didn't live up to Ranney's claim, in an ad published in *Frank Leslie's Illustrated Newspaper* in 1855, that "agents do better with his publications than with those of any other publisher" and made an average of twenty dollars a day.[15] Ranney had a habit of lying about money; five years after he hired Josephine, he would be arrested for swindling six young German men out of $50–$150 apiece with promises of work that never materialized.[16] Still, Josephine's sales of Dr. Root's *The People's Medical Lighthouse* were evidently good, because Ranney kept her on the payroll for the following three years, even paying her living expenses in the winters of 1856 and 1857.[17]

Whatever he paid her, Ranney gave Josephine a foot in the door to a new and more exciting job: that of political lobbyist. Among Ranney's publications was *Johnson's Philosophical Charts*, a set of ten charts containing some three hundred scientific diagrams and illustrations that, Ranney claimed, "possess the merit—rarely found in schoolbooks—of being entirely original in Plan and Arrangement." The set of ten mounted charts, along with a bound explanatory key, cost fifteen dollars. Ranney hoped to convince the state schools to add the charts to their natural science curriculum, as in addition to their basic education value they were "highly ornamental to a schoolroom, and obviate the necessity of philosophical apparatus which would cost from $3,000 to $3,500."[18] A deal with the state's public school system would be Ranney's biggest sale yet—but it required the cooperation of the state legislature. And to get the legislators on board with the deal, Ranney needed a talented lobbyist. He chose Josephine.

Today, lobbying is the province of special interest groups, typically seeking to influence public bills by generating broad public pressure on lawmakers. Political lobbies tend to be large groups drawn along ideological lines and interested in bills with sweeping consequences; professional lobbyists make six-figure salaries and raise far, far more in support of bills. But as the historian Douglas Bowers has demonstrated, in the early nineteenth century lobbying tended to focus on small, private bills like Ranney's, with the lobbyist serving the interests of individuals rather than groups.[19] It wasn't a salaried position, either—prior to the 1830s, individuals often approached legislators directly to lobby for the passage of certain bills. The term *lobby agent* reflects this intimate history: it emerged from the image of the statehouse lobby, where businessmen and other influential citizens met personally with politicians to discuss the bills connected to their various enterprises.[20]

By the second quarter of the nineteenth century, however, the work of lobbying had passed into the hands of professional lobby agents, whose job, as Bowers explains, was to apply all the necessary social graces to shepherd a bill through the whole legislative process:

> Agents sought out legislators wherever they could be found—on the floor, in committee, on the street, or in their rooms at night—so they could use their persuasive skills most directly. To soften the suspicions surrounding interested parties, they sometimes held lavish dinners and welcomed members with free drinks in hotel rooms rented for the purpose.[21]

In general, the agents carrying out this work, which relied on an expert blend of social charisma and legal acuity, were men. Sometimes the agents who gathered in the lobbies and hotels of state capitals were retired lawmakers themselves, or lawyers interested in turning their professional knowledge to a different job. But, as Bowers writes, all the job really required was "political savvy, manipulative skill, and personal acquaintance with enough legislators to enable him to make an effective case." Women could possess those qualities as easily as men and might draw on a different and even expanded toolbox of manipulation tactics. Besides, it was the Jacksonian era: the age of anti-elitism and the celebration of democracy. Lobbying, the new culture said, was rightly the province of all Americans, not just those already in the elite circle of state legislatures. Buoyed by this spirit of democracy, lobbyists' power grew throughout the 1840s and 1850s—and so did corruption, as legislators began to realize that "money could be made on almost any bill that would financially benefit its backers."[22] In other words, the new lobbyists didn't always care about the bills they supported; they just wanted to get paid.

The lobbying profession of the early to mid-nineteenth century, Bowers writes, attracted "skilled manipulators bent on making quick money."[23] In the winters of 1856 and 1857, Josephine McCarty hoped to do just that. She spent both winters in Albany lobbying state representatives for the passage of a bill for the adoption of Johnson's philosophical charts in New York's public schools.[24] While there, she rented rooms at the Congress Hall and Delavan House hotels, both upscale haunts of local and state politicians. Rumors began to swirl—and maybe they were true—that Josephine's tactics of persuasion relied as heavily on the private hotel room as on the proverbial lobby.

Ranney promised her a massive fee—thousands of dollars—if the bill passed, but Josephine couldn't count on that money.[25] In between legislative sessions, she began carving out a third enterprise for herself:

a career as a physician. Selling Dr. Root's medical manual had likely given her the idea. In the mid-nineteenth century, earning a living by practicing medicine didn't require a medical degree—something Root made clear in the preface to *The People's Medical Lighthouse*. In fact, he proudly declared that he had "cut loose from the technicalities of medical schools, and from the professional jargon (entirely unintelligible to all general readers) behind which the ignorant in the science endeavor to hide their want of knowledge." Instead, "with an earnest desire to *understand* and *successfully pursue* the great science of medicine, and with ardent feelings of sympathy for the afflicted," he had "traveled over various parts of the country, visited numerous places where medical information is to be obtained, and attentively considered and candidly weighed all the prevailing systems and doctrines of medicine." The result was the *Medical Lighthouse*, stuffed with nearly five hundred pages of detailed medical advice and needing, Root believed, "no apology."[26]

In the mid-1850s, most medical schools wouldn't admit women. But just years before Josephine's return from Europe, a group of Quaker reformers in Philadelphia had established the nation's first degree-granting medical school exclusively for women.[27] Other medical colleges in the area allowed women to attend classes as nonmatriculated students. While selling Ranney's book in Philadelphia, Josephine started attending some of those lectures, in between trips back to New York to see her mother and visit the state legislature at the Delavan House.[28]

On one of her visits home, she brought up her new career plan: if the Ranney bill failed, she would become a doctor. Tom didn't approve. In fact, he hated the idea so much that he offered Josephine a thousand dollars to start a mercantile business instead—the same kind of cash infusion that gave so many of upstate New York's nineteenth-century businesswomen their start.[29] But Josephine turned him down. Maybe she balked at the prospect of being financially dependent on Tom; maybe she'd enjoyed her brief taste of medical school enough to want more. Either way, her mind was made up.

Tom wasn't discouraged. Still determined to maintain their relationship, as well as the financial dependence on which it had come to turn, he continued giving Josephine money. On one of his subsequent visits, he found an opportunity to leave a ten-dollar bill behind on the kitchen table. When Josephine asked if he had meant to leave the money or if he'd just forgotten it, Tom smiled.

"You'll need something for postage stamps," he said, and left it at that.[30]

In the end, the bill failed. A few years later, Ranney would be arrested for fraud.[31] But he didn't bring Josephine down with him. She'd already moved on—to the Female Medical College of Pennsylvania and the chaotic profession of medicine.

"From a relatively weak, traditional profession of minor economic significance," sociologist Paul Starr wrote in 1982, "medicine has become a sprawling system of hospitals, clinics, health plans, insurance companies, and myriad other organizations employing a vast labor force."[32] No such system existed when Josephine started medical school. Instead, "medicine" was a hodgepodge of different schools of thought, all fighting for the trust—and the money—of the American public. In that competitive chaos, women and outsiders like Josephine found a window of opportunity.

In colonial America, medicine was a part-time occupation, something that a clergyman, a teacher, a wigmaker, or a mayor might do on the side for a little extra money.[33] The United States had no organized medical schools until 1765. Instead, a young man (and it was practically always a man) who wanted to become a doctor would apprentice for a few years with a practicing physician, learning by observation and lecture. When his preceptor believed he was ready, he could begin advertising his services to patients immediately without passing any kind of licensing. But he couldn't expect to make his entire living off medical fees—in part because physicians weren't the only healers recognized in colonial America. Surgeons and apothecaries were the craftsmen and tradesmen whose work complemented that of doctors, while most of the routine healthcare that sustained Americans in between serious medical crises fell to midwives, folk healers and family members.

In other words, if you got sick in colonial America, you'd go to your wife, your mother, or your neighbor for help before calling a doctor. And with the growing popularity of home medical manuals like Dr. Root's, starting around 1769 with the publication of William Buchan's *Domestic Medicine*, taking care of the sick at home became even easier. American doctors, in the 1700s through the early 1800s, were neither essential workers nor established experts; they were a last resort to which many people, particularly in poor families or rural areas, might never actually turn.

That started to change around the middle of the eighteenth century. American students started traveling abroad to study in the medical schools of Britain and France, and they returned with two things:

first, a formal education based on standards agreed upon by the whole profession rather than the priorities of an individual preceptor; and second—and far more important—a sense of the social status that an organized medical profession could claim.

Seeking that status, American physicians began organizing schools and medical societies. The University of Pennsylvania opened the country's first medical school in 1765, and five years later physicians in New Jersey established the first medical society. The local medical societies that started springing up across the country quickly adopted lobbying as one of their most important roles. Newly banded together, physicians lobbied their state legislatures for licensing laws that would restrict the ability of untrained individuals to practice medicine. New York City passed the first of these laws in 1760, and many states followed.[34]

Of course, creating medical schools and professional associations couldn't prevent individuals without that elite training and membership from caring for friends, neighbors, and family—but it could prevent them from making money by doing so. In 1806, New York's state legislature passed a law prohibiting unlicensed practitioners from suing their clients for unpaid fees. Two decades later in 1827, at the urging of the state medical society, the legislature passed a new law making the unlicensed practice of medicine a misdemeanor, subject to a fine and imprisonment.[35]

Just like the abortion statute passed in New York two years later, this 1827 licensing law wasn't regularly enforced—and there's reason to believe that it wasn't intended to be. It was a symbolic bill more than a practical tool: the mere act of convincing the state legislature to pass a law upholding their professional standards gave a major boost to the authority of New York's organized physicians.

By the 1830s, thirteen state legislatures had passed licensing laws similar to New York's.[36] But the tide turned abruptly in the second quarter of the century. The physicians' professionalizing project ran up against an upsurge of negative public opinion, as Americans began to spurn intellectualism as a form of antidemocratic elitism. It wasn't just Enlightenment politics or a desire for democracy in the practice of medicine that turned the public against organized medicine. Many Americans also doubted the efficacy of professional physicians' remedies—and, to be fair, they had good reason.

The majority of the therapeutic measures taught in organized medical schools at this time were what scholars term *heroic medicine*: that is to say, they were dramatic treatments intended to produce dramatic effects on the body. Medical theory in this period tended to favor the idea that all disease could be explained by an imbalance of physical systems or forces.[37] One of doctors' go-to treatments was bloodletting, which they imagined could reduce fevers by relieving vascular tension or restoring the balance of the humors. Another was calomel, a mercury chloride mineral that doctors relied on as a laxative and a medication for just about any condition, even though the massive doses many physicians favored could cause mercury poisoning, making patients' teeth loosen and even fall out as their gums rotted. "Perhaps the most extraordinary aspect of the use of calomel," William Rothstein writes, "was that physicians recognized its side effects, and yet continued to give it in large doses."[38]

The vast majority of Americans in the early nineteenth century hadn't attended medical school, but they could see for themselves that heroic medicine wasn't working. Among the loudest critics of heroic doctors was Samuel Thomson, the son of a farmer in rural New Hampshire, who in 1805 invented a system of medicine that would most fully capture the notice of Americans suspicious of medical elitism. As a teenager, Thomson found a small flowering plant growing on his father's farm, and convinced a companion to eat it.[39] The man promptly began vomiting profusely—but after he recovered from his illness, he regained a healthy appetite and announced that he felt better than ever. The plant was *Lobelia inflata*, alternatively known as Indian tobacco or, more evocatively, "puke weed."

The medical possibilities of puke weed didn't present themselves immediately to Thomson. Only after watching his mother and wife suffer at the hands of professionally trained physicians did it occur to him that the little *Lobelia* plant he'd found on the farm might be a better medicine than anything that professional doctors had in their bags. Thomson observed the use of heroic measures by his mother's doctors with disapproval: "The doctors gave her over," he wrote in one autobiographical account, "and gave her disease the name of galloping consumption, which I thought was a very appropriate name; for they are the riders, and their whip is mercury, opium and vitriol, and they galloped her out of the world in about nine weeks."[40]

Thomson became convinced not only that the treatments prescribed by professional physicians were more harmful than they were effective but also that he and other untrained individuals could become better healers just by looking to nature. *Lobelia* became the foundation for the system of medicine he developed, which revolved around a course of treatments that alternated emetics, laxatives, cayenne pepper, and steam baths. Heat, Thomson argued, was life, and all illness was caused by an imbalance of heat. By purging the system and restoring its heat, any person could cure their illness far more effectively than a doctor wielding a scalpel or a bottle of blue calomel pills. In 1812, Thomson published his findings in a pamphlet that in 1822 was expanded and published as a book. Over the following decades, Samuel Thomson's *New Guide to Health: or, Botanic Family Physician, containing a Complete System of Practice, on a Plan Entirely New; with a Description of the Vegetables made use of, and Directions for Preparing and Administering Them, to Cure Disease, to which is Prefixed, a Narrative of the Life and Medical Discoveries of the Author* went through thirteen editions, including one translation into German.[41]

The popularity of Thomson's work might seem surprising. After all, treating a fever with a series of emetics, laxatives, and solutions of cayenne pepper doesn't sound remotely pleasant. But when the alternative was bloodletting to the point of unconsciousness or a calomel pill that might cause the same and worse, cayenne and puke weed appeared by comparison gentler, more natural, and in some cases more effective. Still, an important part of the appeal of Thomsonian medicine had nothing to do with what the treatment actually did to the body and everything to do with the politics of knowledge in the first half of the nineteenth century. At the core of Thomson's medical philosophy stood not *Lobelia* nor the equation of heat with health but an uncompromising blend of Jacksonian democracy and capitalism. Thomsonianism, as the movement inspired by his book was called, presented a radical challenge to the gatekeeping efforts of professional physicians. His vision for American health was, as sociologist Owen Whooley puts it, "nothing less than a system of medicine without doctors."[42] Available at a low price, easy to understand and to memorize, and transmitted through lectures and the social gatherings of his "Friend Botanical Society" as well as through printed text, Thomson's system of medicine promised to give ordinary Americans the same authority over illness that professional physicians were trying to claim through legislative means. No one needed to go to an expensive medical school to understand and cure illness; they didn't even need to be literate. Health was something to be purchased from Samuel Thomson and his 167 field agents, in the form of a book or a lecture ticket—and the price was cheap.[43]

Thomson wasn't the only maverick offering an alternative to the bleeding and purging of professional medicine. Among the numerous sects that gained popularity in the open market of ideas that was early nineteenth-century American medicine was homeopathy, a system created by the disgruntled German physician Samuel Hahnemann and transported to the United States in the 1820s by one of his students. Like Thomson, Hahnemann disapproved of the heroic treatments favored by professional physicians, but the homeopathic approach, based on the doctrine that "like cures like" and characterized by strongly diluted tonics, differed from Thomsonian medicine in a few crucial ways. For one thing, it was "a decidedly cosmopolitan medical system," based in urban centers in the Northeast; poor farmers like Samuel Thomson's family in New Hampshire weren't calling homeopathic physicians in the 1830s.[44] But that was another thing that distinguished the impact of homeopathy from that of Thomsonian medicine: it preserved the hierarchy of doctor and patient. An ordinary farmer couldn't become a homeopathic healer without attending a homeopathic medical school, the first of which was founded in Allentown, Pennsylvania, in 1836.[45] Homeopathy had its own medical societies, its own schools, and its own organizational structures, just like its counterpart—which the homeopaths called "allopathic" medicine.[46] Within a decade of the system's introduction in the 1820s, homeopathic practitioners were already posed to become "the most persistent and successful challengers to allopathy."[47] But the licensing laws passed in the first twenty years of the century remained in place: by law, allopathic physicians still retained the highest authority in the land to diagnose, cure, and teach about disease.

Then cholera hit.

Cholera was unlike anything else American doctors had ever seen. When it first appeared in the Five Points neighborhood in 1832, carried from Canada by an Irish immigrant named Fitzgerald, physicians had no idea how to treat it. The symptoms were as horrific as they were bizarre: copious watery diarrhea often described as "rice water" for its color and consistency; violent intestinal cramps and labored breathing; and finally, in the late stages of illness, a blue pallor over the face, earning the disease the name "blue death."[48] Cholera came on suddenly; it killed with disgusting violence; and then, perhaps most terrifying of all, it disappeared, only to pop up again months or years later. Unlike endemic diseases such as malaria or dysentery—the former so prevalent in the United States that, Rothstein writes, "it was regarded as a natural part of life"—cholera was an epidemic illness, coming and going in out-breaks that nobody could predict or control.[49]

Bloodletting didn't help. Neither did calomel, the allopaths' favor-ite remedy. Very little, in fact, could treat cholera effectively, although massive hydration, which is still the primary treatment method in the twenty-first century, had the best chance of offering relief, if not ensur-ing survival. And so it may not be surprising that, while allopathic doctors floundered in the face of cholera and published their con-sternation and confusion in their professional journals, homeopaths, and to a lesser extent Thomsonians, claimed a higher rate of success in treating cholera with diluted solutions and botanical remedies. The factual basis of those claims is somewhat questionable: certainly no medical sect in the mid-nineteenth century had a truly success-ful approach to cholera, and not until later in the century would the disease be securely linked to contaminated water.[50] But whether or not homeopaths and Thomsonians were actually more successful in curing cholera mattered a great deal less than the striking contrast between their confidence and the public failure of allopathic medicine to curb the recurring epidemics.

Within the first decade following the initial 1832 outbreak, all thir-teen states that had passed licensing laws in response to the spate of lobbying by medical societies had repealed them.[51] "By mid-century," the medical historian Regina Morantz-Sanchez writes, "dissatisfaction with established medical practice had reached astonishing propor-tions."[52] In response, a general health reform movement sprang up, teaching that men and women could and should be responsible for their own health, rather than depending on the elite physicians whose treatments were so often vicious and whose knowledge had proven catastrophically inadequate in response to cholera. Medicine, so long a part-time practice split between home and office, housewife and physi-cian, was changing. And instead of the elite, exclusive profession the allopaths wanted it to be, it was becoming a democratized business open to anyone able and willing to undertake a little bit of study. As home medical manuals flourished and patent medicines grew into a thriving industry, alternative medical schools opened across the coun-try, inviting Americans outside of the traditional medical elite to make a living in the profession of healing.[53]

Among those who jumped at this new opportunity were women. Women had long been involved in medical care, both as family members responsible for childcare and the treatment of household illness and as folk healers and midwives.[54] But although midwifery in particular "remained unquestionably women's work" throughout the colonial period, Regina Morantz-Sanchez writes that "women who practiced medicine in the colonies were never considered part of the medical profession."[55] Both their training and their practice took place within the context of the household and of female social networks, and women were de facto excluded from the professional organizations, educational institutions, and apprenticeship structures that defined allopathic medicine in early America.

In 1847, Geneva Medical College in the Finger Lakes region of New York became the first allopathic medical college to admit a woman as a medical student. Her name was Elizabeth Blackwell. She had already been rejected by multiple medical schools in Philadelphia by the time of her admission at Geneva. In fact, it was more or less an accident that she was even admitted to Geneva. The male student body voted to let her in as a practical joke on the school's administration, who had put her admission up to a vote in the first place as an attempt to avoid responsibility for the decision. But, joke or not, the result was the same: Blackwell completed the required two years of study at Geneva, and though the school quickly closed its doors to women after her graduation, the historic precedent was set. In 1849, Elizabeth Blackwell became the nation's first woman M.D.[56]

There was no going back. The year after Elizabeth Blackwell graduated, a collection of Quaker physicians and reformers led by Bartholomew Fussell, Joseph Longshore, and William Mullen rented space at the back of 229 Arch Street in Philadelphia to open the nation's first medical college exclusively for women.[57] The founders assembled a faculty of seven physicians willing to lecture to women, most of them recent graduates themselves.[58] The Female Medical College of Pennsylvania (FMCP) opened to students in Fall 1850, with Mullen, "an unlikely combination of watchmaker, dentist, businessman, philanthropist, women's rights advocate, and future prison reformer," as its first president.[59] Just five years later, Josephine Fagan—she was using her maiden name again—became a member of the FMCP class of 1857.[60]

The early years of the FMCP were marked by chaos as lecturers came and went, paying for supplies out of their own pockets, and the school's administrators struggled to pay the rent on the Arch Street space. Had its founders not viewed the FMCP as a reform effort rather than a revenue source, it would doubtless have failed. For one thing, finding faculty was difficult: "Few established male physicians," the institutional historian Steven J. Peitzman observes, would risk association "with the highly unorthodox undertaking of training women in medicine." In fact, the founders later discovered that one of the founding faculty members didn't have a medical degree at all. And trouble came from the outside as well: at the graduation of the FMCP's first class of eight women, police assembled in anticipation of violence from Philadelphians outraged by the project.[61]

Though no such violence broke out, the concern wasn't misplaced. Many Americans, particularly allopathic physicians, expressed serious doubts about the wisdom of allowing women to study medicine. Just like the female seminary students of previous generations, the majority of the FMCP's first students came from middle-class Northeastern Protestant families; all were white. In other words, they came from the same class as most male allopathic physicians, who had vested economic and personal interests in drawing boundaries between their careers and the lives of their wives, daughters, and sisters. The white middle-class ideology of gender came into play as a rejection of women's medical colleges: women, conservatives argued, were naturally pure and passive. Studying the human body—even observing dissections, as students at the FMCP did weekly—would "harden women's hearts and leave them bereft of softness and empathy."[62] If women became "hardened" at school and work, how could they perform the roles their husbands and children needed them to at home?

Such objections would keep the training clinics of Philadelphia hospitals closed to FMCP students for over a decade. Pennsylvania's state medical society would not admit FMCP graduates until 1871, and in 1860 passed a resolution banning members from consulting with either alumnae or faculty from the school.[63] Yet, despite these rebuffs from the organized profession, the FMCP's curriculum more or less followed the guidelines laid out by the allopathic American Medical Association at its founding in 1847: students were required to attend two terms of lectures, each starting in October and lasting between four and five months; the second term generally repeated the same lectures from the preceding year.[64] In addition to lectures, the FMCP required dissection, clinical training in the small dispensary attached to the school, and two years of supervision by a "respectable practitioner." After completion of the necessary lectures and clinical requirements, students wrote a short thesis, took an oral exam, paid a fee of twenty dollars, and, subject to a faculty vote, received their M.D.[65] Even for a single woman like Josephine, all a medical degree at FMCP required was a flexible job that paid enough to cover the cost of lecture tickets and that final graduation fee.

And in return for that investment of time and money, a career in medicine offered Josephine the prospect of steady pay better than what she could make in sales or teaching—but that might not have been her only motivation for choosing the FMCP. Many early women doctors, attending medical school in the wake of the 1848 women's rights convention at Seneca Falls, saw themselves, if not as feminists, then certainly as pioneers. As Regina Morantz-Sanchez writes, they "hoped to reform society by feminizing it." The women who first enrolled at the FMCP did so for a variety of reasons, but many early women doctors viewed their pursuit of the M.D. in essentially ideological terms, sincerely believing "that they had their own special contribution to make to society" that differed meaningfully from that of male doctors. After all, the critique of women's medical education as dangerous to "female modesty" went both ways: if modesty was under threat, "then why should men—even medical men—*ever* be allowed to treat women?"[66] The medical historian Thomas Bonner notes that "nearly all" of this first generation of woman doctors "were interested in problems of women's health," a topic that they believed male physicians incapable of fully understanding or treating appropriately.[67] A degree from a respectable school like FMCP, which adhered closely to the professional standards set and followed by allopathic medical men, gave a dose of professional authority to this feminist project.

But feminism wasn't the only reason for a woman to attend medical school in the 1850s. Morantz-Sanchez acknowledges that many women who went to medical school in the early years "even saw medical practice as a lucrative means of self-support."[68] Her use of the word *even* suggests that making money was less important, or less often important, to early female medical students, but it might have played a bigger role than we realize. Women who attended medical lectures in the 1850s often did so for immediate and mundane reasons. As Steven Peitzman observes, many women "simply wished to (and did) enter a profession and earn an independent living by practicing medicine."[69] After all, becoming a doctor required less starting capital (and less support from male relatives and partners) than opening a general store or a bookshop—and it could pay better.

One thing that suggests that profit was a more powerful motive for Josephine than feminist progress is the fact that she didn't just attend one medical school. In the four years she spent as an itinerant book agent, lobbyist, and medical student, Josephine went beyond the halls of the FMCP to sample the varied offerings of Philadelphia's medical schools. At the FMCP, where she attended lectures during the 1855–56 and 1857–58 terms, she received training in the allopathic theory and practice of medicine.[70] But she also spent three terms at the Penn Medical University, an eclectic school founded in 1853 by FMCP founder Joseph Longshore when he was kicked out of that institution because of his interest in occultism, mesmerism, and eclectic theories of medicine.[71] The Penn Medical University taught both men and women, though they studied in separate departments, and the Boston *Liberator* reported in 1857 that the Female Department, "in every respect equal to that of the Male, evinces a liberality . . . not to be found in most medical schools." The *Liberator* wrote that in addition to teaching "thoroughly and extensively the regular or prevailing practice"—in other words, allopathic medicine—the Penn school "also gives to every other system of the day a liberal appreciation; it rejects no newly discovered truth, because it may be identified with a proscribed dogma."[72]

Like Harmon Root, Josephine never graduated from medical school. By the spring of 1857, with courses at two different medical schools under her belt, she started giving public afternoon lectures on physiology to women in Philadelphia, something that many FMCP graduates did to supplement their income.[73]

But there was one step left to take before she could start making real money. In the spring of 1857, on her way home from Philadelphia to her mother's farm, Josephine stopped at Bagg's Hotel in Utica.[74] Tom came alone to meet her at the hotel, and while they talked, she mentioned to him an idea that had been on her mind for some time: she wanted a divorce from Robert.

CHAPTER 4

"A Woman's Remedy"

Divorcing Robert McCarty meant more to Josephine than emotional freedom. She'd tried being a teacher, then a wife and mother. Neither one had proved profitable, and the second had ended in tragedy. After three years of supporting herself through medical school, Josephine was now poised to begin a career in a lucrative and respectable profession. But Robert was a problem. He still held their marriage certificate, legally binding her to him even over thousands of miles of ocean. This wasn't just a frustrating technicality: through that certificate, Robert retained his legal right to her earnings. He knew where to find her; without a permanent residence elsewhere, Josephine still spent much of her time at Phebe's farm in Augusta. If Robert McCarty, struggling inventor, heard that his wife was making good money as a doctor in New York, he could easily return to the states to claim what was legally his.

Tom agreed that a divorce was "very desirable" and started to make some inquiries on her behalf to determine the best way to get a trans-atlantic divorce.[1] It was a complicated question. While the US had once followed England's common law precedent where divorce was concerned, the rules were changing as local legislatures grappled with complex questions about the role of marriage, the protection of vulnerable subjects, and the place of the family in American life.[2]

In England, Josephine had tried and failed to file for a divorce in London's ecclesiastical court. But in the United States, divorcing Robert was a real possibility. Had Josephine and Robert separated half a century earlier, the situation might have been more difficult. In the words of the feminist legal historian Norma Basch, the world of early America was "a virtually divorceless one," at least in legal terms. US divorce law, like abortion law, followed the English common law precedent, which effectively made divorce illegal for any but very wealthy, very patient men. On the other hand, extralegal forms of divorce, in which spouses simply separated and remarried either through mutual agreement or through desertion, were common.[3]

As the eighteenth century came to a close, however, the same Enlightenment ideals that reshaped Americans' thinking on childbearing led to a reevaluation of divorce law. As the North American colonies engineered their dramatic divorce from the British Empire, lawmakers grew sympathetic to divorce on the domestic level. Through what Basch calls "the easy interchangeability of family and state in Enlightenment thinking," state legislatures began revising common law, passing new statutes that allowed for fault divorce with a right to remarry.[4] These laws varied from state to state, but by the end of the eighteenth century, there was broad agreement in legislatures across the country that if one party in a marriage violated the terms of that contract, especially by committing adultery, the wronged spouse should have the right to end the marriage.

Josephine faced one major problem: New York was notoriously one of the strictest states on this subject. Its first divorce statute, passed in 1787, stressed that divorce should be avoided whenever possible; it guaranteed the right only in cases of adultery. While many women obtained divorces in New York on the grounds of adultery—so many, in fact, that by the mid-nineteenth century the state's printed divorce forms defaulted to "she" as the pronoun referring to the plaintiff, requiring clerks to cross out the "s" whenever a man filed for divorce—many others turned to the alternative of legal separation. Not only was legal separation much easier to obtain in New York, but Basch points out that separations actually "tended to provide women with far more favorable financial terms than a complete divorce." Legal separation protected a woman's earnings and property from her husband, and while adultery remained the sole grounds for complete divorce, women could point to a husband's cruelty or desertion as justification for a separation. Josephine would have no trouble proving that Robert had deserted her; his cruelty might be harder to demonstrate, but state courts were increasingly expanding the definition of cruelty to include "mental cruelty" in addition to physical abuse.[5]

Separation was cheaper, it was easier, it was quicker, but it had just one drawback: it didn't grant the plaintiff the right to remarry. Robert wasn't the only man who factored into Josephine's decision to end her marriage: there was also Tom, waiting in the wings with his regrets and his careful financial attentions. A divorce from Robert opened the door to a new potential future with Tom if he divorced his own wife—or if, under New York law, she divorced *him* for unfaithfulness.

Without material proof of Robert's infidelity, Josephine had no choice but to travel out of state to get a divorce—and in 1857, there was one place in the country where divorces were easier to get than anywhere else. That spring, she bought a ticket on the Ohio & Mississippi Railroad and boarded a train bound for Seymour, Indiana.

Why Indiana? "By some mistake or liberal design," the *History of Jackson County* states, "the early statute laws of Indiana on the subject of divorce were rather more loose than those of most other States in this Union."[6] Val Nolan, Jr., a legal scholar writing in the 1950s, argued that no combination of social and legal factors "can have been so peculiarly operative in Indiana as to account for its peculiar residence law," which permitted anyone to file for divorce, without the presence or knowledge of their spouse, simply by claiming to live in the state.[7] The burden of proof of residence on out-of-state applicants was so light as to be nonexistent, as reflected in a humorous account in *Putnam's Monthly Magazine* in 1858. It told the story of "one Billy Jones" who, determined to divorce the wife he'd married in Michigan, "started off on a tour of inquiry among the neighboring states. A day in Indiana and a brief inspection of its statutes, satisfied him that that was the state likely to be spoken of thereafter in the history of legal divorces. One night's lodging at the hotel made him a citizen of the state."[8]

Though it may have been the country's most famous "divorce mill" state, Indiana reflected broader regional trends in divorce law, which was most liberal in the states now known as the Midwest, with tighter restrictions in the Northeast and South. In the mid-nineteenth century, midwestern states like Indiana granted complete legal divorce on three grounds: adultery, desertion, and cruelty. By contrast, New York's adultery-only statute reflected the stricter model common in the Northeast; and in southern states like South Carolina, where widespread acceptance of the rape of enslaved women by married white men undermined traditional conceptions of sexual exclusivity in marriage, courts might be reluctant to accept even adultery as grounds for divorce.[9]

South Carolina's situation is a good reminder that divorce laws served different purposes from state to state—and that the evolution of divorce law across the United States was about more than just divorce. Increasingly, American lawmakers in the mid-1800s envisioned divorce as a "woman's remedy," a release valve designed to grant freedom to women trapped in marriages with unfaithful or violent husbands. In other words, legal divorce acted as a formal mechanism through which women could do what white men already did with ease—pick up and start a new life when the old one fell apart. As Basch points out, a growing national transportation network meant that, as the century progressed, "it became ever easier for *men* to find new companions and start all over again," the way Robert had in England.[10] For women, with greater childcare responsibilities, limited economic independence, and fewer legal protections, starting over was often simply not feasible. Many early feminists, including Elizabeth Cady Stanton, began to frame the right to divorce as a key part of the "woman movement."

Josephine's divorce from Robert leveled the legal playing field between her and Tom and allowed her to begin her career as a physician without fear that her selfish and violent ex-husband would swoop in to claim her earnings. Unfortunately, it wasn't quite as easy to get as the humorists for *Putnam's Monthly* would suggest. A night in a hotel wasn't enough to grant Josephine legal residence: according to her trial testimony, "a residence of six months in Indiana" was required for the divorce she eventually received in August 1857. Tom gave her a hundred dollars to cover her living expenses for the waiting period, and by the fall of 1857 she was able to return to her mother's farm.[11]

But she didn't marry Tom. Josephine was a free agent now; he was not. Unless he found out that his wife was having an affair, he had no legal grounds to divorce her. If he and Helen had reached a mutual agreement, she could have filed a suit on the grounds of *his* infidelity—which is exactly how many couples in the 1850s chose to amicably end their marriages, since the charge of adultery had far fewer social consequences for men. But Helen didn't divorce Tom after Josephine returned from Seymour, so we can safely assume that she didn't share her husband's interest in dissolving their union.

Of course, Tom could still have done what so many other men did: he could have simply left Helen and married Josephine somewhere else, where anonymity could protect them both from charges of bigamy.

But Tom had stakes in Utica. He was in business with his brothers; his career relied on a social network based in New York. Remarrying would have required him to abandon not just his wife but also his financial and social success. Far easier than legal or extralegal divorce was the option that Tom, and many other men in his position then and now, chose. Without divorcing Helen, he simply kept seeing Josephine.

At the same time that Josephine was navigating the country's complex divorce laws in order to begin her medical career, other American physicians were concerned with another set of laws bearing on marriage, family, and the rights of the husband: abortion laws.

Early calls for the restriction of abortion—like the public outcry that followed the death of Mary Rogers—were tied inextricably to fears of uncontrolled female sexuality: specifically unmarried women's sexuality. But the tenor of lobbying changed as the country inched toward civil war in the 1840s and 1850s. Physicians and moralists now voiced their concern that abortion posed a threat to marriage by enabling relationships like Josephine and Tom's to go undiscovered and unchecked.

Prior to the 1840s, abortion in the United States existed in two forms: in everyday life, as one of the oldest and most effective means of preventing childbirth; and in public discourse, as a marginal practice employed by single women with something to lose. Many of the women who visited Madame Restell's office in New York City fit into the former category. Their procedures were routine, minimally invasive, and private. Women in the second category, like Mary Rogers, often came before the public eye only in death. Whether or not Mary Rogers actually died as the result of a botched abortion was irrelevant to the anti-abortion crusaders who took up arms after her death. The suggestion alone allowed her story to function as a morality tale, warning against the dangers of unguarded female sexuality in a world where the reassuring network of family and community ties were being stretched to breaking point by urbanization and economic reorganization.

In the 1840s, however, opponents of abortion identified a new trend: increasingly, the majority of women seeking (and having) abortions in the United States were married, middle- or upper-class, and Protestant.[12] Many of them were already mothers, turning to abortion not as a desperate means of avoiding public censure but as an increasingly well-known family planning technique. What had once been either an unspoken practice or a plot point in a specific genre of morality tale now became, according to the historian James Mohr, "an obvious social reality," a booming business, and "one of the first specialties in American medical history."[13] Shifts in social life, along with the splintering and commercialization of the medical industry, were making abortion a less private affair. Instead of asking a neighbor, a family member, or a local midwife for advice on how to restore her menstrual cycle, a woman living in a city could now turn to any number of doctors, patent medicine salesmen, botanical physicians, homeopaths, or home medical manuals for abortifacients or other treatments.

Everywhere in the nation, ads for abortifacient medicines proliferated on newspaper pages, many of them naming their audience directly in giant block capitals: "MARRIED LADIES." Private clinics like the one Madame Restell ran on Greenwich Street opened in cities all over the country, promising sure results and discreet care—but women could also avail themselves of a range of products to administer at home without the more expensive and more public option of going to a clinic. Drugstores carried botanical pills and extracts of the same plants known by ancient and early modern women to produce abortions; tansy, rue, savin, and pennyroyal were among the most common and effective ingredients. But for women who discovered a pregnancy later in its course, they also sold instruments, such as douching syringes and uterine sounds, designed to help women end pregnancies at home.[14] A nationwide network of peddlers, book agents, and patent medicine salesmen distributed texts on reproductive control to women in both urban and rural environments. Above all, the postal system became a crucial means through which married women received both information about abortion and the materials to carry it out. In the early nineteenth century, middle-class white women took on the role of chief purchasers for their households—so we can conclude from the widespread and continued sale of all of these goods and services that women were indeed buying.[15]

For their husbands—that is, white middle-class men—the implications of the abortion industry's success could hardly have been more disastrous. The most basic value of reproductive control products, in the form of both birth control devices and abortifacients, was the ability to separate sex from reproduction. In many cases, then as now, men and women in companionate marriages employed these tools together, discussing their mutual needs and desires and planning reproductive control in a collaborative fashion. But in marriages where husband and wife did not see eye to eye on matters of reproductive control, the widespread availability of abortion materials meant that, in theory, a wife could end a pregnancy without her husband's knowledge, either in a female physician's private office or in her own home. That possibility threatened men's authority on two fronts. First, on the domestic level, the practice of abortion by married women raised the possibility of concealing adultery more effectively. A wife who could buy pennyroyal pills at the local drugstore was a wife who could, in theory, have an affair with the neighbor without fear of being betrayed by an unexpected pregnancy. As the business of abortion moved increasingly out of the private sphere and became a commercial enterprise, female physicians, druggists, and book agents selling *The Married Woman's Private Medical Companion* all took on the character of marital interlopers, conspiring with nice Protestant wives to deceive and ultimately cuckold their husbands.

But the threat of married women's abortions also extended beyond the home. Just as pre-Revolutionary Americans had celebrated the reproductive capacity of white women in the context of a colonizing project, some mid-nineteenth century Americans feared that the dereliction of white middle-class mothers from their reproductive duty would allow other groups—particularly Catholic immigrants and free and enslaved Black Americans—to overtake the birth rate of the white Protestant ruling class.[16] Reformers repeatedly contrasted the high rates of abortion among native-born Protestant women with the comparatively low rates of abortion among Catholic immigrants. And it wasn't just birth rates that mattered; the prevalence of abortion among white Protestants seemed to say something bad about their sexual mores. "All the voices in favor of marshaling the law to stop abortion," the historian Rickie Solinger writes, "implicitly or explicitly defined abortion as a crime against the chastity of white women."[17]

Nativist concerns about "race suicide" collided at mid-century with the professional concerns of a particular group of white, largely Protestant middle- and upper-class men: the allopathic physicians. Already concerned with demonstrating their value and authority to a skeptical public, organized physicians in the mid-1850s took up the cause of abortion to further establish themselves as both medical and moral experts. And there was probably no allopath more concerned with the restriction of abortion than a passionate Bostonian named Horatio Robinson Storer.

Horatio R. Storer was a man with a rich inheritance of upper-class Protestant anxieties. Born in 1830 to an elite Boston family, Horatio followed closely in the steps of his father, the natural scientist and physician David Humphreys Storer.[18] David Humphreys Storer had studied medicine under John Collins Warren, the first dean of Harvard Medical School, and his influence played repeatedly in his son's favor, allowing Horatio to enroll at Harvard at age sixteen and at Harvard Medical School at age twenty.[19] As chair of obstetrics and medical jurisprudence at the medical school in the mid-1850s, David Humphreys obtained a position for his son as one of three attending physicians at the Boston Lying-In Hospital in 1855.[20] At the lying-in hospital, Horatio had the opportunity to expand his knowledge of women's health—and to observe the social consequences of extramarital sex. During this period, Horatio learned the contours of a biological process that had been the subject of debate within medical science and philosophy for centuries: fetal development.

Today, the basics of fetal development are common knowledge: sperm meets egg; fertilized egg grows into an embryo; embryo becomes a fetus; at nine months, fetus becomes a baby. This simple chronology forms the bedrock of the "pro-life" movement against abortion, which argues that the just-formed embryo is the same thing, philosophically speaking, as the baby born nine months later—and that destruction of that entity at any point in the developmental process constitutes murder. This articulation of fetal rights, however, depends on medical knowledge uncovered in the mid-nineteenth century through an intricate process of research and debate. Ancient scholars like Hippocrates and Aristotle, when attempting to describe the reproductive process, imagined the fetus as a product of the combination of seminal fluid and menstrual blood. Aristotle, within this framework, argued that fetal development was a gradual process characterized not just by growth but also by change: he believed that the "embryon" created by semen and blood took forty days to become a fully-formed male fetus, and ninety to become a female fetus.[21] In this construction, the question of when life begins might have more than one answer; certainly, Aristotle's theory left room for the idea that the thing that would become a baby was not, in the early stages of pregnancy, simply a smaller, equally human version of the ultimate product. The concept of quickening, which underpinned early American understandings of pregnancy and early anti-abortion legislation, largely agreed with this Aristotelian theory of fetal development.

By contrast, the school of preformationism, which gained popularity in the eighteenth century, argued that the development of the fetus was only a process of growth. William Harvey, in the mid-seventeenth century, had demonstrated that eggs and sperm, not blood and semen, came together to create embryos; preformationists argued that these embryos already existed, "pre-formed," inside the sperm, waiting to grow to their full size in the womb. The development of cell theory in the 1830s and the identification of the mammalian egg cell in 1827 allowed critics of preformationism to advance the account of conception we know today: a single sperm cell and a single egg cell combining to create something new, which develops over time into a fully-formed fetus.[22]

By the 1850s, most allopathic physicians in the United States agreed on these basic facts, which put them in a complicated position. As more and more women turned to their doctors for assistance in restoring their menstrual cycles prior to quickening, doctors' knowledge increasingly taught them that quickening was, in fact, medically meaningless. According to the allopaths' new understanding of fetal development, a woman who took tansy or savin to treat her amenorrhea was not treating a disease state, but actually destroying an embryo that would, if left untouched, eventually develop into a fetus and then into a living child. As the field of embryology matured in the nineteenth century, physicians had to confront a fairly chilling philosophical proposition: that abortion, despite its long history, was actually tantamount to murder. If that was the case, it would mean that American physicians were murdering their own on a daily basis.

One of the first physicians to call for action was David Humphreys Storer, Horatio's father. In a lecture at the Massachusetts Medical College in November 1855, he warned his audience that the "recent sharp increase in uterine disease" was "the result of a similar increase in the frequency of criminal abortion." He had hoped that "some one of the strong men of the profession . . . would have spoken, trumpet-tongued, against an existing, and universally acknowledged evil." But, he continued, "I have waited in vain. The lecturer is silent, the press is silent, and the enormity, unrebuked, stalks at midday throughout the length and breadth of the land. It is time that this silence should be broken. It is time that men should speak."[23]

And not just any men—doctors. Of all the men in the country, David Storer believed that "no one can exert a greater influence than the physician." No one else, he argued, had had a greater opportunity to "witness the misery, to see the distress which is acknowledged by the sufferer to have been thus produced, to hear the disclosures as they reluctantly fall from the lips of the dying penitent." Armed with that burden of knowledge, and with "the affections of the community," Horatio's father told his audience, "We can do much—we can do all."[24]

In calling for a physicians' crusade against abortion, David Humphreys extended the existing allopathic effort to shore up professional authority into the realm of American morality, suggesting that medical men's scientific knowledge could place them, as Janet Farrell Brodie puts it, "in the forefront of a movement to restore morals."[25] Advocating for the criminalization of abortion would accomplish the goals of middle-class Protestant medical men on a number of scores. By preventing the separation of sex and reproduction, laws against abortion would defend their sexual authority within their marriages. By increasing, or at least stabilizing, the white Protestant birth rate, it would fortify their political and economic supremacy. And by creating legal restrictions on the practices of "irregular" practitioners and medical entrepreneurs, it would reduce competition for their business and ensure that their jobs and clients went not to midwives, female physicians, or any other "irregular" practitioner who provided abortion care, but to men from their own class.

Of course, not all of these motives were conscious—and not every doctor who opposed abortion in the mid-nineteenth century acted on the same principles. For some, stamping out competition was the primary goal; others took the charge of "intra-uterine murder" seriously based on new theories of fetal development.[26] For others still, the goal of restricting medical practice to "the right class of people" reigned supreme. Indeed, part of the reason that so many physicians rallied to the anti-abortion cause was because it pushed so many different buttons. Marriage, male authority, sexual ethics, the protection of the unborn, and profit: all these concerns, separately and in combination, motivated the medical men who joined the fight against abortion.

For Horatio Storer, the man who would become probably the single most vocal opponent of abortion in the United States by the time of the Civil War, there was another probable motivating factor that had nothing to do with sex, marriage, or professional authority. It's difficult to look at Horatio Storer's career, which followed so closely the cues set by David Humphreys Storer, without seeing in it a son's impulse to make his father proud. Within months of David Humphreys's call for a "trumpet-tongued" doctor to champion the anti-abortion cause, Horatio began corresponding with a Boston lawyer to learn everything he could about the nation's laws on the subject of abortion. In February 1857, he made a presentation on the subject to the monthly meeting

of the Suffolk District Medical Society and proposed the formation
of a committee to investigate the need for further legislation "and to
report to the Society such other means as may seem necessary for the
suppression of this abominable, unnatural, and yet common crime."[27]
Three months later, he submitted a report to the society in which he
argued that abortion was "clearly MURDER" and, what was worse, it
was no longer confined to poor, unmarried women with "the excuse of
shame."[28]

Although the proposal and report both met with some controversy,
Horatio found more supporters than detractors in Boston's medical
circles. But the scope of Horatio's ambition extended beyond the Massachusetts legislature: he hoped to launch a nationwide campaign for
new anti-abortion laws. "Between March 20, and April 6, 1857," Storer's biographer Frederick Dyer writes, "Horatio received letters from
physicians in twenty states and territories providing information on
their laws related to criminal abortion."[29] At the national meeting of
the American Medical Association in Nashville in May 1857, he helped
to oversee the formation of a Committee on Criminal Abortion, tasked
with researching the extent of the crisis and drafting new statute recommendations to be sent to state legislatures. As women and men
continued to grapple with heavy questions about their sexual and
reproductive experiences in divorce courts and bedrooms and doctors'
offices across the country, Horatio Robinson Storer had succeeded in
bringing the allopathic medical men's most powerful organization into
the national debate on behalf of the fetus.

The physician's war on abortion was underway as Josephine wrapped
up her medical education, but she had not yet entered that particular
battlefield. Before she could practice as a physician, she needed more experience. As Horatio Storer and his colleagues began a furious program
of letter-writing and legal research, Josephine traveled back across the
Ohio River Valley to Phebe's farm in Augusta. After a brief reunion with
Tom, still married to Helen and with no apparent prospects of release,
she went south to Philadelphia, where she spent the winter attending
lectures at Penn Medical University, preparing notes for a second series
of afternoon lectures on "physiology" to women in Pennsylvania.[30]

Josephine's physiology lectures were probably more than just a source
of medical curiosity. Although the word "physiology" could carry a
range of meanings, in the 1850s it often functioned as coded language
applied to practices of reproductive control. According to Janet Farrell

Brodie, public lectures on physiology were yet another way—along with mailers, newspapers advertisements, and home medical manuals—that American women learned about birth control in the mid-nineteenth century. Some physiology lecturers stuck to a broad overview of the functions of the reproductive system, offering their listeners a basic theoretical understanding of the topic without any practical specifics. But other lectures went more in-depth, furnishing their audiences with explicit tips to prevent and end pregnancies. In so doing, both types of lecturer "legitimized ideas about fertility regulation and spread physiological and anatomical information that would facilitate contraceptive practices."[31]

If she was, indeed, lecturing on reproductive control to middle-class wives in the City of Brotherly Love, Josephine was beginning to embody medical men's worst nightmares in more ways than one. Not only was she providing the women of Philadelphia with information they could use to conceal and terminate pregnancies, but she was engaged in an extramarital affair of her own.

According to Josephine, her relationship with Tom between her return from England and her divorce was entirely platonic. They went on long rides through the countryside and talked for hours about his regrets that he'd married someone else; he gave her money; they exchanged letters. But that was all—there was no sexual element to their relationship, she claimed, until after her legal ties to Robert were severed. Whether or not this was true is a toss-up. On the one hand, she had plenty of reasons not to have sex with Tom, from personal scruples to the social stigma applied to women (not men) who broke their marriage vows. And on the other, she had plenty of motivation to lie about when they became more than friends.

Here's Josephine's version of the story.

In the spring of 1858, while staying on her mother's farm, Josephine took a trip to Oswego, a town about seventy-five miles northwest of Augusta on the banks of Lake Ontario. The reason for the visit is unclear. Oswego has never been a major tourist destination, but among its draws in the 1850s was a water cure establishment following the principles of the alternative medical school of hydropathy.[32] Maybe Josephine had encountered the water cure in her classes at Penn Medical University and wanted to see it for herself. Whatever her interest in Oswego, Tom accompanied her on the trip, and the two spent five days there together. Then, on their return journey, a mistake in the train schedule left them stranded for the night in Syracuse, midway between

Oswego and Utica. Tom suggested that they get rooms at the Globe Hotel. Josephine agreed, taking a parlor bedroom while Tom rented a separate suite for himself.

Then, as night fell, Tom appeared at Josephine's door with a bottle of wine in his hand. "I was not then accustomed to drinking wine," she later remembered, but when Tom poured her a glass and toasted to her health, she drank it. They split the bottle between them, and Tom spent the night in her bedroom. According to Josephine, it was then, and only then, that she and Tom slept together for the first time. "He had never lodged with me before," she claimed, but now "he said that I was his wife and that he had loved me so long." Recounting this story in tears from the witness stand years later, Josephine recalled, "He said he would be all to me that a husband could be."[33]

But nothing came of Tom's professions. The following morning, they returned to Utica; Tom went home to Helen, Josephine went home to her mother, and their relationship continued as it had begun: an illicit romance conducted mainly through correspondence and financial loans.

From a twenty-first century perspective, Josephine's story raises some troubling possibilities. The setup is obviously sketchy: a wealthy man and a divorced woman go to a hotel; he gets her drunk; sex ensues. Josephine made a point of mentioning that she wasn't used to drinking alcohol—was she sober enough to consent to sex? Depending on the details, you might call it coercion or date rape.

Recognizing those troubling contours in Josephine's narrative isn't wrong, but it is anachronistic. Josephine's story *is* troubling—maybe even intentionally so—but it doesn't fit nineteenth-century definitions of sexual assault. At the start of the nineteenth century, US law recognized only one major form of sexual assault: forcible (that is, violent) rape. A woman who came to court accusing a man of sexual assault would have to prove both that he had penetrated her and that she had resisted to the full extent of her ability.[34] Being able to show the physical marks of violence on her body would enhance the likelihood of a conviction. Some states required accusers to produce multiple witnesses to the rape. Moreover, courts expected women who accused men of rape to be able to prove their own sexual purity, leading to the extensive use of character witnesses to establish the defendant's trustworthiness (and, maybe, the extent to which she deserved the law's protection).[35]

These high standards of evidence served to protect what Estelle B. Freedman, in her history of sexual assault in the United States, calls "white men's sexual privileges." As a result, not only did comparatively few women even charge their attackers in court, but even fewer—just under one third—actually won their cases. Overwhelmingly, those women who did succeed in rape cases were middle-class white women, and the men convicted were non-white, especially Black and Indian, or, less often, poor white itinerants.[36]

Within this framework, what happened between Tom and Josephine at the Globe Hotel was not sexual assault in any sense: there was no violence, no proof of resistance, and no witness. But as the early decades of the nineteenth century saw a surge of moral reform movements that addressed the inequality of gendered life in America, white women "sought legal remedies to make it easier to prosecute coercive but non-violent sexual relations with acquaintances."[37]

The primary remedy that reformers fought for was the passage of laws to punish the crime of seduction. Today, "seduction" refers generally to sexual enticement; it carries a connotation of manipulation, but not necessarily of unwelcome or criminal behavior. By contrast, in the nineteenth-century United States, the legal concept of seduction referred to cases where men "enticed women to consent to premarital sex on the false promise of marriage or by using other duplicitous means, such as a drugged drink."[38] It was close, but not identical, to the modern concept of "date rape." In practical terms, the category of seduction offered white women a legal framework for dealing with cases of sexual coercion or manipulation that didn't fit neatly into the narrow definition of rape codified by state laws.

In particular, reformers worried about the consequences of extramarital sex when the man refused, or possibly never intended, to marry the woman afterwards. In earlier generations, when economic production was mainly based in the household, local social networks created more pressure on men to marry the women they slept with and provided more support for those women who might have had premarital sex without afterwards getting married. But as more and more women, like Mary Rogers and Josephine Fagan, moved out of small towns and into cities, responsibility for women's sexual purity passed increasingly from the community to the individual. "Chastity," Freedman writes, "became a survival strategy for those women who embraced middle-class ideals, seduction a threat to maintaining it."[39]

In 1834, acting on concerns similar to those that drove physicians to organize against abortion in the 1850s, anxious New Yorkers formed a "Female Moral Reform Society" dedicated to raising awareness of the crime of seduction and to caring for pregnant single women to prevent their exploitation by the sex trade.[40] Similar societies sprang up nationwide, pushing state legislatures to pass laws for the prosecution of men who seduced and abandoned women, as well as those who coerced women into sex through non-violent means.

And when anti-seduction laws failed, unwritten laws often came into play: women, their fathers, and their brothers all found themselves favored by juries when they killed seducers who had abandoned them or their family members.[41] As in the case of divorce, Americans dealt with sexual violence by midcentury through a patchwork of legal and extralegal measures that differed based on the place, the nature of the harm, and the social status of the parties involved.

The justice afforded by anti-seduction statutes and unwritten laws, however, was available on a limited basis. The average conviction rate in seduction cases hovered around 16 percent—twice as high as that for forcible rape cases, but still tellingly low. And those convictions went overwhelmingly to a specific type of victim. Seduction was imagined as a crime against white women, especially young, chaste white women from an upwardly mobile middle class. Women who accused men of seduction were still required to prove their own purity of character in court, and they were rarely the ones to actually bring suit against seducers: that role went to the fathers whose daughters had been impregnated and abandoned. Not until the late nineteenth century would states begin to redefine the injured party as the woman rather than her father. In this sense, the legal tool of seduction existed not to protect women against sexual exploitation and violence from acquaintances but to reinforce patriarchal authority: it was, as Freedman puts it, "a remedy that flowed from a framework of inequality."[42]

Within the framework of inequality governing seduction laws, Josephine occupied an ambiguous position. She was white, and her financial success and education placed her in an upwardly mobile middle class, but she wasn't quite the innocent victim that anti-seduction laws existed to protect; she had already been married once. Josephine's father and stepfather had both died years ago, and she was newly divorced; Tom's seduction hadn't really threatened any men's rights to her. Perhaps more important, Tom, a white business owner, was not the kind of man whose sexuality such laws existed to punish. Had she wanted to pursue a legal remedy for Tom's behavior in 1858, Josephine would likely have failed.

But whether or not she wanted a legal remedy is a bigger question. While Josephine's account of the night at the hotel hits some undeniably troubling notes—from a twenty-first-century perspective as well as a nineteenth-century one—it's almost too neatly constructed. In fact, one of the most striking features of her story, told to a jury at her murder trial years later, is how closely it echoes Part 4, Chapter 1, Title 2, Article 2, section 23 of the 1830 New York Criminal Code:

> Every person who shall have carnal knowledge of any woman Knowing above the age of ten years, without her consent, by administering to her any substance or liquid, which shall produce such stupor, or such imbecility of mind or weakness of body, as to prevent effectual resistance, shall, upon conviction, be punished by imprisonment in a state prison, not exceeding five years.[43]

Josephine may have invented the story of her and Tom's night at the Globe Hotel to sway the sympathies of a jury years after the fact. If she'd had consensual sex with Tom before her divorce, it would make her as culpable of adultery as him. But if he'd seduced her only after her divorce and with the aid of alcohol, she came out on top as the victim of his manipulative tactics.

Ironically, what this episode suggests about Josephine is her own talent for manipulation, a talent she would soon put to good use to make the difficult jump from the lecture hall to the hospital operating room. Making that jump as a woman in 1858 was extremely difficult. At its founding in 1847, the AMA had agreed upon a set of guidelines for medical schools. According to these guidelines, every doctor should have at least three years of study with a faculty of at least seven physicians before starting to practice—and those three years of study should include dissection experience and clinical training. While the FCMP ticked the other boxes on the list, getting clinical and dissection experience for graduates was an uphill battle in the early years. When Josephine attended, finding an operating room in Philadelphia willing to let in female students—let alone a formal clinical post—was nearly impossible. "If women were somehow able to enter a medical school," historian Thomas Bonner writes, "the hospitals were closed to them; if hospital experience was permitted, then internship opportunities were denied; and later, in many places, they would be virtually banned from consulting with experienced male practitioners."[44]

Over the years, steady advocacy by FCMP deans would grind down resistance to women's clinical training, but Josephine was never one to wait for the gears of change to turn. Instead, once she'd had her fill of classroom instruction, she headed for Philadelphia's most chaotic hospital, determined to inveigle herself into a clinical position by any means necessary.

CHAPTER 5

"I Went There to Perfect Myself"

In the summer of 1858, a newly divorced Josephine Fagan McCarty returned to Philadelphia. Like most female medical school graduates, she faced the overwhelming challenge of finding hands-on clinical experience.[1] But she hadn't technically graduated from the FCMP—she never paid her twenty-dollar graduation fee or wrote a final thesis. Without a diploma, Josephine was at a further disadvantage. To get experience in hands-on patient care, she would need to find an institution as desperate for her services as she was for training—somewhere where administrators were willing to overlook some formalities and take on people whom other hospitals would turn away.

Shortly after arriving in the city, Josephine took a ferry ride across the Schuykill River from Philadelphia's city center, where four tall brick buildings surrounded by a high board fence stood on a hill overlooking the river. The complex, built in the 1830s, was home to Philadelphia's public almshouse: a sprawling institution that was at once workhouse, hospital, jail, and asylum.[2] The people of Philadelphia called it Blockley Hospital. "I went there," Josephine later said, "to perfect myself."[3]

Blockley Hospital was not the kind of hospital that exists today.[4] Today, hospitals are the places we go for major medical procedures, for emergency care, and for long-term treatment. They are, more often than not, the places where we expect to die. Most Americans in the twenty-first century will go to the hospital at some point in their lives, whether for an ER visit or an extended stay. Not so in the 1800s. "Most Americans in 1800," medical historian Charles Rosenberg writes, "had probably heard that such things as hospitals existed, but only a minority would have ever had occasion to see one."[5] That minority was decidedly unlucky. Those who could afford to do so sought professional medical care at home when serious illness or injury struck. Before the development of specialized medical technology that required a centralized space for healing, doctors could provide the same treatments in the comfort of a private home that were available elsewhere.

But what about those who couldn't afford a private home visit—or, even worse, those who had no home to call a doctor to? Illness, old age, and disability among the poor and indigent posed a serious problem for the medical establishment and for city governments—a problem addressed by the institution of the almshouse. "By the first decades of the nineteenth century," Rosenberg writes, "every American city had established an almshouse; the larger the city, the greater the number of rootless and dependent who were its natural clients."[6] Almshouses combined multiple functions: theoretically a shelter for those with nowhere else to go, by the late eighteenth century they operated essentially as a combination of municipal hospital and city jail.

Established in the 1730s, Philadelphia's almshouse comprised three main components—a workhouse for the employment of vagrants, a jail for the incarceration of people arrested on minor charges such as prostitution or drunkenness, and an almshouse which functioned as a hospital for those without family or money to care for themselves.[7] The hospital section of the almshouse grew steadily, adding a lying-in department for pregnant women in the late eighteenth century and an insane department not long after.[8] After the 1830s, when the Philadelphia almshouse outgrew its earlier quarters on Spruce and Pine Streets and moved to the meadows above the Schuylkill, Philadelphians knew it best by the name "Blockley Hospital."[9]

The almshouse coupled medical care with the punishment and reformation of a variety of social and moral transgressions, and the exploitation of cheap labor. Although Blockley also had a jail, the hospital section housed some patients who, in the words of Charles Rosenberg, "occupied a gray area between that of the legitimately (morally neutral) sick and that occupied by the culpable offender." Alcoholics, for instance, made up a large portion of the patient population, and the women's venereal wards treated primarily sex workers. Such patients, Charles Rosenberg writes, along with the Black and the elderly, also seen as suspect, "fared particularly badly even in an institutional context in which no one fared particularly well." For women, the punitive function of the almshouse was reflected in housing and treatment strategies. Policies such as giving female venereal patients blue sheets instead of white and dividing the ward based on patients' perceived willingness to reform baked the reformatory impulse into treatment methods for patients deemed morally compromised.[10]

But another approach to moral rehabilitation involved putting inmates—including women—to work. "Women," the historian Monique Bourque writes, "were a particularly problematic category of relief recipient, both because they were potential mothers of more paupers, and because they were considered especially vulnerable to the moral ill effects of institutional life." In part to combat the potential damage to women's character from their stay in the almshouse, and in part to harness the value of their labor, Blockley administrators put female inmates to work at everything from mending clothes, cooking, and manufacturing textiles to caring for the sick and assisting with routine births. "Labor," Bourque explains, "became an important component of the 'cure'" for poor or criminal women.[11]

The women of Blockley, who made up a majority of the institution's workforce by the 1850s, did not always accept their exploitation without question. Rather than engaging in organized resistance, however, women employed at Blockley pushed back in small, individual ways: for instance, "leaving the institution without permission, drunkenness, and appropriating goods for their own use."[12] An example of such small-scale resistance comes from Charles Lawrence's 1905 *History of the Philadelphia Almshouses and Hospitals*, which recalls the case of a "Nurse Welsh," who left her duties abruptly on August 15, 1848, came back the following Monday to attend a labor and pick up her paycheck, and then left again, taking with her a large number of flatirons and bedclothes. Theft was, apparently, Nurse Welsh's way of reclaiming some of the value taken from her by the almshouse, and to many it seemed to also reflect administrators' worst fears of the effects of almshouse life on women's morals. "To show the character of Nurse Welsh," Lawrence concluded the story, "it need only be said that she was afterwards sent to the Penitentiary for throwing vitriol in a young man's face and destroying his sight."[13]

Nurse Welsh, it turned out, didn't act alone. An investigation into the matter revealed that a member of the almshouse board of guardians,

Mr. William Abbott, had assisted her in absconding from the premises with her stolen goods.[14] But rather than pursue punishment against either Nurse Welsh or Mr. Abbott, the board let the matter drop.

It wasn't the first time the Blockley board had turned a blind eye to wrongdoing by its members. Just three years prior to the Welsh-Abbott scandal, the board of guardians had declined to take action against local medical students' practice of stealing bodies from Blockley's graveyard to dissect in their lectures. "If the supply from the Almshouse was cut off," board members argued, "the bodies would be stolen from the cemeteries"; far better "that those who died without friends or relatives to mourn for them should go to the dissecting rooms than that the doctors should have the graves, in which so many living persons felt an affectionate interest, *robbed of their contents.*" Sometimes the corruption was more blatant: in 1856, rumors suggested that board members had used almshouse funds to host private banquets and purchase cigars and brandy.[15] Similar episodes of corruption, embezzlement, and theft by the board and their associates tarnished the almshouse's reputation; by the 1850s, the administrators of Blockley Hospital were popularly known as the "board of buzzards."[16]

But for all its problems, Blockley Hospital offered bright promise to one group of people in particular: medical students. Although it was a less desirable posting than a job at a private hospital or a personal practice, Blockley provided a solid training ground for young physicians. What it lacked in social status and a pleasant environment, Blockley made up for with the "sheer volume of clinical material" it presented to such trainees—including, yes, the corpses that the board allowed students to dig up for dissection.[17]

In the 1850s, Blockley's administrators were still resistant to making that clinical material available to women. The almshouse would not open its clinics to female medical students until 1868, and the private classes offered by the hospital remained closed to women until 1878.[18] But the administrators' opposition to women wasn't monolithic. In 1851, when the medical graduate Sarah Adamson applied for "such a situation in the Blockley Hospital as will afford me the opportunity of seeing its practice," the board agreed, making her the nation's first woman intern.[19]

Unlike Sarah Adamson, Josephine wasn't hired as a doctor. Adamson had succeeded in her application thanks to the sponsorship of two male physicians; Josephine, by contrast, didn't even have a medical degree. In fact, it's possible that she made her way to an appointment in the hospital's insane department by entering the almshouse at first as an inmate. It's not clear exactly when or how she came to Blockley: by her own account, she spent the entire summer of 1858 there, but hospital officials later reported that she wasn't assigned to the insane ward until that September.[20] Maybe she was in a different position at first—or maybe Josephine, recognizing her lack of credentials, took advantage of the porous distinction between inmate and staff in an institution defined by its opportunistic exploitation of poor women's labor and voluntarily got herself admitted to Blockley in hopes of moving up the ranks.

Whatever the circumstances of her arrival at Blockley, her stay was relatively short, and ended in scandal. In January 1859, an article appeared in Philadelphia's daily *Dollar Newspaper*, headed "Almshouse Disclosures."[21]

> It appears that some two or three months ago, a young woman, named Josephine Fagan, was introduced into the institution for the purpose of receiving medical instruction. The woman being of prepossessing manners and appearance, attracted the notice of the Guardians, and she was appointed to the position of night nurse. She had not held the situation long before some of the Guardians considered it necessary, for the welfare of the institution, that it should be abolished.

According to the article, "Mrs. Fagan" had left Blockley with "an unusual quantity of bundles, trunks and band-boxes, containing a large amount of wearing apparel and other articles." When her landlady, a Mrs. Bunker, suspected that "her boarder had not come honestly by the goods," she told a friend, who reported Josephine to the board of guardians, who procured a search warrant.[22] Upon searching Josephine's room at Mrs. Bunker's house, the police found an assortment of goods, including undergarments, nightgowns, buckets, a clock, "a foot stool in the shape of a big pumpkin," and several anatomical charts engraved on steel plates.[23] On the evening of January 21, Josephine was arrested on charges of larceny, the alleged stolen goods seized, and a hearing convened at the office of the alderman James Freeman.

The proceedings at the alderman's office were well-attended. On top of the usual whiff of corruption that surrounded Blockley's operations, this incident had its own flavor of scandal. "As everybody knows who is familiar with the business of the Guardians," the *Daily Pennsylvanian* reported, Josephine "had been allowed special privileges at the Almshouse by the Chief Resident Physician for a period of some months," including "that of being present at the medical operations that took place in the lecture room." When the board finally forbade her attendance, the paper explained, "Mrs. Fagen [*sic*] was accommodated with a position in a room adjoining, a hole being cut in the door for her express accommodation, through which she could observe anything without obstruction."[24]

Eventually, this arrangement also fell through. Josephine had been dismissed, going to board with Mrs. Bunker, whose house the *Pennsylvanian* called "a peculiar institution of modern times." There, living under the name of Mrs. Thomas, she "had a gentleman friend who had access to her room at all hours." Although she initially introduced him as her husband, she later said that his real name was Dr. Preston. Mrs. Bunker later learned, however, "that instead of being 'Dr. Preston,' the friend in question was Dr. Smith, Chief Resident Physician at Blockley Almshouse."[25]

The story of Josephine's clandestine clinical training, intertwined with and enabled by a clandestine love affair with the chief resident of the hospital she worked at, drew public attention. So did the accused herself, whom the *Daily Pennsylvanian* described as "a woman of considerable attractiveness, [who] is said by those who know her, to possess cultivation of no ordinary character." In particular, the paper noted, "with some members of the Board of Guardians, she appears to be a great favorite." One board member, Mr. Kames, bet the *Pennsylvanian*'s reporter a cool hundred dollars that Josephine would prove that all of the property had been given to her as a present by Dr. Smith. "It is a fair inference," the reporter wrote, "that his wager was offered upon a certainty."

The bet would have to wait: rather than deciding the case on the spot, Freeman held Josephine to five hundred dollars bail and sent her to jail to await trial. Within days of her arrest, Josephine had secured legal representation from Frederick Carroll Brewster, the illegitimate son of the Philadelphia attorney and Mayflower descendant Francis Enoch Brewster and the future attorney general of Pennsylvania.[26] Josephine had chosen her attorney well: Brewster was known for "unceasing toil and indomitable energy," perhaps as a result of having to work twice as hard to rise above the circumstances of his birth. "During his career," according to one 1899 memorial, "he managed cases with an application and careful study that rarely failed to secure his purpose."[27] Upon taking Josephine's case, Brewster promptly filed a writ of habeas corpus and paid his client's bail. In mid-February, the "fascinating Mrs. Fagan" walked free to await trial.[28]

While Josephine waited, the Blockley board of guardians launched an investigation of Dr. Robert K. Smith. Smith was not, by all accounts, particularly popular among his Blockley colleagues. He had been briefly elected to the position of chief physician once before, in 1855, but didn't stay in the position long due to controversy surrounding his election.[29] "Whatever may have been the abilities of Dr. Smith," writes the Blockley historian J. W. Croskey, "he seems to have been a man of such temperament as to make himself disliked by a large number of those with whom he was brought in contact."[30] At a meeting on March 15, 1859, Smith himself reported on the progress of the investigation into his misconduct, saying that "nothing had been elicited" of any importance.[31] Josephine had been summoned to appear before the investigating committee, but refused to attend or to testify without the presence of her lawyer. "She says," the guardians' report in the Philadelphia *Press* stated, "she considered the Guardians her enemies."[32]

With the lines thus drawn between her and the board of guardians, Josephine came to trial in early April in the Court of Quarter Sessions. "The court room was filled to overflowing at an early hour," the *Philadelphia Inquirer* reported, "while many persons heaving sighs of disappointment . . . contented themselves with leaning against the wall outside the Court room, enjoying the pleasant sunshine."[33] For a minor larceny case, Josephine's trial had certainly attracted a lot of public interest.

The first witness to testify before this disgruntled crowd was William Hoops of the board of guardians, who displayed so much confusion that the audience could have been forgiven for thinking that he had never been to Blockley Hospital or heard of Josephine Fagan. He had come to examine the alleged stolen property at the alderman's office, but could not remember what he had seen beyond "a piece of carpet"; he couldn't be sure the anatomical plates belonged to the almshouse; he was unsure when Josephine had come to Blockley and claimed not to know she was a medical student. At every question, Hoops denied as much knowledge of the case as he could get away with, and retired from the stand having provided the jury with almost no usable information.

The court's second witness was Dr. Smith. Smith promptly identified one of the stolen articles that Hoops had equivocated on: "I know the plates," he said; "they were in the Almshouse library, and were the property of the city." He had not seen the plates in the four or five months since he loaned them to Josephine. "I did not give her permission to take them away," Smith stated, adding that the stolen drop light and bucket also belonged to Blockley; he hadn't given her permission to take them, either. "When we give goods" to employees, he explained, "it is not personal property; for when people leave the institution they can be stripped of all goods given them." The staff had evidently forgotten to strip Josephine of her goods, because the only thing that belonged to her among all the items found at Mrs. Bunker's house was a calico dress. "The clock," Smith admitted, "belongs to me." When asked why Josephine had left Blockley, though, Smith avoided giving a direct answer. "I know Mrs. Fagan became objectionable to the Board," he said, "and they desired me to dismiss her." Asked if he had visited Josephine after her departure, he claimed not to know how many times he had called on her, but admitted that he had done so once, "and went as far as the door."[34]

From Smith's testimony, the facts seemed clear: whatever the nature of his relationship with the defendant, she had stolen from the almshouse. But the court's third witness told a different story. Mary Williams, who worked at Blockley, stated that the stolen muslin came from Smith's office, and that after Josephine's departure Smith had ordered her to make up three dresses and three nightgowns to be sent to Josephine. "The goods in court," she said, "look like those I made." In the end, Judge James R. Ludlow dismissed the case, stating that "there was not sufficient evidence to constitute a larceny."[35] He dropped the charges, Josephine was set free, and the crowd went home.

Approximately nine months after her arrest in late January, Josephine's son Louis Napoleon was born. Later in life, Josephine would claim that Louis was adopted. His mother, she claimed, had been her attendant at Blockley, and after her death Josephine brought Louis up as her own. But two factors call this story into question. First, the dates don't line up: according to immigration documents created later in his life, Louis was born on November 2, 1859, several months after Josephine was fired from her position at Blockley and accused of stealing from the institution on her way out.[36] While she might have gone back to attend his birth as Nurse Welsh had done, it seems unlikely.

Second, even if we assume that Josephine simply mixed the dates up—that through accident or design she assigned Louis a birthdate months after his actual birth—the records of childbirth kept at Blockley give no evidence of a boy being born during her time at the almshouse that could plausibly be Louis. The almshouse birth register, now held in several volumes at the Philadelphia City Archives, is a surprisingly rich and detailed record. In each hefty volume, Blockley's physicians wrote down the names of mothers who gave birth in the hospital, along with their age, marital status, birthplace, the number of children they'd given birth to in the past, and the number of abortions, if any, they had had.[37] They recorded the length and weight of every infant and the duration of both gestation and labor, and many doctors added marginal comments noting interesting factors in each case.[38] All of them signed their names to the record of the delivery.

This record turns up no trace of Josephine, Louis, or Josephine's attendant, whom Dr. Smith identified at Josephine's larceny trial as a woman named Mary McDevitt. A baby boy *was* born at Blockley on November 2, 1859, but to a woman named Margaret Merchant, who named him Samuel.[39] Of course, it's possible that Dr. Smith remembered the wrong name or deliberately lied to the judge; it's also possible that Josephine adopted that baby and renamed him ("Louis Napoleon" was more her style than "Samuel").

But sometimes the simplest explanation is closest to the truth. Newspapers reported that Dr. Smith had been visiting Josephine on a daily basis immediately prior to her arrest in late January, at all hours of the day and night. Louis Napoleon was born nine months later—and the spring of 1859 was the first spring in years that Josephine didn't spend on her mother's farm. Instead, she stayed in Philadelphia through the spring and summer, without any indication in her own accounts or the historical record of what she was doing for those nine months.

In fact, the only indication of what Josephine was doing in mid-1859 comes from the *National Police Gazette*, the same tabloid newspaper that got its start reporting on the "demon murderess" Madame Restell of New York. Years later, in July 1859, the paper printed a piece on "Mrs. Fagan" of Philadelphia.[40] The article opened with an account of Josephine's recent time at Blockley, where, the *Gazette* explained, "she at first was a seeker of knowledge, and afterwards a nurse, and all the time the friend and confidant of the chief resident physician, Dr. Smith." Now, the *Gazette* announced, Josephine had "been doing a little in a line evidently new to her—cowskinning an editor or publisher."[41] To give the full account, they printed a letter purportedly written by Josephine herself to the editors of the *Gazette*.

According to this letter, Josephine had called on John S. Jackson, the editor of Philadelphia's *Sunday Transcript*, "to remonstrate with him upon the unwarrantable use he made of [her] name in his issue of Sunday last." Evidently the novelty of the scandal surrounding Dr. Smith's recent "confidant" had not yet faded. Jackson protested that the target of the paper's scorn was Smith, not Josephine—but she found his excuses unsatisfying. "I could scarcely reconcile myself to be sacrificed," she wrote in the letter, to "be torn in pieces in the mad play of men's bitter animosities." But Jackson offered no apology. "Incensed beyond all self-control," Josephine continued, "I sprang upon him with a gutta-percha whip," raining blows on Jackson until he managed to wrap the whip around his hand and wrestle it away from her.[42]

> He then threw himself into an attitude of attack, but I looked at him, and told him to strike if he thought best . . . Had he have offered me personal injury I should have called into requisition a more deadly weapon than a gutta-percha riding whip. As it was, I had inflicted the personal indignity he merited, and with a very insignificant weapon, and I told him he was quite welcome to the whip.[43]

Upon departing, Josephine discovered that she had forgotten her umbrella, and when she stepped back in to retrieve it, Jackson followed her, using foul language. Josephine broke her umbrella in two over his head, and left for good. "It will no doubt be said," Josephine's letter concluded, "that my attack upon this Jackson was unfeminine and unladylike—the usual stereotyped cant of people who talk but never think." As a single woman, without father, brother, or sons to defend her, she saw herself with no choice but to defend her own honor against a man "beneath the grasp of the laws." "Outraged and maddened beyond endurance by these unmerited and public insults," she wrote, "I offered in return the most humiliating insult in my power . . . it is time that woman should find some protection from the coarse ribaldry and defamation of men, and if no other means are offered let them protect themselves."[44]

In the spring and into the autumn of 1859, as Josephine dealt with scandal and unemployment, Horatio Robinson Storer ramped up his efforts to convince fellow physicians that the issue of abortion deserved their attention and outrage. In January 1859, the same month that Josephine was arrested in Philadelphia, Storer published the first of a series of nine articles that ran in the *North American Medico-Chirurgical Review* on the topic of "Criminal Abortion." In this series, Storer laid out the most thorough medical argument to date for the criminalization of abortion.

The central claim of Storer's abortion series was that the current legal framework failed by working too hard to protect mothers and, in doing so, disregarding the life of the fetus. "The whole question of the criminality" of abortion, he argued, "turns on this one fact, the real nature of the foetus in utero." The public's general understanding of the fetus, he wrote, was that it was not alive prior to quickening, and that the contents of the womb prior to quickening "might be thrown off and expelled from the system as coolly and as guiltlessly as those from the bladder and rectum."[45]

Yet, Storer wrote, "common sense" indicated that the fetus was alive from "the very outset" of pregnancy. He based his reasoning on the argument that the embryo, even in the first weeks of pregnancy, is separate from the mother's body. The connection between mother and embryo, he believed, was "wholly broken" as the ovum traveled through the Fallopian tube to the uterus—and therefore, he reasoned, it must remain separate from the mother thereafter.[46] Based on this novel understanding of the mechanics of conception, Storer believed, a fetus was "from the very outset, a human being . . . existing independently of its mother."

To Storer, the implications of this new view of conception were clear. "The offence becomes, in every stage of pregnancy, MURDER." The problem with American laws, Storer concluded, was that "they are so worded as almost wholly to ignore foetal life."[47] Today, this argument is familiar: in fact, the rights of the fetus are the foundation of the modern anti-abortion movement that developed in the mid-twentieth century. But in 1859, it was a more radical claim.[48] Horatio Storer wasn't the first person to argue that abortion is murder, but he was among the first Americans to advocate loudly for the passage of laws to codify and punish what he saw as widespread murder of fetuses.

The novelty of the argument meant that Storer had to go much further to convince his audience. In the March issue, Storer tried to convince the physicians reading his essays of the sheer scope of the abortion problem. Drawing on statistics from European countries and New York City indicating an overall decline in population and a rise in fetal deaths, Storer decided that "from these figures there can be drawn but one conclusion, that criminal abortion prevails to an enormous extent in New York, and that it is steadily and rapidly increasing."[49] Not only was abortion on the rise, but it was specifically increasing among the wrong kind of people. "This crime prevails in our midst to an almost incredible extent," Storer wrote, "among the wealthy and educated and married; we are compelled to admit that Christianity itself, or at least Protestantism, has failed to check the increase of criminal abortion."[50] Worse still, in places like Massachusetts where populations were growing, the increase in births was "almost exclusively among its resident foreigners, Catholics."[51] Storer's use of the word "foreigners" signaled that his concern was with race as much as with religion. The "problem" with Irish Catholic immigrants was not just a doctrinal difference, but a cultural one that became racialized as native-born Protestants worked to distance themselves from those outsiders. In fact, scholars Nicola Beisel and Tamara Kay, in their study of race and abortion in the nineteenth century, argue that "Protestant" and "Catholic" are perhaps better understood as racial or ethnic categories than as strictly religious ones.[52] Storer's writing reflected the commonly held fear of white Protestant Americans that Catholic immigrants would soon outnumber them and challenge their social and political authority.

For readers who doubted the seriousness of abortion's threat to the white Protestant majority, or those unconvinced that life began at conception, Storer's series continued in the May issue with an essay on abortion's "victims." The first victim in Storer's mind, of course, was the fetus, but he also emphasized the dangers of abortion for the mother. Criminal abortion, he stated, nearly always ended in the death of either the fetus or the mother—or both. But, he cautioned, death was "by no means the most common or the worst result of the attempts at criminal abortion." An attempted abortion that failed to terminate the pregnancy could lead to "epilepsy, paralysis, or idiocy" in the child, while the mother might suffer from hemorrhages or infections brought on by a failed operation.[53] Abortion, he argued, could even endanger women who didn't actually go through with the procedure:

> We have seen that in some instances *the thought* of the crime, coming upon the mind at a time when the physical system is weak and prostrated, is sufficient to occasion death. The same tremendous idea, so laden with the consciousness of guilt against God, humanity, and even more natural instinct, is undoubtedly able, where not affecting life, to produce insanity . . . Were we wrong in considering death the preferable alternative?[54]

As strenuously as he fought to prove that abortion was unthinkably dangerous, Storer did acknowledge that the operation could be accomplished safely in some cases. Specifically, when abortions were performed by professional physicians for reasons of absolute necessity, "not one was fatal."[55] But, of course, few respectable physicians would perform abortions: Storer dismissed any claim to the contrary as "wickedly false."[56] The primary guilty parties in the crime of abortion, he believed, were women. Female physicians, he stated, "frequently cause abortion openly and without disguise"; by contrast, "of male abortionists we have less to say."[57] As far as Storer was concerned, men rarely forced women to get abortions: such cases were "so rare, that in a general statement they may be assumed not to exist."[58] In his view, it was the woman, whether with or without the co-conspiracy of a male partner, who sought out, consented to, and ultimately was most guilty of, the crime. "Such ladies," Storer wrote, "boast to each other of the impunity with which they have aborted, as they do of their expenditures, of their dress, of their success in society. There is a fashion in this, as in all other female customs, good and bad. The wretch whose account with the Almighty is heaviest with guilt, too often becomes a heroine.[59]

The woman, in Storer's view, was always most guilty, "yet as laws now stand, she can scarcely ever be reached."[60] Even New York State's law—one of the few that defined getting an abortion as a crime—wasn't strict enough, or enforced often enough, for Storer. After all, New York's law defined abortion as either manslaughter (in the case of the practitioner) or a misdemeanor (in the case of the mother). In other words, New York law treated abortion as a crime without malice or criminal intent.[61] Nothing less than a law that treated abortion as premeditated and cold-blooded murder would answer, Storer believed, for the enormity of the crime.

The only people capable of addressing the spread of "criminal abortion," Storer argued, were doctors. "Medical men," after all, were "the physical guardians of women and their offspring; a proposition that none can deny."[62] Every doctor, Storer advised, ought to "reflect that upon himself more than on clergyman or legislator, often rests the standard of public morals."[63] Not only did physicians have the power, and indeed the duty, to influence public morality, but their expertise rendered them alone capable of determining when, if ever, an abortion was truly necessary. At a minimum, Storer wrote, "two competent medical men" should be consulted in every case before permitting a woman to get an abortion.[64] New York State had previously had a clause requiring just that, but the 1845 revision of the state law did away with the so-called "therapeutic exception."

Above all, Storer argued in the final essay of the series, physicians had a duty to make "a bold and manly utterance of the truth" and uphold the rights of "the unborn child." Medical men, he wrote, must "stand, irrespective of personal consequences, in the breach fast making in the public morality, decency, and conscience, and, to the best of our strength, defend them."[65] Abortion, in his view, was a threat not only to unborn children and their mothers; it also posed a threat to the moral and social authority of men like him—white, middle-class Protestant husbands and fathers.

He wasn't alone in his views. In May of 1859, the American Medical Association held its annual meeting in Louisville, Kentucky, and adopted a set of resolutions on abortion put forth by a committee chaired by Storer himself.[66] "The committee, along with Storer, took up the stance that abortion was "no simple offence against public morality and decency, no mere misdemeanor, no attempt upon the life of the mother, but the wanton and murderous destruction of her child."[67] In order to combat this crime, the AMA's first resolution was to "publicly . . . enter an earnest and solemn protest against such unwarrantable destruction of human life." Second, the AMA resolved to bring their concerns to state legislatures and advocate for the passage of laws designed to address the crime as physicians saw it: that is, to define abortion as murder. Finally, the AMA called for state medical societies to take up the cause and lobby their local legislatures. Only physicians, the statement insisted, could be expected to accomplish this aim. "The case is here of life or death," the committee wrote—"the life or death of thousands—and it depends, almost wholly, upon ourselves."[68] The members of the AMA gathered in Louisville, compelled by the argument laid out by Storer's committee, voted unanimously to adopt the resolutions.

While all this controversy played out, Josephine was busy being fired from her first medical post, beating up an editor, and quite possibly carrying and giving birth to the child of the man who had caused the trouble in the first place. But after Louis's birth, things settled down. Within a year of the AMA committee's first meeting, Josephine began giving consultations under the assumed name Emma Burleigh, M.D. The pseudonym was probably an attempt to separate herself from the scandal surrounding her name in Philadelphia, but she went farther than that—in fact, she went all the way to Ohio.

On June 1, 1860, the *Cincinnati Daily Press* printed an ad headed "WANTED—PATIENTS—IMPORTANT SECRET FOR MARRIED LADIES."[69]

> Mrs. Burleigh, M.D. will lecture to ladies every afternoon at four o'clock, at her office, Room 28 Pike's Opera-house. Admission fifteen cents. Consultation hours from one to four o'clock P.M., and through the Post office. Prolapsus Uteri is treated by a method which affords immediate relief. Irregularity, Leucorrhea and Ulceration are permanently cured.

Women reading the ad would have understood, from the emphasis on "secret" treatment for married women, that abortion was among the services offered by Mrs. Burleigh, M.D. Josephine's choice is interesting: she used her mother's maiden name. Whether the trip out west was intended to evade the watchful eye of the Philadelphia medical establishment or that of her own mother, it is clear that Phebe Burleigh Williams was on her daughter's mind.

Josephine didn't stay long in Cincinnati. Throughout the remainder of 1860, she moved through the Midwest, stopping in various cities to give public lectures on women's health and to offer consultations. At some point that year, she passed through Louisville, where the AMA had recently adopted its anti-abortion resolutions, to deliver a lecture on "the preservation of female beauty" that proved so popular with local ladies that she stayed to give it four more times.[70] By the end of the year, with sectional tensions heating to an unbearable pitch, she moved south to St. Louis, where in early December the *Daily Missouri Democrat* advertised an upcoming lecture by "Mrs. Dr. Burleigh, a lady of high recommendation, and a Virginian by birth," on the subject of female diseases.[71] She was supporting herself, in defiance of the AMA's condemnations of both abortion and female physicians, and making her way as a single mother.

In 1861, however, the path of Josephine's career diverted sharply in the face of the American Civil War. The war would also put the physicians' campaign against abortion on hold. When the regional and moral debates that had gripped the nation for years finally erupted in violence in South Carolina that spring, doctors across the nation began reorienting their priorities. For the following five years, battlefield medicine, with all its demands, horrors, and discoveries, would command the attention of medical minds, relegating the abortion issue to the back burner. But for Josephine, the war offered the thing she was always looking for: an opportunity to make some fast money.

CHAPTER 6

The Blockade Runner

The Civil War changed everything. The years between 1861 and 1865 remain the deadliest in US history, with military deaths alone totaling around 620,000—approximately 2 percent of the country's population.[1] It's hard to overestimate the impact of a conflict with that kind of death toll. By the war's end, everyone knew someone who had died. Many knew several, including close family and loved ones: brothers, husbands, mothers, wives.

It wasn't just the overwhelming number of fatalities that altered the landscape of America, or the physical destruction of the land, particularly in the South, that changed things for Americans on all sides. The war redrew state boundaries, challenged social divisions, and, with the Emancipation Proclamation, ushered in a new era of racial politics. In the shadow of the Civil War, Josephine McCarty would endure imprisonment, escape a murder attempt, give birth to two children, and emerge on the other side as a professional abortionist.

For women like Josephine—that is, white women living in the North—the war presented a unique set of challenges and opportunities. Clara Barton, founder of the American Red Cross and probably the war's most famous woman, argued in 1888 that the war had advanced women's "position" in society by "at least fifty years."[2] Elizabeth Cady Stanton, one of the feminist leaders who organized the Seneca Falls Convention for women's rights in 1848, remarked in the 1880s that the Civil War "created a revolution in woman herself."[3] Barton and Stanton's comments suggest that, whatever losses women suffered on a personal level—and for many women, they were substantial and painful—the Civil War had produced changes in white women's social status and even the way they thought about their own roles in American society.

The historian Judith Giesberg has argued that the departure of men for the war front "sent women into motion, driving them from home to support their families" and blurring the imagined boundaries between home and public—and, in this case, home and war.[4] Women displaced by war sought aid from charitable organizations and governments; they also lent their labor to the war effort, whether in munitions factories, field hospitals, or the field of battle itself. Libra R. Hilde argues that women's work as nurses both responded and contributed to "an emerging nineteenth-century female politics."[5] Daneen Wardrop, in her study of women's narrative accounts of wartime nursing, argues that the Civil War provided women with an opportunity to put into practice the feminist rhetoric developed at the Seneca Falls convention.[6] As the war destabilized gender relations and economic structures along with every other facet of American life, women found more options for work outside the home, and many connected that fact, either at the time or later on, to the developing movement for women's rights.

In the field of medicine in particular, the war created the conditions necessary for a major reorganization of gendered labor. The historian Margaret Humphreys has argued that the Civil War was a moment for reform in medicine generally, as it "brought surgeons and bodies together in unprecedented numbers," leading to new developments in surgery and other forms of medicine. But she also agrees with Clara Barton, writing that the war "was clearly a vehicle that carried women from the home into the public sphere."[7]

The vehicle of war carried few women farther than the controversial Dr. Mary Edwards Walker. Raised in a progressive family in Oswego, New York, Mary Walker graduated from medical school in 1855 and spent the first three years of the war pushing stubbornly for a position as a surgeon in the Union army. Her mulish efforts were eventually rewarded: after working as an unpaid surgeon for two years, she finally received the title of "Contract Acting Assistant Surgeon (civilian)" in the fall of 1863. She was eventually awarded the Medal of Honor, the highest decoration available in the US Armed Forces; to this day, she's the only woman who ever received it.[8]

Walker's story demonstrates that it was possible—if only barely—for a female physician to turn the demands of battlefield medicine to her advantage. Far more women took the path of least resistance and entered the wartime medical field as nurses. In the early months of the war, the historian Jane E. Schultz observes, "the zeal with which young men enlisted . . . was matched by women seeking hospital positions." These women were motivated, Schultz says, by the same things that pulled young men into the war: "patriotism, self-sacrifice, the prospect of adventure, and, of course, money."[9] By her estimate, over twenty thousand women from both North and South served as hospital workers between 1861 and 1865, laboring in positions from battlefield nurse to laundress in one of the city hospitals that met the growing demand of war-related injury and illness.

In the first two years of the war, the Union army attempted to control the influx of women by appointing the mental health and prison reformer Dorothea Dix as general superintendent of nurses, with the authority to reject, hire, and assign women to positions in the various hospitals serving the army.[10] Dix put in place strict criteria for her nurses: they had to be at least thirty years old and ideally between thirty-five and fifty; they should be neat, sober, and industrious. In addition to these requirements for age and character, all applicants should be able to produce two letters of reference. It was a hard checklist to complete; as the war ground on, up to half of the women who served in hospitals did so not by passing Dix's muster but simply by showing up and making themselves useful.[11]

Some Americans objected to the idea of women working in hospitals, using the same arguments that had been employed in recent decades to discourage the medical education of women. Military hospitals, just like the public almshouse hospitals of the antebellum years, were places of squalor and suffering; the sight of gore and sounds of misery, critics argued, would "strain" the "delicate constitutions" of middle- and upper-class white women.[12] On top of these conditions, to be expected in civilian and military life alike, some opponents of women's war work suggested that women serving in military hospitals faced a heightened risk of sexual assault.[13] Yet, as Margaret Humphreys demonstrates, those twenty-thousand women who worked in Civil War hospitals proved these notions false.[14] As more and more women entered the medical field of war, both with and without the approval of a formal body such as the Union Army's general superintendent of nurses or the United States Sanitary Commission, they demonstrated that women could, in fact, endure hospital conditions without a fatal blow to their health, psyche, or moral character.

Josephine, for her part, had already proven this before the war broke out. Her few months at Blockley, although they ended in scandal, demonstrated that she was capable of withstanding the difficulties of hospital work. She might have been expected, with her medical training and ambitious drive to support herself through her own labor, to have joined the throng of women traveling to Washington to apply to Dorothea Dix for a post in a hospital. Certainly, she would have had a good chance of qualifying. She was thirty-five years old; she had professional training and hospital experience. Unlike the many women who, without connections in the professional world, turned to friends, pastors, and even strangers for letters of recommendation, Josephine could presumably have reached out to her former medical professors, her clients, or even to Milton Thomson, an established businessman, for references. Although her reputation could have endangered her application if rumors from Philadelphia reached Dix in Washington, it's hard to doubt that Josephine could have worked in a military hospital as a nurse or assistant had she chosen to do so.

But she didn't. Evidence from the war years suggests that, from the outbreak of hostilities until the conclusion of the conflict in 1865, Josephine never worked in any capacity in a military hospital. There isn't even anything to show that she cared for the sick and wounded in the less formal sites of healing—civilian homes, emergency field hospitals—that sprung up around battlefields in the North and especially in the South. The Civil War did not advance her medical career in the way it did for women like Mary Edwards Walker. Nonetheless, the war changed her.

What it changed, specifically, was her relationship with Milton Thomson. When the war began, Josephine and Tom had been seeing each other regularly for about seven years, and sleeping together since at least 1858. Up to this point, it seems as though their relationship was amicable and mutually beneficial, if not mutually passionate. The two continued to correspond through the late 1850s, and they spent time together whenever Josephine's restless travels brought her back through Utica. Either one could have walked away without a significant loss or risk to their social status if they'd decided that the relationship was no longer meeting their needs. They chose, then, to stay together.

That changed in the second year of the war. Two things happened in 1862: first, Josephine traveled south from Utica to Washington, ostensibly to apply for one of the coveted nursing positions in the capital's military hospitals. Upon her arrival, however, Josephine was arrested for espionage before she could even make it to Dorothea Dix's office. When she finally saw Dix, it was to charge her jailors with rape, rather than to apply for a job. Around the time of her release from the Old Capitol Prison, Josephine discovered the second thing that would transform her life in 1862: Milton Thomson had gotten her pregnant.

Tom was at Josephine's side in January 1862 when she boarded a train in Utica, bound eastward on the first leg of her journey to Washington.[15] The couple traveled to Albany on the first day, spending the night in a shared room at the Stanwix Hall hotel before heading on to New York City. In New York, Josephine recalled, "we always stopped at the Brandreth House," a swanky but seedy hotel built by the patent medicine magnate Benjamin Brandreth.[16] Here, Josephine and Tom lingered for two or three days, booking separate rooms but "lodging" together, enjoying a last moment of private intimacy before Josephine embarked for the front. Setting out for Philadelphia next, Josephine traveled with Tom on the Perth Amboy ferry, but here he seemed to get cold feet. "He met a Mr. Churchill," Josephine remembered, "an old gentleman from Utica." Churchill's presence made Tom skittish: when Josephine asked him to come with her, "he whispered and said he was afraid to go, as Churchill was there; he wished Mr. Churchill somewhere else."[17] When the boat reached Philadelphia, Tom turned around and headed back to Utica and his wife, while Josephine pushed on alone.

In Philadelphia, she bought a suit of men's clothes. After buying the suit and getting a haircut, Josephine had a photograph taken and mailed it up to Tom in Utica; she had promised him a picture of her new look. In her new disguise, she completed the final portion of her trip, arriving in Washington sometime in early February. Rather than going straight to a hospital or to Dix's office, Josephine rented a room at an establishment called the Union Club House on Thirteenth Street. The Club House, run by a New Yorker named Barney Donnelly whose sympathy for pro-slavery Democrats was a matter of public record, was also the unofficial Washington headquarters of the Excelsior Brigade, a New York unit led by the wealthy politician Daniel E. Sickles.[18] In other words, the Club House on Thirteenth Street was home to some of the most notorious names in New York Democratic politics. Josephine had made connections during her brief stint as an Albany lobbyist for Adolphus Ranney. Among the lodgers staying at Donnelly's club house in February 1862, she recognized Colonel Lewis Benedict, a former city attorney and state assemblyman, although he didn't recognize her in her disguise.[19]

What happened next is unclear. Josephine later claimed that she had been in Washington for only a few days before she was arrested and that she had not left the city since her arrival, but when she answered a late-night summons to the Provost Marshal's office, army officials claimed that she had been seen visiting secessionist families across the river in Port Tobacco, Maryland—her former teaching post. Josephine denied the charges, but even the suspicion of rebel sympathies was enough to justify imprisonment in early 1862. Josephine was sent to the Old Capitol Prison, where she spent at least six weeks in captivity for a crime that she always insisted she did not commit.

The evidence, however, seems to stand against her. Josephine admitted that, when she made her trip south, she had in her possession "a bottle or two of quinine given me in Blockley Hospital."[20] If her goal was to join the forces of nurses at the front, bringing quinine might make sense, but her male disguise would not. But if she came south hoping to bring medical aid to the Confederacy, drawing on her connections in Port Tobacco, both the medicine and the disguise would be logical choices.

A voice from inside the Old Capitol Prison suggests one more reason for Josephine's trip behind enemy lines. Rose O'Neal Greenhow was probably the most famous prisoner the building housed in the war's early years, and she remembered Josephine. Greenhow, a fixture of the antebellum social scene in Washington, grew up in her aunt's boarding house in the capital, where she brushed shoulders with congressmen, lawyers, and other stars of the DC scene from a young age.[21] Greenhow's parentage remains up for debate.[22] Most historians agree that she came from a slaveholding family somewhere in Montgomery County, Maryland, and the journalist Ishbel Ross, in her 1973 biography of Greenhow, claimed that her father was killed in her early childhood by one of his enslaved workers.[23] This legend, nowhere substantiated by any particular evidence, seems designed to provide a psychological explanation for Greenhow's fervent support of the Confederacy in adulthood. But there's an easier explanation: Greenhow, as a member of the white Southern elite, had as much invested as any other Confederate in her defense of slavery and repudiation of "abolition rule."

By 1862, Greenhow's work for the Confederacy was already notorious. Although the Civil War espionage expert Edwin C. Fishel calls her skills as a spy into question in his book *The Secret War for the Union*, other writers have accepted uncritically the Confederate General P.T. Beauregard's claim that she was instrumental in his army's victory at the First Battle of Bull Run in the summer of 1861 by reporting the movements of Union troops before they happened.[24] Shortly after that battle, Greenhow was arrested in Washington and held for several months in her own home. In January 1862, just before Josephine's arrival in the city, Union officials made the decision to transfer Greenhow to the greater security of the Old Capitol Prison. Greenhow's daughter came to the prison with her, as did several other women accused of treason against the federal government. On February 9, *Frank Leslie's Illustrated Newspaper* reported that Greenhow and a "Mrs. Braxley" had been transferred to the Old Capitol Prison. "We infer," the paper stated, "that they will not suffer much except from their inability to 'gad about,' since it took a large army wagon, drawn by six horses, to convey their baggage to their new abode."[25]

Greenhow had only been at the Old Capitol Prison for a few weeks when she met Josephine. In her memoir *My Imprisonment and the First Year of Abolition Rule at Washington*, recalling the early weeks of her stay at the prison, Greenhow writes, "Quite an excitement was created throughout the prison, about this time, by the arrest of a woman in male attire."[26]

> She was apprehended at the hotel of a man named Donnelly, in Washington . . . Her object had been to go to Richmond with the proffer of a projectile which her husband, who was in England, had invented, the model of which she had in her trunk. Donnelly was to have forwarded her over. She was very handsome, and was a woman of some cultivation and scientific attainments. She was a keen observer, and both spoke and wrote well. Her room was adjoining mine; and, although there was a double door between, I was enabled to converse and pass communications through the keyhole . . . Mrs. McCartney was the name of this person, and, apart from her *costume*, there was nothing about her but was calculated to inspire respect, as her conduct was marked by great modesty and propriety.[27]

Greenhow was clearly impressed by Josephine, seeing in her an equal in both talents and politics. "She was a monarchist," Greenhow noted, and "had supreme contempt for the Abolition Government, and sneeringly enumerated its lawless acts in support of her thesis—that sooner or later all republican forms of government resolved themselves into unlimited despotisms."[28] Whether this position was a genuine expression of Josephine's views or an act she put on to win Greenhow's favor isn't clear. She certainly had Confederate connections, and Louis Napoleon's name is probably sufficient proof that she had some monarchist sympathies. But her sympathies were also to the region where she was born: in her recent speaking tour of the Midwest, conducted during the height of sectional frictions leading up to the war, she had advertised herself as "a Virginian by birth," suggesting that her Yankee upbringing hadn't stamped out her loyalty to the South.[29]

Yet Greenhow's mention of Robert's gun underscores a motivator that was probably at least as strong as politics or sectional loyalty: money. Robert himself would attempt to sell the gun to the Union army the following year.[30] Maybe Josephine's disguise was an effort to pass as an arms dealer.

Whatever scheme landed her in prison with Rose Greenhow in March 1862, Josephine didn't stay there long. By her own account, she was released about six or eight weeks after her arrest by General John Adams Dix, one of two men appointed to a commission in early 1862 to review the cases of political prisoners in Washington.[31] The reasons for her release, just as with her arrest, are murky. Both Josephine and Rose Greenhow claimed that the disloyalty charges were dismissed for lack of evidence, and the fact is that the Union simply had too many political prisoners to manage at that time. Dix and his colleague Edwards Pierrepont had been ordered to review their cases in order to relieve the strain on a disorganized system.

Greenhow's memoir, however, suggests another possible reason for Josephine's release. Before Josephine left the prison, Greenhow wrote, "this lady laid before the Government the most horrible outrage committed in that Old Capitol Prison—too dreadful, too revolting, to be mentioned here." Even without mentioning it, Greenhow made her meaning clear: Josephine had accused the prison guards of rape. "She also wrote to Miss Dix with whom she was well acquainted, describing the foul act," Greenhow stated, and the army undertook an investigation, which was, in Greenhow's view, "a humbug, gotten up by the Superintendent Wood for the purpose of clearing himself, and allaying the excitement consequent upon the dark deed."[32]

Was Josephine's rape allegation true, or merely an attempt to stir up trouble and secure her release? For decades, historians insisted that the Civil War was an "anomaly" in the history of wartime sexual violence—the only war in human history where rape was extremely rare.[33] Despite the seeming ludicrousness of this claim—rape is common enough outside of violent conflicts that destabilize communities and bring soldiers into contact with unprotected women outside of their social circles—it has had remarkable staying power. As late as 1994, Thomas Lowry devoted an entire chapter to rape in his book *The Story the Soldiers Wouldn't Tell: Sex in the Civil War* but concluded that the crime was comparatively rare and dismissed the women whose cases he listed in the book as "the unlucky exceptions."[34]

In recent years, scholars have started to push back against this outdated argument, but actual evidence of rape during the Civil War remains thin on the ground—in part because in many cases no record was made at the time. In the records of the Old Capitol Prison, held today at the National Archives in Washington, there's no surviving evidence of the investigation Greenhow described in her diary. Josephine's case was not among the roughly 250 sexual assaults tried by military courts during the war.[35] However, Congress did not declare sexual assault a military crime until 1863, meaning that any accusation made in 1862 would not have resulted in a court martial.[36] And even after the military started trying rapes, not every accusation went to trial. Although E. Susan Barber and Charles Ritter have argued that "women who brought assault charges to Union officials came with the expectation that their accusations would be heard," most women already knew that US law placed a higher burden of proof on them than on their accusers, making a rape charge very difficult to prosecute successfully.[37] Indeed, if Greenhow's account is accurate, Josephine's case demonstrates that even a middle-class white woman—theoretically the most likely to get a fair hearing from the military establishment—could expect to have her claims dismissed by a "humbug" investigation.

Taking Greenhow's story at face value, there's no reason not to believe that Josephine did endure some form of sexual harassment or assault while at the Old Capitol Prison. The article in *Frank Leslie's Illustrated* suggests the contempt in which many Northerners held the "crinoline-cased rebels" at the prison, and the circumstances—male guards for female prisoners—were ripe for abuse.[38]

But that wasn't the only hardship Josephine had to deal with during her brief incarceration. "Before I left the prison," she said, "I discovered that I was pregnant."[39]

The baby was Tom's. Neither Josephine nor Tom ever questioned this. The timing, after all, was right: they had had sex at the end of January, at Albany's Stanwix Hall and again at the Brandreth House in New York City. A few months later, Josephine was pregnant. Four or five weeks after her release in late April or early May of 1862, Josephine met up with Tom in Philadelphia. She had come to the city to retrieve Louis from the family he had been staying with and to consult a doctor about her pregnancy, then presumably approaching its fourth month. Tom, who had learned of Josephine's condition via letter weeks earlier, came to convince her to get an abortion.[40]

She refused. After all, she was at least four months along. Even today, over 88 percent of abortions in the United States occur earlier in pregnancy, and with Josephine's training she understood better than most the risks of an operation at this point—including the risk that it might simply be unsuccessful.[41] Instead of an abortion, she agreed to return to Utica early that summer to negotiate with Tom's agent over the terms of child support.

In Utica, things went badly. Josephine could not reach a satisfactory agreement with Tom's lawyer, Thomas Spriggs, and she went home to Augusta empty-handed, now nearly seven months pregnant. Shortly after her arrival, an agent of the Thomson family came to Augusta and began knocking on doors, asking neighbors if they knew Josephine McCarty and informing them of her condition. Outraged and determined as ever to address an assault on her public reputation, Josephine hired a lawyer and sued Milton Thomson. Although she won the suit, it plunged her deeper into legal troubles, as her lawyer pocketed most of the money.

But money was, for once, the least of Josephine's troubles. Phebe had not taken the news of her daughter's pregnancy well. "It caused a great deal of trouble between us," Josephine said, and she was forced to leave the farm in Augusta in late summer.[42] Locked in a legal battle with Tom, she couldn't turn to him for support, and so she traveled to New York alone to find a place to wait out the final weeks of her pregnancy. She found a place to board with a large family on the East Side, just above Union Square, and settled in to wait for the baby.

Ernest Judson Seymour arrived in October. When her labor pains came on, Josephine called for a doctor named Alanson Jones, whom she had met on the ship back from England in 1854. Jones kept an office on West 26th Street, not far from where Josephine was boarding, and on October 12, 1862, he delivered her fourth son, to whom she gave a new surname: Seymour.[43] Unlike her professional title (Dr. Burleigh), Seymour was not a family name. In fact, it was the surname of Horatio

Seymour, the Democratic candidate for governor of New York, then campaigning on a staunch anti-Lincoln platform.[44] The name, she later said, was Tom's idea. She called the baby "Juddie."[45]

The birth wasn't easy. Assuming that Louis was indeed her biological child, Juddie was Josephine's fifth, and she was sick for several weeks afterwards.[46] When she recovered, she began searching for a lawyer to help her recover the money she'd lost in the suit against Tom that summer. She managed to track down an old friend from her school days in Cazenovia, a man named Dodge, and with his help, she sued her old lawyer. With the new lawsuit underway, she packed her things, took Louis and baby Juddie on the Perth Amboy ferry, and found a farmer's family in New Jersey willing to take the boys in while she returned to Washington.

Josephine's movements in Washington in 1863 are difficult to track. She claimed, once again, that her plan was to apply to a hospital for employment, but once again, she failed to secure a job, and there's no evidence that she ever applied in the first place. She did, however, travel repeatedly back and forth between the capital and Union-occupied Port Tobacco, ostensibly to visit old friends.

What was Josephine doing in Port Tobacco? Why did it suddenly become so urgent, in the midst of a war, to visit families she hadn't seen in almost two decades? The roads to and from Port Tobacco were tightly patrolled; Josephine's stagecoach was stopped more than once on the journey.[47] Josephine's visits were surely more than social calls, but what remains unclear is which side she was spying for. On the one hand, Rose Greenhow's recollections and Josephine's own choice of surname for her newborn child suggest that she had Democratic sympathies—which, in 1862, was all but synonymous with Confederate sympathies. But after the war was over, a newspaper reporter published a story allegedly told by the former superintendent of the Old Capitol Prison that suggests Josephine changed sides in the winter of 1863.

Josephine knew Colonel William P. Wood as a prison superintendent, but his actual duties were more complex.[48] In addition to his post at the Old Capitol Prison, obtained through his close friendship with Secretary of War Edwin M. Stanton, Wood managed a network of spies and confidants who delivered information to him throughout the war.[49] At the war's end, he was sworn in as the first chief of the Secret Service, which was founded in July of 1865 not to protect the president (that ship had sailed), but to combat the widespread counterfeiting of money. According to his obituary in the *New York Press*, Wood had a "pleasant personality" and was "jovial even with the prisoners intrusted to his care, and as popular among them as with the guards."[50] Even Belle Boyd, a teenage Confederate spy imprisoned at Old Capitol later in the war, once said of Wood that "beneath his rough exterior there beats a warm and generous heart."[51]

Seven years after the war, the *New York Sun* printed a story purporting to come from an interview with Colonel Wood, which claimed that Wood had hired Josephine McCarty to spy for the Union after her release from the Old Capitol Prison. "There is one man in Washington," the *Sun* stated, "to whom the secret history of the rebellion is a living record," and that man was Colonel Wood. Even years later, Wood remembered Josephine clearly: "A very bright, intelligent woman, of superior attainments, and possessed of plenty of grit"—and, the *Sun* noted, "a good figure."[52]

Just as Greenhow reported, the paper stated that Josephine had been released from the prison for lack of evidence, but rather than leaving town as ordered, she lingered. Wood "thought it proper to KEEP AN EYE ON HER MOVEMENTS," and a few days later tracked her to the home of a "Charley Butler," whose son was serving in the Confederate army.[53] Determined to discover her motives, Wood demanded, "Come, now, tell me what game you are up to here?" "If you don't leave me alone," Josephine replied, "I will shoot you like a dog!" Colonel Wood, evidently, was not intimidated. "The bullet ain't made to kill me with," he said, and warned her that if she continued her suspicious movements, he would be compelled to keep following her. Josephine promised to leave the city—and, sure enough, Wood stopped seeing her around Washington within a few days.

But not long after this conversation, the *Sun* reported, Wood received a visit from "a prim, sanctimonious looking man, dressed in glossy black clothes, and wearing a sedate, pious air—for all the world like a Presbyterian Deacon." The man began by asking after a woman arrested wearing men's clothing, warning Wood that the woman in question was "A VERY DANGEROUS CHARACTER" and should be watched closely. Wood, suspicious of his visitor, demanded to know his name and motives, and the man confessed that "his name was Milton H. Thomson, of Utica, N.Y.," and "he had had an object in hunting down Mrs. McCarty." Josephine, he informed Wood, was his former mistress, but "she was so extravagant and ungovernable and gave him so much trouble that he had been forced to throw her off." Not only had she cost him a considerable amount of money but she had also "borne him a child or two" whom he had no desire to support, and he was now determined to get rid of her by any means possible. Thomson asked Wood if he would do the job for him: "He produced the cash," the *Sun* reported, "and offered to plank down $10,000 if he would undertake the job."

By all accounts, there was nothing William P. Wood disliked more than a mercenary. As prison superintendent, he had nothing but "contempt" for Confederate prisoners who took an oath of allegiance to the Union in exchange for their freedom. Presented with a man attempting to clear away the evidence of his own indiscretion by paying for his mistress's murder, he was indignant. Thomson, he said, "had mistaken his man, and he had better take the money he coolly offered for her blood and provide for her and his children." Showing Thomson the door, he "told him that if he did not take himself out in a hurry, he would aid him with his boot."

Shortly afterward, Wood ran into Josephine again, this time at a public lecture in Washington. After hearing about Thomson's visit to Wood, Josephine was moved to tears, pouring out to him the whole history of her troubles with Thomson. After all her years of loyalty, "it was now the old story, he kicked her out to battle with the world for herself and little ones." But she said that "she would not lead the life of an abandoned woman." Alone, penniless, but not yet defeated, she "thought she would be of service to the Union cause as a spy." Wood hired her on the spot.

The story, as printed in the *Sun* in 1872, is almost certainly not true—or, at least, not all of it. For all the *Sun*'s protestations regarding Wood's astonishing memory, upon which names, dates, and other trivial details were "seemingly written indelibly," the narrative contains a suspicious level of detail and embellishment nearly a decade after the fact.[54] The *Sun,* in general, was not known for its dedication to sober accuracy. Upon the death of the paper's editor, Charles Anderson Dana, a writer for the *Seattle Post-Intelligencer* remarked that "editorially [*The Sun*] is ever interesting, if seldom convincing."[55]

That said, the tabloid story served up by the *Sun* may have been based largely on the truth. First, an appointment by Colonel Wood to spy for the Union would explain why, despite being stopped and searched on the road to Port Tobacco, Josephine was never arrested in the two months she spent there, when just a year earlier she'd been thrown in jail after only a few days in the city and a whisper that she might be making social calls to Confederates.[56] As strong as her medical resume was, she had an equally excellent set of qualifications for espionage: in addition to her valuable Port Tobacco connections, the skills she employed as a lobbyist in Albany would have served her well as a spy. She was intelligent, eloquent, and, above all, persuasive. During her stay in the Old Capitol Prison, Wood would have had an opportunity to observe these characteristics in Josephine. If their paths crossed when she returned to Washington after Juddie's birth looking for work, he might well have brought her on as part of his spy network.

The story of Tom's attempted murder bribe seems more far-fetched, if not for one crucial fact: Josephine reported hearing the same rumor at the time. In the summer of 1863, she met with Tom at the Continental Hotel in Philadelphia, where she confronted him with the rumors that he had "offered money to Col. Wood to put me out of the way." Tom, she said, "treated it as if it was a falsehood," claiming that he had gone to Washington that spring only to make sure that she stayed out of trouble. "He threw himself on his knees," she recalled, "begged my pardon for his ill usage, and implored me to forgive him." Evidently, Tom's explanation and his apology satisfied Josephine; after a long talk about the past and the future and a mutual agreement not to expose the other's shame again, they reconciled. They slept together again at the Continental, Tom gave her money, and, as Josephine put it, "we parted friendly."[57]

This time, Josephine didn't return to Washington. She spent the autumn in New York State, first in Utica and then in New York City, where she obtained work as a traveling sales agent for two different businesses: a sewing machine company based in New England and a patent medicine for the cure of headaches and menopause symptoms.[58] As autumn deepened into winter, she traveled up the Hudson to the capital region, and from there into western Massachusetts, where she moved from town to town, hawking sewing machines and patent medicine powder. By Josephine's own account, her sales weren't good, but she found something else in the town of Pittsfield that kept her there until May 1864: a married furniture dealer named Thompson, with whom Josephine had a brief affair sometime in the spring of 1864.

That spring, she discovered that she was once again pregnant. Years afterward, she would claim that the child was Milton Thomson's. After all, she continued to see him through the latter half of 1863 and the beginning of 1864; according to Josephine, their last "criminal intimacy" was in May 1864—just a few months after her child was conceived in February.[59] But either she believed at the time that Thompson, not

Thomson, was the father, or she simply saw an opportunity to make a little money—either way, she filed a paternity suit against the Pittsfield Mr. Thompson, claiming that he was the father of her unborn child. Her attorney obtained a settlement for $500, only $300 of which Josephine actually received, and in the summer of 1864, she returned to New York State.

She couldn't go back to Utica. She and her mother had never reconciled their dispute over her previous pregnancy, and Phebe died in 1864. But Josephine had another reason to stay away from Utica: she may have wanted to hide her condition from Tom, who had reacted so badly to the first pregnancy. By the summer of 1864, it was clear to Josephine that, whatever promises he'd made at the Continental in Philadelphia, she could not count on Tom's protection or his loyalty. Nor could she rely on sales commissions to pay the bills for her and her two—soon to be three—children. Her best route to independence lay through the practice she'd dropped at the beginning of the war: medicine. In particular, as the anti-abortion crusade of the AMA stalled in the war years, the business of terminating pregnancies, still legal in New York if the operation was performed before quickening, presented a potentially lucrative opportunity. And so that summer, pregnant with her sixth child, Josephine McCarty moved to Albany to open an abortion practice.

CHAPTER 7

Mrs. Burleigh, M.D.

In the summer of 1864, as the Civil War entered its final months, Josephine retreated north and settled in a house at the corner of North Second and Catherine Streets in the area of East Albany known, on account of its lush riverbank views, as Greenbush.[1] That fall, attended by a local physician named B. P. Staats, she delivered her second daughter.[2] Following her mother's example, she named the baby after two different empresses: Josephine Cleopatra.[3] She also gave her the same surname—Seymour—that Milton Thomson had suggested for their son Ernest.

In Albany, Josephine McCarty became Virginia Seymour: a widowed mother of three, trying to support her family on the outskirts of the state capital. For the past few years, the combined income derived from sewing machine sales, her alleged espionage for the Union army, and her relationship with Milton Thomson had been enough to keep Josephine and her children housed and clothed. But making money as a sales agent or a spy meant moving around frequently, and the money wasn't steady.

With two young children, a newborn, and a waning faith in Tom's willingness to provide, Josephine needed a more stable income—and a place to live. Undaunted by the fact that she'd never technically graduated from medical school, she began advertising her services as a women's doctor: Mrs. Emma Burleigh, M.D. Josephine's abortion practice in Albany allowed her to settle down with her children for the first time. Unfortunately, the years immediately following the Civil War saw a remobilization of physician's efforts to outlaw abortion—and this time, they had increasing support from both lawmakers and the press.

The story of Pamela Wager, another abortionist operating in the Albany area in the 1860s, shows the shifts taking place in public discourse on abortion at the time. Pamela, unlike Josephine, was an Albany native: born in 1812 in Albany County, she raised three children in nearby Troy with her husband Michael, a leather worker. Also unlike Josephine, Pamela probably had no formal medical training. By the time medical education began opening to women in the 1850s, she had already been a wife and mother for twenty years. Nonetheless, she listed her profession on the 1855 state census as "doctress," and in the 1857 Troy business directory she advertised her services as a "botanic physician"—a kind of catch-all category for eclectic physicians, usually those who hadn't graduated from medical school.

It's not clear whether abortion was Pamela's only service or whether she offered her neighbors more general healthcare, but it was abortion that made her name briefly notorious to some newspaper readers in New York in the 1860s. In November 1866, the *New York Herald* reported on "a terrible case of death produced by abortion" in Troy.[4] The victim, the *Herald* told readers, was Elizabeth Dunham, a widow with "a high character for religion and fidelity to virtue." Edward Martindale, her lover, took the role of a minor villain, but the primary antagonist in the *Herald*'s narrative was "that scourge of unfortunate women known as the female abortionist," embodied in the person of Pamela Wager. Pamela, the paper reported, had "carried on her nefarious practices here for years." After charging "a heavy fee in advance," she had attempted a surgical abortion on Elizabeth Dunham "without the slightest approach to success, but with great and constantly increasing pain to the deceased," whom the *Herald* concluded "must have died a fearfully agonizing death."

In the *Herald* article, Wager appears as a caricature of violent greed, a woman so unscrupulously bent on making money that she'd attempt a dangerous operation just to make a buck. It was an ironic choice by the newspaper editors in light of the fact that 61 percent of the *Herald's* medical ads in the 1860s were for either abortion or birth control.[5] Profiting from the "nefarious" practice was apparently well and good for the *Herald*, but not for Pamela Wager. The paper described her as a woman "of a stout form, an intelligent but, to the close observer, a sinister countenance. She looks the abortionist and the bad woman."

After this colorful report, the *Herald* provided no updates on the Troy abortion case, probably because the denouement was unsatisfying: Pamela Wager, whether through a lack of clear evidence, a lack of motivation on the part of the courts, or her own persuasive powers, was never convicted of any crime in connection with Elizabeth Dunham's death. But her name cropped up in the *Herald* again the following year. Another of her patients had died—and once again, the paper painted a moving portrait of the victim, Carrie Hubbard: "Rarely," the *Herald* declared, "has a more beautiful corpse been looked upon."[6] Pamela and her servant John Henry were accused of throwing Carrie Hubbard's beautiful corpse out the window of a carriage, presumably in an attempt to dispose of evidence. Evading punishment would be more difficult this time, and Pamela knew it. She fled Troy, but was captured at her brother's house in nearby Kinderhook on the last day of summer. "She appeared to exhibit a vast deal of contrition," the *Herald* reported, "and finally went off in a swoon."

Pamela Wager's name spread rapidly. By early September, the *Courrier de Etats-Unis*, the Western hemisphere's most famous French language newspaper, had picked up the story of "Le Meurtre de Lansingburgh."[7] The public outcry over the Hubbard case was so great that Robert A. Lottridge, the district attorney of Rensselaer County, and John H. Colby, who had held the position before him, felt compelled to make a public statement exonerating themselves from responsibility for Pamela's latest crimes. "Justice to ourselves," they wrote, "compels us to say that no indictments were ever found against Mrs. Wager, nor were any such indictment or indictments upon the records of the criminal courts in this county during the terms of either of us as prosecuting officers of this county." They had, of course, "no desire to screen or shield Mrs. Wager from punishment for any offence she may have been implicated in," but in the face of editorials accusing them of corruption, "we should do ourselves great injustice to allow such charges to remain uncontradicted so far as we are concerned."[8]

Despite the attorneys' protestations, however, the *Herald* pointed out that Pamela had been indicted for abortion as far back as 1860, although only a *nolle prosequi* was entered in the court records—that is, a formal notice of the dismissal of charges by the prosecution. "At first there was apparently little feeling in the matter," the article stated, "but now the greatest excitement prevails in all this section of the country, and is constantly on the increase." The author of the *Herald's* report seemed to view this increase of excitement over an abortion trial as a welcome development, and Pamela's current predicament as an opportunity: "It is sincerely and earnestly hoped that the law will make an example of the person who may be guilty, and the people, outraged and scandalized by this affair, seem to demand that swift retribution shall be visited upon those who have committed this terrible crime."

Not interested, apparently, in being made into examples, both Pamela and John Henry pled not guilty before a grand jury to the charge of second-degree manslaughter under New York State's abortion law.[9] Although Pamela's family attempted to secure her bail—"on the pretense," the Albany *Argus* reported, "that she was in feeble health"—Judge Gilbert Robertson refused, and Pamela was forced to wait out the six months before her trial in the county jail. When the Hubbard case finally came to trial in March 1868, the jury deliberated for only half an hour before returning a guilty verdict.[10] In light of Pamela's age, the judge sentenced her to only half of the maximum sentence: six months of imprisonment at the state penitentiary. "This announcement," stated the *Albany Evening Journal*, "caused the prisoner and her daughter to burst into a flood of tears."

After her stay at the penitentiary, Pamela returned to Troy, but not, apparently, to her practice. Certainly, her name never appeared again in the local newspapers with news of a botched abortion. A state census seven years after her trial found her living in Kinderhook with the family of Mary, the daughter who had burst into tears with her at her sentencing. Pamela Wager, mother of Mary E. Harder, is listed in the 1875 New York Census as having "no occupation."[11]

What changed between the early 1860s, when Pamela Wager apparently performed many abortions without any serious legal consequences, and 1868, when the death of Carrie Hubbard finally landed her in the penitentiary? It would be easy to conclude that the disturbing details of Hubbard's death, especially her "violent ejection into the street" by John Henry, caused sufficient outrage to put her behind bars. But an important discourse on abortion was unfolding in New York State in those years—one that would bring the debate into the public spotlight and lead the state legislature to pass the country's most stringent anti-abortion law in 1869.

At the forefront of efforts to sway public opinion on the issue of abortion was none other than Horatio Storer. In the same year that

Josephine moved to Albany, the American Medical Association held its annual meeting in New York City, where a delegation from Michigan presented a resolution offering a prize for "the best *short and comprehensive tract* calculated for circulation among females, and designed to enlighten them upon the criminality and physical evils of forced abortion."[12] The AMA adopted the resolution, and the following year the association's prize committee, chaired by Horatio Storer's father David Humphreys Storer, award the prize—one hundred dollars and a gold medal—to an anonymous submission titled "The Criminality and Physical Evils of Forced Abortion."[13] In 1866, the winning author published his prize-winning essay as a book, entitled *Why Not? A Book for Every Woman*.[14] The author was none other than Horatio Storer, the foremost champion of the anti-abortion campaign and son of the prize committee chair.

Why Not? laid the groundwork for the anti-abortion movement for decades to come. In the book, Storer framed abortion as a selfish and morally degrading act—and a dangerous one, both for the woman who undertook it and the society that tolerated it. Calling himself "one who has given more thought to the subject than probably any other person in the country," he implored his imagined female readers to read his book so that "an immense deal of ill-health would be prevented, and thousands of maternal as well as foetal lives would annually be saved" (13).

In his articles on criminal abortion in the *North American Medico-Chirurgical*, Storer focused on the importance of protecting fetal life. But in *Why Not?*, maternal life and health were at the center of the book. Women, after all, were Storer's intended audience, and he wanted to convince them of the importance of his argument. He also needed to offset public suspicions about the reasons behind the AMA's campaign against abortion. In the introduction, Storer acknowledged that public opinion had already begun to allege that anti-abortion doctors like him were "actuated by a selfish motive" (12). Although much of the intracommunity discourse on abortion in medical journals and conference proceedings did focus on the role and authority of doctors in society, Storer drew his readers' attention away from the needs of the profession and toward the needs and rights of patients. And so, he wrote, it was for the sake of women as much as their unborn children that "the profession thus transcends, almost for the first time . . . the barrier which for mutual protection, both of science and the community, has always been allowed to stand" between doctor and patient (13).

Women, after all, should be supremely interested in the topic of abortion, Storer argued: "It is one that affects, and more directly, perhaps, than can anything else, their health, their lives"; their "discretion," "conscience," "moral character," "peace of mind," and sanity, as well as "all the elements of domestic happiness" and "conjugal love" (13–14). Although the first reason Storer gave for opposing abortion was that abortion is "a crime against life, the child being always alive, or practically supposed to be so," he followed this argument up quickly by adding that abortion was also a crime "against the mother," as well as against nature and public morality. But, he concluded, "barring ethical considerations, and looked at in a selfish light alone, [abortions] are so dangerous to the woman's health, her own physical and domestic best interests," that the decision to have an abortion "should almost be looked upon as proof of actual insanity" (15).

Since the book was intended for a lay audience, Storer offered a detailed explanation of the mechanics of conception and pregnancy as best understood by allopathic doctors at the time. "Many women suppose," he wrote, "that the child is not alive till quickening has occurred, others that it is practically dead till it has breathed" (32). Both beliefs, he cautioned readers, were wrong: "Quickening is in fact but a sensation" (32). Not only was the embryo in motion long before the four-month mark when quickening generally occurred but physicians, with the aid of professional equipment and training, could perceive fetal movement early on in pregnancy when their patients could not. Miscarried fetuses, he told his readers, had "been seen to move when born, during miscarriage, at a very early period" (33). It's easy to hear, in certain passages of *Why Not?*, echoes of the billboard messages that line many US highways today with images and slogans about fetal movement and heartbeats.

In 1866, however, Storer evidently didn't expect his audience to be swayed solely by the idea that an unborn baby could move. Rather than dwelling on the question of fetal life, Storer spent the better part of *Why Not?* detailing the range of negative consequences he believed abortion had for women's physical and mental health. Women were already afraid of dying in childbirth—with good reason. Childbirth has always carried serious medical risks: risks that multiplied in the days before germ theory and modern obstetric practices. In fact, for some women, a risky illegal abortion might have been preferable to the possibility of a painful death at the end of an unwanted pregnancy. But in *Why Not?* Storer claimed—without offering any supporting evidence—that the risk of death was "infinitely" increased in cases of criminal abortion (40–50). Even if women survived the operation, he warned that having abortions could lead to lifelong invalidism, a higher risk of cancer, infertility, and profound mental anguish. "If life still remains" after an abortion, he wrote, "it is too often rendered worse than death" (46). So great were the dangers of abortion, Storer argued, that a woman didn't even need to actually *have* an abortion to suffer from these effects: "We have seen that, in some instances, the thought of the crime, coming upon the mind at a time when the physical system is weak and prostrated, is sufficient to occasion death" (49).

Despite these concerted efforts to convince women of the dangers of abortion, Storer cautioned his readers that they should not trust themselves to make decisions about abortion. "If each woman were allowed to judge for herself in this matter," he wrote, "her decision upon the abstract question would be too sure to be warped" (74). His reasoning derived from his recent research on insanity. "Woman's mind," he explained, "is prone to depression, and, indeed, to temporary actual derangement, under the stimulus of uterine excitation" during puberty, menstruation, pregnancy, lactation, and menopause—in fact, during most of women's adult lives (74–75). Storer argued that instead of leaving pregnancy decisions to women, "at least two competent men" should review the case of anyone seeking an abortion (71). "Submitted to such a tribunal," Storer wrote, "seldom indeed would the sanction be given" (71).

But abortion wasn't just a threat to individual women, Storer cautioned. Like others at the time, Storer had noted an increase in the popularity of abortion among middle- and upper-class Protestant Americans—or, at any rate, greater openness about the practice. A "wanton disregard for foetal life," Storer wrote, had "in the main been confined either to savage tribes, or to . . . the Chinese," but that was clearly no longer the case (16). If the "American and native element" of the population kept getting abortions at such a rate, he worried, poor Catholic immigrants and other less "civilized" groups would soon outnumber them (63). Abortion, Storer concluded, "strikes a blow at the very foundation of society itself" (64).

Horatio Storer wasn't the only white Protestant worried, in 1866, that the foundations of his society were shaking. Immigration to the US hadn't yet hit the peak it would at the turn of the twentieth century, but the rate was beginning to climb, and the demographic effect of every new arrival was magnified by the monumental losses of the Civil War. Storer put the problem plainly to his readers:

> All the fruitfulness of the present generation, tasked to the utmost, can hardly fill the gaps in our population that have of late been made by disease and the sword, while the great territories of the far West, just opening to civilization, and the fertile savannas of the South, now disenthralled and first made habitable by freemen, offer homes for countless millions yet unborn. Shall they be filled by our own children or by those of aliens? (85)

Only white Protestant women, Storer concluded, could come to the rescue of their race: "Upon their loins depends the future destiny of the nation" (85).

Why Not? wasn't just compelling to Storer's father and the rest of the AMA prize committee. The book sold well over the first five years and remained in print for the rest of the century, becoming a key text for the mobilization of public opinion on the issue of abortion.[15] The journalist who reported on Elizabeth Dunham's death for the *Herald* in 1866 might well have bought a copy. The judge and jury that found Pamela Wager guilty of manslaughter two years later might have been influenced, in part, by the arguments put forth in Storer's book. The patients who visited Dr. Emma Burleigh in Albany might have arrived at her door less frequently or with more trepidation than before, Horatio Storer's voice whispering in the backs of their minds.

But Horatio Storer wasn't the only doctor pushing for abortion reform in the years following the Civil War. While he brought the conversation to the public with *Why Not?*, and the AMA continued to adopt resolutions and research initiatives on the subject, the Medical Society of the State of New York began taking steps in 1867 to put their state at the forefront of abortion legislation.

In February 1867, the state medical society met at Albany's city hall, just blocks away from Josephine's new office on Broadway. At that meeting, Dr. James Anderson of the New York Academy of Medicine presented the following resolutions on abortion:

> *Whereas,* From the first moment of conception there is a living creature in process of development to full maturity; and,
> *Whereas,* Any sufficient interruption in this living process always results in the destruction of life; and,

Whereas, The intentional arrest of this living process, eventuating
in the destruction of life (being an act with intention to kill), is
consequently murder; therefore,

Resolved, That this Society do express their abhorrence, and
deprecate in a most emphatic manner the growing increase of
that demoralizing aid given and practice rendered in procuring
criminal or unnecessary abortion.

Resolved, That this Society will hail with gratitude and pleasure the
adoption of any measures or influences that will entirely arrest
this flagrant corruption of morality among women, who ought
to be, and unquestionably are, the conservators of morals and of
virtue.

Resolved, That the publication in newspapers and by secret circulars
of ostensible remedies for female diseases, that suggest abortion,
is highly detrimental to the public health and morals, and that
the Legislature ought, by the enactment of a suitable law, to
forbid such publications.[16]

In other words, the medical society of New York State agreed in 1867
that abortion was always murder, that abortion was on the rise, and
that the increase in this practice was due to the "flagrant corruption of
morality among women." But who had corrupted the nation's women?
The press. Rather than calling for a tighter ban on abortion—which
was, as the words "criminal and unnecessary" imply, occasionally necessary and legal—the medical society resolved to lobby the state legislature for a law banning the advertisement of abortion and abortion
remedies through newspapers and circulars. "The most pleasing part of
the whole matter," Dr. Anderson stated, "was, that the two last resolutions had been appended to the original at the suggestion of a promi-
nent senator."[17] Despite this cooperation, the state legislature failed to
get to the issue of abortion in their 1867 session. And so the following
February, while Pamela Wager awaited trial just miles away in the Rensselaer County jail, the medical society took up the topic of abortion ads
once more.

In his opening address to the society, John P. Gray, president of the
state medical society and superintendent of Utica's State Lunatic Asylum, stated that "more effective legislation is needed to guard the public in the sale and dispensing of medicines by unqualified persons, and
especially of substances which may be used for criminal purposes."[18]
Even though he did not specify which criminal purposes, exactly, he

was concerned with, his audience would have recognized the rhetoric of the anti-abortion campaign. Later in his remarks, Gray became more direct: "Again, it is now notorious that the laws intended to prevent or punish the procurement of abortion, are openly disregarded or evaded by druggists and others calling themselves respectable." Newspaper advertisements, he charged, gave publicity to such unscrupulous pharmacists while at the same time "pretend[ing] to *caution* women in a certain condition against taking them."[19]

In addition to calling for new laws restricting the advertisement and sale of abortifacients, Gray read aloud portions of the 1845 state law concerning abortion and proposed a specific revision: the omission of the phrase "pregnant with a quick child," which left "room for quibbling and evasion."[20] Under the 1845 statute, state law only treated abortion as second-degree manslaughter—that is, as the taking of a life—if it occurred after quickening. In practice, this made convictions overwhelmingly rare. After all, who could prove after an abortion was completed that the patient had actually been "quick" with child? At best, abortionists could be convicted of a misdemeanor and a short stay in the penitentiary. Pamela Wager's story shows that the milder penalty was sometimes an effective deterrent, but Madame Restell's long career is proof that it often wasn't.

At the medical society's 1868 meeting, the committee on the president's inaugural address presented two resolutions summing up Gray's proposals: one calling for the passage of a law controlling the sale of drugs, and one for the revision of the 1845 abortion law "to cover the whole period of gestation." Abortion, the committee stated, "is of such frequent occurrence, and is so lightly regarded by the community in general, that its wickedness and enormity, and destructiveness to health can only be made apparent by the united expression of the medical profession."[21] Sure enough, both resolutions were adopted unanimously.

This time, the state legislature responded. In 1868, New York State passed a law banning advertisements for contraceptives and abortifacients.[22] Anyone found guilty of "sell[ing], or offer[ing] to sell, or giv[ing] away, or offer[ing] to give away, or hav[ing] in his or her possession with the intent to sell or give away" any materials that mentioned abortion or contraception could be sent to jail for up to a year, fined one thousand dollars, or both.[23] The law broke down in great detail how the fine was to be distributed: one third would go to the school department in the county where the conviction was made, and one third to the local orphan asylum or the superintendent of the poor—or, in New York

City, to the treasurer of the Female Guardian Society, the new name of the "Moral Reform" organization formed in 1834 to raise awareness of seduction and shelter pregnant single women. But the final third of the fine—up to $330 dollars—was to be paid to the informer upon whose evidence the person so offending shall be convicted."[24] With this clause, the state offered New Yorkers the chance to turn in neighbors, friends, enemies, girlfriends and ex-girlfriends, wives and ex-wives, and anyone they knew who possessed or sold medicines, books, pamphlets, or any materials related to the prevention or termination of pregnancy—for a reward. The law, in other words, mobilized the public's greed in the fight against abortion.

The following year, New York made the most important revision yet to the state's abortion laws, amending the 1845 statute to remove the reference to quickening as requested by the medical society's resolution.[25] "Any person," the new law read,

> who shall administer to any woman with child, or prescribe for any such woman, or advise or procure her to take any medicine, drug, substance or thing whatever, or shall use or employ any instrument or other means whatever, with intent thereby to produce the miscarriage of any such woman, unless the same shall have been necessary to preserve her life, shall, in case the death of such child, or of such woman be thereby produced, be deemed guilty of manslaughter in the second degree.[26]

Anyone who administered medicine or used instruments to produce an abortion at any stage of pregnancy could now be convicted of second-degree manslaughter in New York State. That included regular physicians, but it also applied to midwives, to botanical physicians like Pamela Wager, and to fake MDs like Dr. Emma Burleigh. Under the new law, the death of the patient or a successful abortion could mean up to seven years in prison—if the authorities found out.

The new statute also made provisions for the arrest and conviction of pharmacists and patients, but those penalties were lighter. To "unlawfully supply or procure" any medicine or drug with intent to procure a miscarriage was a misdemeanor under the law, punishable by three to twelve months in a county jail, a thousand-dollar fine, or both.[27] But here, again, the legislature stamped out any chance at quibbling and evasion. Supplying or procuring abortion drugs was a misdemeanor whether the woman in question "be or be not pregnant." A druggist who'd sold abortion pills to a woman couldn't dispute the charge by

claiming that he didn't know she was pregnant: as long as the intent to abort was there, so was the crime. Finally, the third section of the law gave courts the right to compel any party guilty of either charge to testify against other participants in the act. Any "testimony so given," the law stated, "shall not be used in any prosecution or proceeding, civil or criminal, against the person so testifying."

Together, the three sections of the 1869 law gave courts unprecedented leverage against abortionists. Just five years into Josephine's abortion practice in Albany, politicians and doctors in that city had crafted the harshest abortion law in the nation.

She could have retired. After all, that's what Pamela Wager did, retreating to her daughter's house in Kinderhook. But Josephine didn't have Pamela's support network. She'd left home at age sixteen and lost one person after another: her husband and children in England, her friends in Philadelphia after the affair with Dr. Smith, her mother after her scandalous extramarital pregnancy. Her old boss, Adolphus Ranney, was in prison for fraud; her tryst with Mr. Thompson in Massachusetts had ended in a lawsuit. Even Milton Thomson, once her biggest supporter, had threatened to have her killed during the war. Without the support of a husband, a family, or a local community, Josephine's medical training remained her best means of earning a living and supporting her three children.

Instead of retiring, she did exactly what the organized physicians of New York State had tried to prevent: she began to advertise.

In the 1870–71 issue of the Gazetteer and Business Directory of Albany & Schenectady County, Mrs. Emma Burleigh, M.D., ran a half-page ad addressed, in large block capitals, "TO LADIES."[28] Much of the ad copy was occupied in listing the many procedures Josephine promised to perform, and the conditions she claimed to be able to cure: "All maladies of the UTERUS," up to and including "Entire Prolapsus," as well as painful menstruation, spinal diseases and neuralgia, bronchitis, and catarrh—the common cold. Through "Chrono Thermal Remedies," Mrs. Emma Burleigh promised the ladies of Albany that their suffering could be relieved and their health restored.

More pointedly, Josephine advertised her ability to "[remove] all obstructions to the Monthly Courses at one interview." This phrasing was exactly the kind of coded language the doctors' 1868 advertising bill had been designed to outlaw: every woman (and most men) reading the text of Mrs. Burleigh's ad would have no question as to the kind of obstructions she meant. This was, unmistakably, an ad for abortion services, and Josephine promised swift results and "strictly private" care.

The part of the ad not devoted to describing Dr. Burleigh's discreet services was in essence an advertisement for herself as a reputable female doctor. "There is so much connected with this subject of woman's health," the ad read, "that all women should consult a physician, herself a woman and conversant with all the improvements and discoveries of science." American women, Mrs. Burleigh believed, were "very ignorant" of the role of science in preserving beauty as well as health, while she had "made herself familiar with the habits and customs of distinguished women in France and elsewhere." She neglected to mention that she had been in France to search for the children her husband had kidnapped and claimed instead to have spent "four years in France in the study of Midwifery, and the various modes of treating female diseases, in which the French are so superior." If readers were unconvinced by her own account of herself, they could read the testimonial appended to the ad, purportedly from the editor of the *Louisville Journal*, stating that "Mrs. BURLEIGH is a lady of the finest intellectual powers and very uncommon literary attainments, and, as she has had very great advantages in the study and practice of medicine, both in this country and Europe, we cannot doubt that she is a skillful physician." Those interested in consulting Dr. Burleigh were asked to write to her new address at 62 Howard Street, with one dollar enclosed "to ensure attention."

Every line of this advertisement flies in the face of the efforts of the New York State medical society, many of whom opposed the education of women in medicine and who had been concentrating so much of their collective energy in recent years on banning the practice and advertisement of abortion. And it is hard to imagine that Josephine McCarty—literate, engaged in the medical field, and out of necessity aware of the laws on abortion—didn't know all of this when she took out the ad immediately following the passage of the 1869 abortion law. We can only guess at her intentions. Maybe her primary motivation was financial: after all, as the legal crackdown on abortion drove longtime practitioners like Pamela Wager out of business, a well-timed ad in the business directory could put her on the radar of patients whose options were suddenly thinner on the ground. If women who'd read *Why Not?* were now afraid to get abortions for fear of risking death or permanent disability, they were more likely to come to a respectable woman doctor with years of French training and bona fides from male physicians. But

Josephine's ad might have been a political choice as well as a shrewd business move. In another ad elsewhere in the directory, she wrote, "We are glad to learn that ladies of the best minds in our land are giving attention to the study and practice of medicine. There is a wide field open before them and the pioneers are deserving of special credit for their perseverance against obstacles which few men would overcome."[29] It's not hard to read a proto-feminist message in those words, especially taken together with her advice to women to consult someone familiar with their problems both as a woman and as a doctor.

By 1870, the state's challenge to her woman-centered medical practice was extremely close to home for Josephine—literally. On April 7, 1869, she'd signed the deed for a two-story brick and clapboard house located at 62 Howard Street, just around the corner from the capitol building.[30] The house cost $4,545; in order to afford it, Josephine turned to Milton Thomson, who agreed to loan her $1,000 and assisted her in taking out a mortgage on the property for a further $1,000.[31] It was in this house, just two years later, that the greatest crisis of her medical career would begin when she received a visit from a young woman calling herself Fanny Wright.

It wasn't her real name. Fanny Wright was a Scottish-born lecturer and reformer known, among other things, as an advocate of sexual freedom and women's involvement in medicine; she was a close friend and colleague of Robert Dale Owen, whose *Moral Physiology* (1831) presented an early argument for birth control.[32] The real Fanny Wright died in Cincinnati in 1852. The woman who came to Josephine's office on Howard Street in the summer of 1871 was just twenty-two years old, the child of Irish immigrants in the Albany suburb of Troy. Her name was Maggie Campbell, and she needed an abortion.

Maggie Campbell is a difficult woman to find in the historical record. Even at the time, journalists had trouble learning anything about her beyond her name. "Her history is obscure," one commentator observed.[33] In, fact, beyond her hometown (Troy) and her age (twenty-two), he was able to draw only one conclusion about Maggie Campbell: "Evidently she was not of correct moral habita."[34]

This judgment was based, presumably, on the one piece of information we do know about Maggie Campbell as an adult: she was in a sexual relationship with an older man named Peter Mochrie. A bartender turned postal clerk, Mochrie was thirteen years Maggie's senior when he met her in 1870. An ex-army lieutenant who rose on the tide of instant promotions that swept through the Union Army in the final years of the Civil War, Mochrie was thirty-four years old and still unmarried when he met Maggie. The two started up a correspondence in the latter part of 1870, and in 1871, they "had connection" for the first time. For the next five months, the couple continued to meet in Albany, sharing a night in a hotel room and parting ways the following morning. The reason for the relative secrecy of their relationship was probably not the difference in age between the two but the fact that they had no particular intention of getting married, as Mochrie would later state publicly. Maggie Campbell thus had three strikes against her in the eyes of New York's "respectable" Protestant middle-class: she was an Irish immigrant, she was working-class, and, most troubling of all, she was engaged in a sexual relationship outside of marriage.

In the summer of 1871, Maggie left her job as a waitress in the dining room of the Mansion House hotel on Broadway and found a room in the boarding house of the sisters Mary and Elizabeth Cleary at 45 Union Street at the rate of four dollars a week. The Clearys might have wondered where she got the money for room and board—after all, Mary remembered, "she did nothing while she board[ed] with us"—but the answer to that question arrived in the shape of Peter Mochrie, whom Maggie visited on an almost nightly basis. Maggie explained that Mochrie, who spent three separate evenings with Maggie at the boarding house, was her guardian and "had charge of her money and property." Her first husband had passed years ago, she claimed, and her only child died in infancy. Now, alone in Albany, she told Mary and Elizabeth that Peter Mochrie was "the only gentleman" in the city whom she could trust.

Mary Cleary remembered one more thing about their newest tenant. For the first week of her stay at the boarding house, she was taking medicine for "the whites"—that is, leukorrhea, a milky vaginal discharge that can occur at various points in the menstrual cycle, as well as during the early stages of pregnancy. Later, however, "she said it made her sick, and she said that she had discontinued the taking of it."[35]

Around this time, early in August, Maggie announced to the Cleary sisters that she was going away to visit her brother's wife in the country. She left in the morning as anticipated and returned around one in the afternoon, explaining that her sister-in-law had been out visiting friends.[36] This seemed like a plausible circumstance in a world without reliable telephone communication, and the Cleary sisters thought nothing of it. A week later, Maggie left again, this time explaining that she was going to visit her aunt. Once again, she returned in the afternoon: her relatives were out; the visit had been cut short; she would try again next week. By the end of the month, the Cleary sisters might well have wondered why Maggie's family was so socially active as to be virtually impossible to catch at home on a summer weekend—or why she never seemed to reach out beforehand to alert them to her planned visits.

On the evening of Friday, September 1, Peter Mochrie called at 45 Union Street and gave Maggie Campbell sixty dollars, a sum she had requested several days earlier in one of their many letters. The following morning, Maggie announced once again that she was going to the country to visit family. Instead, she went to 62 Howard Street, the white brick residence of Mrs. Emma Burleigh, M.D., who promised private boarding and medical care in her advertisements in the Albany business directory. Maggie gave her name as Fanny Wright, unpacked the few dresses she had brought with her in Mrs. Burleigh's upstairs room, and settled into the house under the pretext that Mrs. Burleigh had hired her as a servant.

What happened in the following weeks is a mystery, but we can make some guesses: Mrs. Burleigh, a trained physician with a long-standing practice in women's medicine, would have examined Maggie and questioned her about the circumstances of her condition. Maggie and Peter had had intercourse in May, and sometime after, Maggie noticed that she had missed her period. The medicine she took in the first week of July, when she was at least two months pregnant, might have come from any number of local druggists: in spite of the new state law against advertising abortifacients, it was still fairly easy to find medication promising to restore the menses.

But the medicine evidently didn't work. Maybe Maggie balked at the side effects and stopped taking it too early, or maybe she'd been sold an ineffective product. Her weekend trips in August were presumably to visit abortionists or midwives, but either their procedures were unsuccessful or, more likely, they refused to treat her. After all, abortion at any stage of pregnancy could be prosecuted as a felony if the patient died, and with every week that went by, the risk of a deadly operation grew. By September, Maggie's pregnancy was far enough advanced that a medication abortion was no longer possible; she needed a surgical option, and that was the most risky from both a medical and a legal standpoint. The vast majority of abortionists convicted in the late nineteenth century had, like Pamela Wager, attempted an instrumental abortion that led to their patient's death.

Josephine was probably not the first abortionist Maggie Campbell approached, but she was apparently the first willing to perform the operation. She gave Maggie an abortion sometime in the first or second week of September.[37] On Monday morning, September 18, evidently satisfied that her patient was recovering, Mrs. Burleigh and her daughter Josie traveled to Vermont to visit her young son, and left Maggie alone in the house on Howard Street. When they returned on Tuesday night, they found her in bed, suffering from severe pain and diarrhea. The following day, Maggie was very ill, complaining of terrible pain and thirst. Mrs. Burleigh, turning to the chrono-thermal remedies she placed her faith in, dipped flannels in camphor, heated plates, and applied these to Maggie's abdomen, hoping that heat would return her body to its natural balance or at least relieve the worst of the pain. At two o'clock that afternoon, she became alarmed: Maggie's abdomen was tender to the touch, she was urinating copiously, and the pains she described were regular and severe.

She grew worse during the night. The pains became more severe, she barely slept, and even the troubling discharge of urine had all but stopped, suggesting that the infection was worsening. Dr. Burleigh couldn't leave her patient and her young daughter alone long enough to call a doctor to give a second opinion, but she sat up all night with Maggie, and when morning came, she finally called for Dr. J. R. Boulware. The doctor arrived at 10 o'clock, made a brief examination of the patient, recommended more frequent administration of morphine to dull the pain, and left within twenty minutes.[38]

That morning, Mrs. Burleigh asked Maggie if she had any relatives whom she could call. She made no mention of a father or mother, but she told Mrs. Burleigh she had an aunt living at 45 Union Street. If anything happened, Mrs. Burleigh could write to her. Later that afternoon, Maggie slipped further into the cloud of fever and pain, and could no longer talk. By that evening, when Dr. Boulware visited again, she was dead.

Someone summoned the undertaker. At Mrs. Burleigh's request, Dr. Boulware asked a colleague of his to assist in a post-mortem examination. It was not, perhaps, standard practice to hold a post-mortem witnessed by two people when a servant died of a stomach ailment, but Dr. Boulware, who by his own admission was long acquainted with Mrs.

Burleigh, did not question the precaution. The post-mortem complete, the doctors and the undertaker carried Maggie's body to an unmarked grave in the upper reaches of the sprawling Albany Rural Cemetery. By Friday night, the only sign that Maggie Campbell had been at Mrs. Burleigh's at all were the dresses she left behind in the upper room.

CHAPTER 8

The Campbell Inquest

On the Tuesday after Maggie Campbell's death, the *Daily Albany Argus* published a brief note on the back page under the heading "Mysterious Affair":

> A young girl named Margaret Campbell died at the house of Mrs. Dr. Emma Burleigh, No. 62 Howard street, in this city on Friday, where it is said she had been employed as a domestic. The circumstances attending her burial were so quiet and mysterious as to arouse suspicions that all was not right, and Coroner Harrigan gave the case his attention. On investigating it he found that the girl died of "inflammation of the bowel;" that two reputable physicians of this city who made a post-mortem examination of the body, gave a certificate that she died from natural causes. Here the case rests for the present.[1]

It's not clear how John Harrigan Jr., the coroner, and consequently the *Argus* got wind of the affair. Maybe the Cleary sisters, to whom Mrs. Burleigh dutifully wrote with the news of "Fanny Wright's" death, started to talk, or maybe someone on Howard Street noticed the comings and goings: first two doctors, then the undertaker, and finally a small party carrying a long bundle under the cover of night. It's possible, for that matter, that anti-abortion advocates in the city were already keeping a wary eye on all activity at 62 Howard Street, where Dr. Burleigh had advertised illegal abortion services. In any case, Harrigan took quick action on Tuesday, ordering three doctors out to the Rural Cemetery to disinter the body and perform a second autopsy. While the doctors cut Maggie Campbell's body open again, Harrigan called up a jury of six honest men: a deputy bank superintendent, a confectioner, a cabinet maker, a shirt and collar dealer, a carriage trimmer, and a draftsman.

The proceeding that John Harrigan convened that evening in the office of the Police Justice at Albany's City Building was not a trial. It was an inquest—that is, an official but non-litigious investigation into the cause of a mysterious death. Inquests are a curious aspect of American legal history. Although they're a familiar part of murder mysteries and true crime dramas, they're comparatively rare in real life, at least in the United States. "Looking only at America," the legal scholar Paul MacMahon writes, "one might be forgiven for assuming that the inquest is a slowly dying anachronism."[2] That slow death, he explains, occurred mostly over the course of the late nineteenth century—and it was orchestrated in part by the same allopathic doctors who called for an end to abortion.

Why would physicians want to see the end of the American inquest? When the United States first separated from the British Empire, the new republic retained the office of the coroner, which was created in medieval England for the purpose of death investigation. In this system, the coroner, an elected official, held the power to direct inquests. Technically, "the coroner could not initiate his own investigation," the historian Jeffrey M. Jentzen explains; "rather, the coroner directed the sheriff to summon ordinary citizens from the county where the body was found."[3] That group—sometimes fewer than a trial jury, sometimes more—would then view the body, consider the evidence at hand, and render a verdict determining the death to be either natural, accidental, unlawful killing, justified killing, or suicide.[4]

Although the role of coroner had existed since the twelfth century, many Americans in the early nineteenth century began to associate the office with political corruption, as lawyers and laymen with no particular qualifications took on the position for personal profit.[5] In particular, allopathic medical men, seeking to demonstrate their authority in the face of cholera, sectarianism, and alternative practitioners, objected to coroners' lack of medical training and their failure to call on physicians for expert testimony at inquests. Horatio Storer and his father weren't the only doctors who felt that physicians should be voices of moral authority as well as scientific knowledge. In 1857, the same year that Storer initiated the physicians' campaign against abortion, the AMA's committee on forensic medicine issued a formal recommendation that elected coroners be replaced nationwide with court-appointed physicians trained in allopathic medicine and subject to removal by their peers.[6]

According to Jentzen, the AMA's attempts to replace the elected office of coroner with physician-led medical examiner systems met with a great deal of frustration and only partial success. By the start of the twenty-first century, only 60 percent of the country's jurisdictions were served by medical examiners with medical training.[7] Today, death investigation practices vary not just state by state, but county by county—and in many places, MacMahon writes, "the inquest was abolished along with the coroner."[8] Because inquests are quasi-judicial proceedings and medical examiners are doctors, not lawyers, coroners—death investigation officials with the authority to hold an inquest—are closer to the exception than the rule in the United States today.

But in 1871, Albany hadn't yet done away with coroners or inquests. The process remained an odd combination of medical and legal inquiry. John Harrigan Jr., who directed the state's investigation into Maggie Campbell's death, was an undertaker with no formal medical training.[9] Although Harrigan called three reputable allopathic doctors to conduct the second post-mortem, Maggie Campbell's inquest was more than a medical inquiry—and more than a legal proceeding. "Inquests," Paul MacMahon writes, "can do things that adversarial litigation is not designed to do: to help the deceased's family come to terms with the death, and to warn the broader community of the dangers of deadly activities while suggesting precautions." Because they are held in public and not bound by the strict rules of criminal trials, inquests have a remarkable freedom to seek truth and respond "to a deep human need to understand troubling events."[10]

Maggie Campbell's death was certainly a troubling event. That she had died at twenty-two, with no known illnesses or enemies, was one thing. That she had died at the house of one of the few doctors in Albany still bold enough to advertise abortion services was sufficient to raise concerns in Albany's medical community, and perhaps among the statesmen who had passed the recent abortion bill. But if Maggie had died even a few months earlier, doctors and lawyers might have been the only people deeply troubled by the abortion angle. After all, even the dramatic death of Carrie Hubbard in 1867 only received a few paragraphs of press coverage—and only after an arrest had been made. By contrast, two of Albany's leading papers—the *Albany Evening Journal* and the *Argus*—covered the Campbell inquest in great detail. For three days running, both papers printed extensive transcripts of witness testimony, including the findings from multiple post-mortem examinations. No one had been arrested and no direct accusations had even been leveled against Josephine McCarty, but the editors of the local papers apparently believed that the inquest proceedings would nonetheless prove interesting to their readers.

They had good reason to think so. Just weeks before Maggie's death, another abortion case had made headlines in New York City. In the summer of 1871, one newspaper in particular took up the anti-abortion cause—and, at exactly the same time, a tragic death provided the perfect case study to illustrate the dangers and moral depravity of abortion to the general public. The paper that broke the abortion story of the century was none other than the *New York Times*.

The *New York Times*'s turn to anti-abortion advocacy reflected a recent shift in the paper's public role as a news source. Founded in 1851 with a mission of serving the public good through journalism, the newspaper had become "indispensable" to readers through its daily coverage of battles and casualties during the Civil War.[11] Henry Raymond, one of the paper's two founders, insisted that the *Times* should maintain a sober, fact-finding role in contrast to the more sensational and openly partisan reporting of its major rivals, the *Herald* and the *Tribune*—but in 1869, Raymond passed away, leaving his co-founder George Jones at the helm.[12] Under Jones's leadership, the *New York Times* reinvented itself as a crusader for truth in the face of corruption and evil. A pivotal moment in this new battle was the July 1871 exposé of William "Boss" Tweed, leader of the Tammany Hall political machine, for extensive fraud and corruption.[13] The *Times*'s reporting on Tweed's crimes helped to kill the Tammany boss's chances in an upcoming mayoral election. Through the Tweed scandal, the *Times* showed that serious reporting could get quick results in real-world politics.

Even before the *Times* published its Tweed exposé, its editors had their eyes on another set of moral "crimes": the practice of abortion by doctors without sufficient medical training. In 1870, after the arrest of Dr. Thomas "Lookup" Evans following the death of his patient Mary Elizabeth Geary, the *Times* printed an article bemoaning the open practice of abortion, with the provocative title "The Least of These Little Ones." Abortion, the article said, was on the rise—and "the hideous traffic" was not limited to the city. "In the rural districts of this State," the article read, "there are quiet, unpretending cottages which seem, amid embowering foliage, the chosen abode of innocence and peace; but from these places wasted baby-forms are carried into nameless graves."[14] Pamela Wager and Josephine McCarty, the *Times* suggested, posed as much of a threat to the collective good as the notorious Madame Restell in her Fifth Avenue mansion.

The 1870 article ended with a call for further action: "The evil that is tolerated is aggressive; if we want the good to exist at all, it must be aggressive too."[15] Within months, a reporter named Augustus St. Clair stepped up to embody aggressive good in the fight against abortion. In the summer of 1871, he visited the New York City offices of several abortionists along with a female companion, pretending to be a couple seeking an abortion. On August 23, the *Times* printed his report, under the dramatic headline "THE EVIL OF THE AGE: Slaughter of the Innocents—Open Trade in Crime—Where Vice is Nurtured—The Moral and Physical Nature Both Destroyed—Scenes Described by Eyewitnesses."[16]

St. Clair might have had a copy of *Why Not?* open on the desk as he drafted his opened paragraph, so closely did it adhere to Horatio Storer's argument against abortion. He framed the problem first in terms of "medical malpractice"—a theme, he wrote, "for most serious consideration."[17] Throughout the article, St. Clair noted the spurious credentials of the practitioners he visited:

> One man procured the diploma of a deceased physician, erased the name by some chemical process, and inserted his own . . . One fellow who appends "M.D." to his circulars was recently a cobbling shoemaker—and a very poor one at that. Suddenly he closed his shop, moved to another part of town, and was metamorphosed into a "doctor."[18]

But abortion wasn't just a matter of malpractice to St. Clair—it was murder. "Thousands of human beings," he wrote in his opening lines, "are thus murdered before they have seen the light of this world," adding in an echo of Storer's warnings to women that "thousands upon thousands more of adults are irremediably ruined in constitution, health, and happiness."[19]

St. Clair and his anonymous female companion visited eight abortionists: the infamous Madame Restell, Madame Grindle, Dr. Ascher ("alias Rosenzweig"), Dr. Selden, Dr. Franklin, Madame van Buskirk, Madame Costello, and Madame Worcester. Two were immigrants: Dr. Rosenzweig, St. Clair wrote, "claims to be a Russian, but his voice has the twang of a German Jew."[20] Dr. Franklin's "real name," he said, was Jacoby; "a German Jew with no scientific and regular medical education." The rest, save Dr. Selden of Ohio, were women, but St. Clair warned readers that these practitioners were double frauds: "Lady patients, of course, prefer to call upon a 'madame' in delicate cases, and are willing to converse freely with her." But as soon as the woman had disclosed the reason for her visit, St. Clair wrote, "the 'madame' calls her 'husband' (?), the 'doctor,' (?) who really then assumes charge of all that is afterward done."

"The Evil of the Age" was more than a titillating peep into the medical underworld. "Enough is here given," read the final line of the article, "to arouse the general public sentiment to the necessity of taking some decided and effectual action."[21] Little did the editors who published St. Clair's piece know how soon the opportunity would come for authorities to do just that. Just three days after the "Evil of the Age" piece appeared in the *New York Times*, a baggage agent at the Hudson River Railroad Depot in Manhattan noticed a trunk emitting "a very offensive odor."[22] Concerned and curious, he opened the trunk to discover the nude and "shockingly distorted" body of a young white woman.[23] Horrified, the baggage master called the police, who dispatched messengers to call one of the city's four coroners. At 9 o'clock that night, the coroner, Herrman ordered a post-mortem examination, and the body was carried away to the morgue at Bellevue.

A post-mortem examination conducted by Dr. Joseph Cushman, a young Russian doctor who served as deputy coroner under Herrman, revealed that the woman had died of "metroperitonitis"—an infection of the uterus and peritoneum caused by a botched abortion. In the days of frantic investigation that followed this revelation, the "Great Trunk Mystery" led police to the door of Jacob Rosenzweig, one of the abortionists St. Clair had visited for his piece in the *Times*. Rosenzweig denied any involvement in or knowledge of the woman's death, but police kept uncovering evidence connecting him to the trunk. First there were some bloody rags discovered along with part of a petticoat under a pile of rubbish. Then police found a chemise "of fine quality," also stained with blood and showing evidence of "a determined effort" to destroy its identity. Then, in a second search, a police captain named

Cameron pulled a linen handkerchief out of a laundry basket, faintly embroidered with the initials "A.A. Bowlsby."[24]

Then there was the question of how the trunk had gotten to the station. The porter who had delivered the trunk to the depot testified to picking it up from Rosenzweig's office, and an undertaker from down the street came forward swearing that Rosenzweig had recently approached him to ask how much it would cost to bury a woman. "It did not matter to him how or when she was buried," the undertaker said, "so that it was done."[25]

As evidence against Rosenzweig mounted, the identity of the woman in the trunk still remained a mystery. Her body, by now heavily decomposed, was put on display at Bellevue Hospital, but so far the public masses marching through the morgue had failed to positively identify her. But as news about Dr. Rosenzweig's guilt emerged in the press, Augustus St. Clair came forward to reveal previously untold details of his visit to Dr. Rosenzweig—details that linked the doctor definitively to the woman in the trunk. Dr. Rosenzweig, St. Clair claimed, had sworn to him that if the mother died in the course of the abortion, "We can do the thing up handsomely, and I can save you lots of expense." Immediately after this damning admission, St. Clair revealed, Rosenzweig had realized that his visitor was a spy, and, "wrought up to the highest pitch of excitement," threatened to kill him—a fate St. Clair escaped narrowly by drawing a revolver and taking advantage of the doctor's momentary alarm to run out of the room. On his way out of the office, St. Clair stated, he had seen a young blond woman standing on the stairs. "It was the same face I saw afterward at the Morgue," he wrote. "I positively identify the features of the dead woman as those of the blonde beauty . . . and will testify to the fact, if called upon to do so."[26]

St. Clair's story seemed to prove beyond a shadow of a doubt that the dead woman had visited Dr. Rosenzweig for an abortion—but he couldn't put a name to the rapidly decomposing face in Bellevue's morgue. It was a dentist from New Jersey, in the end, who came forward to attach a name to the victim. Joseph Parker, upon examining the corpse at Bellevue, recognized his own dental work and identified the body as that of Alice Augusta Bowlsby—the owner of the handkerchief discovered in Rosenzweig's office. The press, looking into the character of the deceased, found that she was "a young girl whose life had apparently never been darkened, and upon whom the breath of suspicion had never fallen." A "respectable" girl with "relatives in the highest circles," she was known for her amiable character and elegant manners, and "her rare beauty surrounded her with many devoted admirers."[27]

The identification of Alice Bowlsby's body provided the press with the final element of a new kind of abortion story. In the past, newspapers had written about abortion as a weapon wielded by greedy and untrained women like Madame Restell against innocent country girls recently transplanted to the city. Now, with a beautiful white woman from upper middle-class society as the victim and a volatile Jewish immigrant as the villain, the story of abortion became the story of racial and class politics. The old abortion stories had no heroes, only incompetent police forces and heartbroken lovers. But in the "Great Trunk Mystery" of 1871, heroes abounded, from the police who chased down Alice's killer to the press, the champions of truth and defenders of the unborn who brought the whole story to light.

Physicians also played their heroic part in the abortion drama. At an inquest held after the identification of the body, physician testimony helped to secure the jury's finding that Alice Augusta Bowlsby met her death by metroperitonitis resulting from an abortion performed by Jacob Rosenzweig, probably on the very day that the *New York Times* published "The Evil of the Age."[28] Rosenzweig vehemently denied the charges, but he was taken into custody anyway and sent to the Tombs prison to await trial.

The Bowlsby case moved the debate over abortion from the private meetings of state medical societies and legislative sessions into the sphere of public discourse. Over the summer and early autumn of 1871, the *New York Times* impressed upon its readership two basic ideas: abortion was a public danger, and thinking about it was a public responsibility. As Tanfer Emin Tunç notes in her study of nineteenth-century criminal abortion narratives, although stories like the "Great Trunk Mystery" dropped off in the press after 1871, "abortion remain[ed] a national obsession in the United States" ever afterward.[29]

In September 1871, Alice Augusta Bowlsby was buried in New York's potter's field on Hart Island while Jacob Rosenzweig waited in the Tombs for his upcoming trial.[30] Later that month, one hundred and fifty miles up the Hudson River, reporters from the *Albany Evening Journal* and the *Argus* attended inquest hearings on the death of Maggie Campbell, no doubt hoping to open a local chapter in the best-selling story begun in New York City. The stakes were clear to those listening: although Dr. Emma Burleigh wasn't on trial, the findings of the inquest would determine whether or not she, like Dr. Rosenzweig, could be charged with criminal abortion. If the jury came back with the verdict that Maggie Campbell had died from an abortion, Josephine would be subject to second-degree manslaughter charges, which carried a possible penalty of up to seven years in state prison.

Josephine was the first witness to testify at the inquest. At 8 o'clock on the evening of September 27, Mrs. Burleigh made a statement before Coroner Harrigan's jury, explaining the timeline of events as she understood them: Maggie had arrived three weeks ago as a servant and had taken ill on Tuesday. All Mrs. Burleigh's efforts could not save the patient, who passed away after three days of severe pain. She had notified the Cleary sisters, since they were the only relatives Maggie had mentioned, and provided for the poor girl's burial. At no time, Mrs. Burleigh stated, had she suspected pregnancy, though the pains her patient described were "somewhat similar in their character to those which would attend labor pains." Yes, she did make a specialty of "private diseases among females," but she would admit to no connection between her line of work and the tragedy of last Thursday. With that, the hearing adjourned for the night.[31]

The following afternoon, the inquest resumed with testimony from the five doctors involved in the case: Dr. Boulware and Dr. Charles H. Porter, who had conducted the initial post-mortem at Mrs. Burleigh's house, and Drs. Henry Haskins, John Lansing, and Albert Vanderveer, who performed the autopsy at the cemetery the morning of the inquest. Dr. Boulware began by stating that he had agreed to do the post-mortem at Mrs. Burleigh's insistence, but only on the condition that another physician assisted and the results were made public. He rehearsed the findings laid out in the official cause of death: "On opening the body we found the peritoneum universally inflamed, and the tissue of the heart fatty and softened: I think death was caused by peritonitis—general inflammation of the peritoneum." Asked about the condition of the intestines, Dr. Boulware admitted that he had found no evidence of diarrhea—the first direct contradiction to the testimony of Mrs. Burleigh, who had told the jury the previous night that Maggie's illness began with severe diarrhea. When Coroner Harrigan asked him what had caused the inflammation that killed Maggie, Dr. Boulware refused to give a definitive answer. "There are so many causes," he said, and listed several possibilities: a physical blow, an injury to an existing wound, or ulceration of the bowels. Of course, none of these possible explanations for Maggie's infection answered the lurking question in the minds of everyone present: *had she been pregnant at the time of her death?*

"[I] saw no evidence that uterus had contained a foetus," Dr. Boulware asserted, "that is, within the last three or four weeks." Even more explicitly, he stated that he "saw no evidence that an abortion had been produced within the last three or four weeks." Though there was, in his opinion, some evidence that the deceased had *at some time* borne a child or children, "there was no positive evidence in the uterus that the woman had or had not been pregnant, except that it was larger than usual; there were no indications that a foetus had recently been delivered." Gaining confidence with each denial, Dr. Boulware swore to the jury that "a dozen [fetuses] might have been removed and no evidence remain in the uterus."[32]

But the uterus was missing. In fact, in performing his post-mortem, Dr. Boulware had removed several parts of Maggie Campbell's body, including the left kidney, a portion of the heart, and the whole of the uterus and most of its appendages.[33] This, he explained, was a routine practice; he removed the organ to dissect it, and after the dissection destroyed it, as he would do in any post-mortem examination. Notably, he failed to elaborate on what he'd found in that dissection.

Yet there was one odd piece of evidence which Dr. Boulware found it harder to brazen his way out of. Maggie's breasts, he informed the jury, had been in "a normal condition" at the time of her death. What kind of normal condition? Well, Dr. Boulware said, "milk escaped on pressure." This, he admitted, was "some evidence that the uterus had contained a foetus within a month" after all.[34] But he cautioned his audience not to put too much stock in Maggie's breasts: the presence of milk only meant *"that the woman had been or was about to become a mother;* she might have had a child and milk be found in the breasts, six or twelve months afterwards."[35] The editors of the *Albany Evening Journal*, recording this evidence, took special care to put this line in italics, flagging its crucial importance for anyone not reading carefully.

Dr. Porter, who testified after Dr. Boulware, largely contented himself with agreeing with his colleague's account. Yes, the peritoneum was inflamed; yes, the cause of death was certainly peritonitis. In fact, Dr. Porter agreed with Dr. Boulware "in every particular, except that I have no recollection of seeing any portion of the intestines laid open." Dr. Porter explained to the jury the phenomenon of puerperal peritonitis, or inflammation of the peritoneum following childbirth. He described the various methods for procuring abortion, including "mechanical injury to the parts," and noted that such an operation was "sometimes necessary to save the life of the patient"—as, indeed, the 1869 state law allowed. But he couldn't say for certain that any operation of that kind had been performed on Maggie Campbell prior to her death. He stated, finally, that he "[did] not think it possible, absolutely, to tell whether a uterus has contained or not contained a foetus three weeks previous to the examination." Dr. Porter retired from the witness stand, and a recess was called for dinner.[36]

The evening session opened with the testimony of Mary Cleary, one of the two keepers of the Union Street boarding house. She related to the jury the story of Maggie's arrival at the house; her association with Peter Mochrie, who had called for her on three separate evenings; her strange trips to the countryside to visit relatives who never seemed to be at home. She and her sister had received the news of Maggie's death from Mrs. Burleigh. "I felt real bad about her," Mary recalled, "and I said that I would tell the girls of the Mansion House." But Mrs. Burleigh, she told the court, had objected to that suggestion, telling her instead "that I had better say nothing about it." When Mary asked Dr. Burleigh what to do with the dead girl's clothing, she answered that the Clearys now owned any clothes Maggie had left at their house. Throughout Mary Cleary's testimony, Josephine was sitting in the audience, listening to the landlady incriminate her again and again.[37]

One of the features of the coroner's inquest that gives it, in Paul MacMahon's view, unusual power is the fact that any concerned member of the public may, if they so choose, take an active role in the interrogation of witnesses and thereby "seek to influence the proceedings."[38] Hearing Mary Cleary tell the jury a story in which Josephine seemed to be encouraging the sister to cover up the circumstances of Maggie's death, Josephine herself took advantage of this right and came forward to ask the landlady a few follow-up questions.

"Did I ask you if she had any relatives?" she asked. Yes, Mary recalled: "I said that she had a moth[er] in Troy."[39] Mrs. B, she now remembered, had been "very anxious to find [Maggie's] relatives." In light of this information, it was easier to imagine that the doctor's admonition not to tell any of Maggie's former coworkers what had happened came from a desire to inform her family first.

After Josephine's cross-examination, the coroner called the next witness: Peter Mochrie, Maggie Campbell's alleged guardian and former lover. He admitted that he had known Maggie Campbell—known her carnally, in fact—for two years off and on. Pushed to characterize the nature of their relationship, Mochrie wavered. "I did not know what I intended doing," he told the jury; "time was needed to tell what would be the result." But his intentions, he insisted, were nothing but "honorable." He described his acquaintance with Maggie, their meeting, and their correspondence, examples of which were produced in the courtroom but not published in the *Evening Journal* as their contents were "too indelicate for publication in our columns." Mochrie mentioned that he had "had suspicions she was going with other parties," but this statement seems flimsy in light of Mary Cleary's testimony that Maggie took no visitors but Peter.[40]

Mochrie insisted that he had no knowledge at all of Maggie's pregnancy. The previous winter Maggie had had a scare of that kind, but it quickly resolved itself, and since then she had "never intimated to me she was in the family way; never hinted at there being anything wrong in that direction." He claimed that he had "no idea of what she wanted with the money" he lent her the night before she went to Mrs. Burleigh's. He had heard of her, he acknowledged, through the newspaper and his coworkers at the post office. "They talked of her," he said, "as a woman who treated for private diseases—as an abortionist." But Maggie "never told me she was going to Mrs. Burleigh's," he insisted, "and I honestly believed she was going to Rensselaerville" to visit her family. "She said she would be back in two or three weeks," he said, "and I honestly believed her." When he learned of her death, he admitted, he "took no steps to see about burying her; felt [he] had nothing to do about it." Whatever his intentions with regard to Maggie in life, he claimed no responsibility for her in death.[41]

Harrigan then pressed Mochrie for information about his involvement with other women, if any—a question Mochrie declined at first to answer, saying that "it would compromise [himself]." The coroner evidently didn't care whether or not Mochrie compromised his good reputation, and Mochrie was finally forced to admit that he had, indeed, "had connection with other women, how many he did not know." He insisted, however, that he was not the father of any child—"that I know of." "Did you ever," Harrigan finally asked, "either by note, personally, or by any means, indicate that you would like Maggie to go to Mrs. Burleigh's?" "Never in any way," Mochrie swore, and with that his testimony in the inquest of Maggie Campbell was concluded.[42]

The groundwork of Maggie's story thus established, Harrigan returned to the medical evidence, calling Dr. Henry R. Haskins to the witness stand. Haskins informed the court that he was a practicing physician and surgeon in the city of Albany and a professor of anatomy at the Albany Medical College. In light of these credentials, he had been called by Harrigan to conduct the autopsy at the Albany Rural Cemetery two days earlier. The body, he recalled, was in "a good state of preservation," with no sign of injury save the inevitable marks left behind by the first post-mortem. "The only part that attracted attention," he said, "was that of the external organs of generation; those parts being very much swollen and engorged with blood and dilated; in the floor of the vagina was found a laceration or wound occupied by a clot of blood."[43]

The jury sat up straighter; this was something new. Dr. Haskins continued: all the blood vessels in the pelvic region "seemed to be unusually engorged with blood," and the breasts were "well developed and contained milk" with "no evidence of recent nursing, or of her having ever nursed a child." This knocked a hole in Dr. Boulware's careful insistence that the presence of milk could simply be evidence of a previous pregnancy, though Dr. Haskins agreed that "the evidence of the breasts in the condition they were, were simply evidences that she had been pregnant sometime." More damning was Dr. Haskins's assertion that he found "no evidence of disease in that part of the peritoneum left in the body," and certainly "no evidences of inflammatory action sufficient to cause death." Indeed, he said, "there was not anything remaining in the body to indicate a disease of the peritoneum."[44]

Those repeated phrases—no evidence left in the body, not anything remaining—reminded the jury of the missing uterus which Dr. Boulware and his colleague had dissected. Without the uterus, Dr. Haskins couldn't conclusively identify the cause of death. Still, the autopsy had revealed two unmistakable signs which could not be ignored: the distinctive dilated condition of the genitalia, and the unusual engorgement of the blood vessels surrounding the missing uterus. These appearances, in Dr. Haskins's opinion, "were evidence of the uterus having contained a foetus a few days prior to her death." This estimate was notably shorter than the "few months" that Dr. Boulware had suggested could have transpired between Maggie Campbell's alleged pregnancy and her death. Haskins allowed that several other factors could conceivably have produced similar signs in the body, but could give no explanation for the external injury and the clot of blood except to say that it was "such an injury as might be caused by the birth of a child."[45]

Dr. Haskins had just placed Josephine in serious danger. If the jury concluded that Maggie had indeed been pregnant and returned a verdict of death as a result of abortion, then a court could find her guilty of second-degree manslaughter. And so, once again, Dr. Burleigh stepped up to cross-examine the witness. She drilled him at length about the peritoneum, asking him to explain to the jury its form and function, and the distinctions between all the many diseases which might affect it. Again and again, her questions chipped away at the mountain of medical certainty he had just raised up. Would the vascularity he observed in the body not be the same in the case of another pelvic disease? Could the condition of the swollen genitalia not be explained by a sexually transmitted infection as easily as by a recent pregnancy? To each of these questions, Dr. Haskins was compelled to answer "yes." Upon re-direct, Haskins reiterated that "the parts taken away might or might not show the disease was puerperal peritonitis," but Josephine's interrogation had undermined that "might."[46]

The remainder of the medical testimony was brief: Dr. John V. Lansing, called to give his account of the autopsy, was happy to simply agree with Dr. Haskins's testimony, and Dr. Albert Vanderveer did much the same, adding only that they had found a woolen cloth covering the intestines, which had helped to preserve them. Like his colleague, he could not give any concrete opinion as to the cause of death. The coroner called Dr. Boulware one last time, and he told the jury that he had no knowledge of the vaginal injury Dr. Haskins had testified to. Asked how such an injury might have occurred, he suggested that it might have been caused when he placed the woolen cloth Dr. Vanderveer described inside the body. He described his dissection of the womb in vague terms without giving details of his findings, and retired from the stand for good. Finally, Mrs. Burleigh returned as a witness, testifying that she had sent word to Mary Cleary on the day of Maggie's death; that Maggie had never given her any money; and that, contrary to Mary's own evidence, she had not requested that she and her sister keep the matter quiet when they talked in the back hallway on that tragic Thursday.[47]

With that, the evidence was complete. Harrigan turned the case over to the jury, who retired for two hours and returned with the verdict that the cause of Margaret Campbell's death on September 21 was peritonitis. The verdict made no mention of abortion and assigned no responsibility for the death. The state had no crime to prosecute. The proper paperwork was signed, the document stamped and filed, and the witnesses left the courtroom.

Why did the Campbell jury rule that Maggie's death was not the result of abortion, while the Bowlsby jury just weeks before had assigned the blame for Alice Bowlsby's death to Jacob Rosenzweig? It would be tempting to imagine that Josephine single-handedly averted a manslaughter charge through skillful interrogation, but even with the doubt she introduced to Haskins's medical findings and to the Cleary sisters' damning recollections of her attempted coverup, the evidence remained fairly conclusive. The missing uterus, the lactating corpse, and, indeed, Josephine's own desperate efforts to redirect attention away from these clues, all pointed to the obvious conclusion that Maggie Campbell died because the abortion Josephine performed caused a fatal infection. Yet, rather than return a verdict along those lines, the six men called by Coroner Harrigan chose to assign the cause of Maggie's death to simple peritonitis.

It wasn't a lack of evidence that made the Campbell case different from the Bowlsby case; it was the abortionists themselves. It's impossible to understand why the two inquests reached such different conclusions without looking at the abortionists whose practice stood at the heart of the issue. Jacob Rosenzweig reflected the worst fears of white Protestant America: a Jewish immigrant whose unauthorized medical practice led to a pretty blonde girl's death. Public reports seemed to keep his national origin vague, perhaps deliberately so. Augustus St. Clair couldn't decide whether he was Russian or German. "He is very bulky in figure," St. Clair wrote, and "is said to know more of the saloon business than of medicine."[48] The official report of the Bowlsby case, published in 1872 by Barclay & Co. of Philadelphia, indicated that he was a Polish immigrant and called him "a fat, coarse and sensual-looking fellow, without any traces of refinement in person or manners," who "does not bear the faintest appearance of the educated physician."[49] Throughout the coverage of the Bowlsby case, the scientific and philosophical debates about the nature of abortion that motivated the physicians' crusade fell away in favor of a horror story that pitted an unskilled Jewish immigrant's greed against the life and purity of a white, Protestant, native-born female victim.

Josephine resembled the victim in this new abortion drama more than the villain. Josephine's gender might have put her at a disadvantage when it came to getting a medical education, but she possessed all the characteristics that the crusade against abortion was meant to protect: that is, she was a white Protestant woman, born in the United States, and, as a result of her successful medical career, middle class. In fact, she fit the profile of abortion victim better than Maggie Campbell, a working-class Irish immigrant. While it's unlikely that anyone present at the inquest saw Josephine McCarty as a victim, her membership in the same broad social classes as the jury meant that she, unlike Jacob Rosenzweig, possessed a special kind of medical legitimacy: she was the kind of woman that middle-class white men wanted their wives to turn to for abortion care.

Horatio Storer had told the nation that abortion was murder. New York State's medical society and legislature agreed. Now the *New York Times* had thrown its weight behind the physicians' campaign. But in practice, abortion remained an accepted part of reproductive life for many Americans. As 1871 drew to a close, Josephine's narrow escape from the law proved that the question of who provided abortions was just as important as the question of whether or not the practice itself should remain legal.

Josephine's privileged social position might have allowed her to evade criminal charges, but it offered her less protection in her personal life. In fact, well before the 1871 inquest, she was already ensnared in an ongoing legal battle with none other than Milton Thomson. Their relationship had soured since the war and the rumors of his attempt to have her "gotten rid of," and by the autumn of 1871, the house he'd helped her to purchase on Howard Street was no longer the refuge it had once been. In fact, it was no longer legally hers.

The trouble had started the same summer that she moved in. Shortly after the purchase of the property and the first $1,000 mortgage, Josephine had gotten Milton Thomson's assistance in taking out a second mortgage for another $1,000 in the name of Thomson's friend Ephraim Chamberlain, treasurer and secretary of the Utica Steam Cotton Mills.[50] At the same time, she started making improvements to the property, hoping to keep her budget within $500—but either she'd underestimated the amount of work needed, or her design goals were too ambitious.[51] By the end of the summer, the cost of repairs to 62 Howard was closer to $5,000, a sum she had no way of paying herself.[52] Throughout the fall and early winter of 1869, she struggled to raise the funds, but failed to come up with the money: in April of 1870, contractors issued a mechanics' lien for failure to pay for repairs made to 62 Howard Street, and the property went up for sale.[53]

In the past, Josephine would have fallen back on Tom's generosity to pay off the debt. He'd been giving her money for years, ever since their reunion at her mother's farm in 1854. Their relationship had not been without its moments of friction, but in recent years the differences between them appeared to have been put aside as they settled into an arrangement in which Thomson enjoyed the occasional intimate company of his old mistress in exchange for financial support for her and his two children, who knew him as "Uncle Tom" and looked forward to his visits to Albany.[54]

But by 1871, the amicable spirit was gone. Maybe Tom had simply grown tired of the risk and financial burden of supporting Josephine's growing family, not to mention the effort of keeping that illicit cash-flow secret from his wife. Maybe he'd genuinely lost all interest in the woman he'd once professed to love like a wife. Rumors also suggested that Thomson's health was failing, leaving his brothers Mortimer and LaMott to take a firmer hand in his business, both professional and personal. Maybe it was Mortimer and LaMott, more than Milton Thomson, who decided it was time for the affair to end. Whatever the reason, the result for Josephine was the same: mired in debt she could never afford to pay off on her own, at risk of losing her home, her livelihood, and her children's safety, and under the watchful eye of the law, she now found herself betrayed by the one person she had always counted on to get her out of exactly this sort of trouble.

But Josephine refused to accept defeat. She convinced her friend, Albany lawyer LeGrand Bancroft, to purchase the house in June 1870 on her account.[55] She and her children could stay where they were; her practice could continue uninterrupted. Still, Josephine's debts were mounting; having emptied her bank accounts into repairs, she still owed money on the original mortgages, and the due dates for those bills were rapidly approaching. Desperate, she traveled to Utica at the end of June to appeal to Tom to purchase the Augusta farm for the sum of $5,000—enough to pay off her debts and take full legal possession of 62 Howard Street without fear of foreclosure.[56] In addition to the sale of the farm, she had two further demands, both of them concerning her and Tom's son Juddie, which she detailed in emphatic terms to Tom's lawyer Thomas Spriggs in a letter dated July 3rd. "It is no use to talk of half-way measures," Josephine informed Spriggs. "This house must be deeded unencumbered to Juddy," and "an insurance of $5,000 put on my life for Juddy, paid up to Milton's death."[57]

Tom refused. Josephine returned to Albany, only to find that in her brief absence someone had attempted to move her belongings out of the house. She wrote to Spriggs with her outrage: "My carpets were taken up and my furniture partly packed." Despite this apparent warning she insisted, "I shall not abate one jot of my demand." By this point, her feud with Tom was about much more than financial security: "The revenge is worth more to me than the money," she told Spriggs, "though it may not be to the child."[58] She ended the letter with an ultimatum:

> I shall wait only until Monday, and if I do not hear from you by Monday night, something more definite than as yet been offered, I shall go with Juddy to New York on Monday Night, and shall call on the officers of the New York Insurance companies there, and on the Physicians who have Mr. Thompson in charge. I shall see Mrs. Thompson, no matter how often she changes residences. If you think I shall not keep my word week after next when I come to Utica, you will assure me differently. I am only carrying out what I received upon [sic] years ago as soon as the end should come. Milt Thompson [sic] shall have a story in circulation that shall carry a deeper meaning than his funeral sermon.

Almost a year later, on May 30, 1871, Warren S. Kelly issued a foreclosure on 62 Howard Street in the name of Ephraim Chamberlain.[59] Once again, Josephine called on Bancroft to intervene on her behalf, but this time the Thomsons were ahead of her. When he arrived at Kelly's office, Bancroft discovered Mortimer Thomson and his brother LaMott already there, ready to sign the paperwork. The house was sold for $5,700 in June to LaMott Thomson in the name of Charles S. Green, a friend of the Thomsons then living on Long Island but happy to allow his name to be used to wrestle the Albany property out from under Milton's troublesome mistress.[60] Within weeks, Green had filed a claim for surplus mortgage on the property.

This drawn-out legal battle was starting to have an effect on Josephine. On the evening of May 31, the day after the final foreclosure on 62 Howard Street, the Albany alderman Thomson Mulhall was standing at the corner of Park Avenue and Philip Street around 7 p.m. when an unfamiliar woman approached him with her servant. Without giving her name, she asked if he knew Mr. Mulhall or where he lived; upon learning that she was talking to the man himself, she explained that she was looking for "a couple of trusty men" to watch her house, and had been given his name.[61] There were burglars coming, the woman went on, and she had no husband at home to defend her. Her name, she said, was Dr. Burleigh, and the house under attack was 62 Howard Street.

Mulhall obliged, calling up a neighbor to help him stand watch at Howard Street. The burglars never appeared, and the men departed after midnight, satisfied that Josephine and her children were safe. Six weeks later, a young boy appeared at Mulhall's office several days in a row. He said his name was Louis Seymour, and he left repeated messages from his mother begging Mr. Mullhall to come back and watch for burglars. After a week's badgering, Mulhall gave in, bringing with him this time a baker named Thomas Merriman. The pair arrived at 62 Howard Street to find the gas lights turned down so far that Mrs. Burleigh and her servant appeared as shadowy masses, indistinguishable from each other. The doctor offered Merriman a pistol, but he declined. He then sat at her kitchen table until 3 o'clock in the morning, but again saw nothing. At 3 a.m., tired of watching, Mulhall and Merriman departed by the back door.

Mulhall was not the only one receiving urgent requests for security from Dr. Burleigh that summer. The day after she first contacted Mulhall, Josephine called on her neighbor Timothy Strong, a printer for the Albany *Argus*, to stand watch at her house for burglars she expected to arrive on the night boat from New York.[62] Like Mulhall, he agreed to watch; like Mulhall, he saw nothing and formed the opinion that Dr. Burleigh had lost her mind. Throughout the summer of 1871, Strong occasionally found Louis crawling through the window connecting his house to 62 Howard, begging him in tears to come over and help his mother fight off the burglars she was sure had been warned of by mail, or seen passing in the street, or heard knocking things around in the backyard.

The burglars never came. The sheriff did. On Thursday, January 4, 1872, Undersheriff John P. Bradt knocked on Josephine McCarty's door and showed her a writ of assistance authorizing him to remove her from the premises. Josephine begged him for more time—by Monday or Tuesday of next week, she said, she could be out of the place. Bradt, who had known Mrs. McCarty for six years, was in no hurry to throw her and her children out into the street, so he agreed to return in a few days' time. He waited until Tuesday, but when he came back to the house that day Mrs. McCarty told him she had not yet found another place to live. She had been packing but had made no arrangements for her belongings or furniture, and implored Bradt to give her another extension. But he refused—this time, he told her, he "should have to go right on." When he returned early on Wednesday morning with a deputy and seven men, Bradt found the house nearly packed up and Mrs. McCarty "excited." When the deputy began directing the sheriff's men in carrying her belongings from the house to the street, Josephine sat down on the sofa and cried. "She thought it hard," Bradt remembered, "to be put in the street in winter."[63]

Sometime between 1 and 2 o'clock, the removal was complete: all of Josephine McCarty's earthly possessions were in the street, and 62 Howard Street was empty. Howard Street itself was full, with spectators and neighbors and people hopeful of picking up a few odds and ends that the doctor couldn't carry away herself. A neighbor, Mrs. Garwin of 60 Howard Street, agreed to take in some of the goods for safekeeping and allowed the evicted family to sleep under her roof on Wednesday night.[64]

On Thursday night, Nancy Scrivens, a friend and former patient of Dr. Burleigh's, opened her door after dinner to find Louis Seymour standing on the doorstep. He asked Nancy if his mother could stay the night. It might have been an odd request—Nancy had only visited Dr. Burleigh two or three times in the year she had known her, and the two were not particularly close—but Nancy had read in the paper that morning about Mrs. Burleigh of Howard Street being thrown out of her home, and with Louis standing in her doorway she could hardly say no. Within a few minutes, Josephine, Juddie, and Josie had come around the corner with a packed valise holding all their clothes. Nancy, who had other company staying at the time, was as gracious as she could be, conducting the family up to bed and doing what she could to make them comfortable under what were undeniably uncomfortable circumstances for all involved. Josephine didn't say much that first night: "she looked tired and said she was tired."[65]

The following morning, while the children ran out in the yard to play, Nancy sat at the breakfast table with Josephine, who was complaining of a headache. "Have you ever felt as if you had water running through your head?" she asked.[66] Nancy could not say that she had, but Josephine did—she made the comment several times, as if she couldn't remember that she had already said it. She felt as though she was coming down with something—inflammation of the brain, or something; the water kept running through her head. Nancy thought she had better stay there until she felt better. Josephine disagreed. She had business to attend to, friends to call on; she had been turned out in the winter with her children, and now her head was full of water and she couldn't think what to do. Sitting at the table with an untouched cup of tea in front of her, Josephine burst into tears so violent she couldn't speak, and ran upstairs to the room she and her children had shared the night before.

Shaken, Nancy went to consult with her husband. Whatever the circumstances surrounding the doctor's eviction, they couldn't throw this woman and her children out on the street. She was afraid to leave Josephine alone in the upstairs bedroom much longer, much less to send her away in this state of mind. After a quick conversation with Mr. Scrivens, Nancy climbed the stairs to check on Josephine, whom she found "crying and taking on in her room . . . wringing her hands, [and] saying she did not know what she would do with herself and children."[67] After ten or fifteen minutes, Nancy had calmed Josephine down enough to bring her back downstairs, but she still seemed distracted. She must go to Utica—she had a friend in Utica—she would go to Utica and consult with the friend about her mother's farm.

Stay another night, Nancy implored her. Better to rest up and recover her energy before setting about any more business. A few days' delay wouldn't make a difference to the friend in Utica; her farm, at any rate, wasn't likely to pick up its feet and run off. "I did not like the looks of her eyes," Nancy recalled later. "There was a marked change in her appearance from what I had noticed about her before; her eyes look[ed] wild."[68] Josephine and the children stayed at Nancy Scrivens's house until Saturday afternoon, a little under forty-eight hours. On Saturday, Josephine got up early, packed a trunk for Louis and another for herself and the two little ones, and loaded her family on board a train bound for Utica. That was January 13.

"The next thing I heard of," Mrs. Scrivens said, "was a homicide."[69]

CHAPTER 9

The Privilege of Murder

Josephine and the children arrived in Utica on the evening of Saturday, January 13. They didn't go to the Thomsons' house; instead, they went straight from the depot to the Butterfield House, a ritzy four-story hotel located in downtown Utica just steps from the insurance agency of M. H. and M. G. Thomson on Genesee Street. She shared one bed with Josie that night; the boys slept together in the other.

In Josephine's luggage was everything she owned. Her things were packed along with Juddie and Josie's; Louis's clothes were in a separate bag. Once she'd resolved things with Tom, she planned to send him west to Niagara Falls, where the Episcopal Diocese of New York operated the DeVeaux College for Orphans and Destitute Children, a military school for boys eight to twelve years old.[1] Louis was the oldest, but he was also the only one of Josephine's children who wasn't Tom's. She couldn't claim child support for him, and without a home or an income, the best she could do for him was to send him away for good.

But first she had to talk to Tom. He wouldn't be in his office over the weekend, so Josephine spent Sunday in her room. She didn't say much to the children; what was there to say? The headache that had started at Mrs. Scrivens's house hadn't abated, and Josephine could feel the sensation of water rushing through her head. While the children played, she paced the floor, her head in her hands, dizzy from a lack of sleep and food.

On Monday morning, Josephine ate breakfast in a private dining room at the Butterfield then went out to see her lawyer, warning Louis to keep the door to their room locked. She went down the block to the office of Robert O. Jones, an attorney she'd consulted in the past, and explained everything that had happened: the long battle over 62 Howard Street, the day she'd come home to find her things half-packed, and finally the sheriff's arrival at her door—once, twice, and a third time with men to force her and her children out onto the frozen street.[2] Jones sent a messenger to Thomson's office to see if he was in, but they returned with the news that Thomson's clerks hadn't seen him since Friday.

Josephine left Jones's office and started down Genesee Street, walking into shops and asking the staff if they'd seen Milton Thomson. Nobody had. Exhausted and overwhelmed, Josephine went back to the Butterfield Hotel to spend another sleepless night with her children.

On Tuesday morning, she went out again, telling Louis once more not to let anyone into the room. Again, she walked up and down snowy Genesee Street, asking everyone she met if they'd seen Milton Thomson go by. Nobody knew; some thought that Mr. Thomson must be out of town. So Josephine started asking a second question: What time did Mr. Thomson usually go to his office? Ten o'clock, someone told her. Every morning, at 10 o'clock, Milton Thomson took the streetcar from his house near Oneida Square to his downtown office.

The following morning, Josephine stood in the snow by Oneida Square, just out of sight of Milton Thomson's house. In the pocket of her heavy winter coat was a revolver; she'd used it before to shoot rats in the backyard at Howard Street and she'd kept it with her on those late nights the previous autumn when she sat up, heart in her throat, waiting for burglars to arrive from New York. Now it rested against her side as she watched Tom emerge from his front door, accompanied by a young man she'd never seen before. She ran after the streetcar that had just passed and got on, shaking the snow from her boots and the hem of her skirt. A few minutes later, the car stopped again—and there, at last, was Tom.

If he noticed her, he gave no sign of it. Josephine watched him settle himself on the seat across from her as if it was a perfectly normal Wednesday morning. As if he—the person who'd comforted her after the loss of her oldest children, the person who'd given her a second chance at life after Robert brought the first one crashing down, the one who once said that he'd love her in every way a husband could—wasn't the reason that she and her children were now homeless.

She got out of her seat and stood in front of him. "Tom," she said loudly. He looked up. "I've brought your children," she told him, "that you turned out in the streets to starve. I cannot support them any longer."[3] Tom looked up at her. "Go to hell with them," he said.

"The next I recollect," Josephine remembered later, "I was standing near the middle of the car." She noticed her revolver on the seat opposite her; there was a smear of melted candy on the barrel. She'd noticed it days ago, and she'd told Louis to clean it. Apparently, he never had. She picked up the gun and glanced to her right. She saw Tom sitting with his face turned away, a ragged hole in his cheek starting to ooze bright blood. She watched in slow motion as his hands came up to clutch at the wound.

Then she was on the platform, in the blasting January air. She was holding onto a stranger, and then he was helping her off the car, walking down the street with her through the trampled snow, away from the streetcar and toward the hotel where Louis and Juddie and Josie were waiting. The police caught up with them midway down Genesee Street. They asked Josephine what had caused the trouble.

"If you knew what trouble that man had made," she told them.

Josephine was taken into custody on the street within minutes of the streetcar's arrival at the Butterfield House. Henry Hall was dead by the time the car stopped outside the hotel. Doctors who had been called there to treat the wounded found that the bullet that failed to kill Milton Thomson had lodged in his nephew's right lung, killing him in less than five minutes.

By the evening of January 17, the *Utica Daily Observer* picked up the story of Henry Hall's death. On the second page, under the sparse heading "The Tragedy," the paper laid out the simple facts of the case: "In the broad light of day, a desperate woman seeking vengeance, wounds her intended victim and kills outright a young man whom she never saw before, and against whom she could entertain no ill will."[4]

The story sold. "The excitement which prevailed in Utica yesterday," the Friday edition read, "growing out of terrible tragedy enacted on our principal thoroughfare, was never surpassed, perhaps never equaled."[5] So great was the public's demand for information that "our double cylinder press, which throws off sixty impressions per minute, was kept constantly at work for many hours to supply the unprecedented demand." Murder was good business for the *Observer*: "The sale of last evening's paper," the article noted, "was twice as large as on any occasion during the war."

Josephine's crime was big news—and so was she. In the days following the shooting, as news of the crime spread from Utica to the rest of the nation, the woman who killed the wrong man became a source of rampant curiosity. By the weekend, all the major papers were trading various versions of Josephine's biography, with an emphasis on her career as an abortionist, her stint as a Confederate spy, and her repeated intrigues with powerful men from Albany to Washington to Philadelphia. The Friday evening edition of the *Observer* was peppered with eye-catching headlines: "MISTRESS OF A NOTED POLITICAL LEADER"; "SMUGGLING QUININE"; "A REBEL SPY"; "BITTER PERSONAL ATTACK"; "THE TERRIBLE LIFE SHE WAS LEADING." In Mrs. McCarty's luggage at the hotel, the paper reported, authorities had discovered "AN INSTRUMENT OF DEATH" made of wire, "*the various threads of which were coated with blood.*"[6]

Josephine wasn't the only one surrounded by swirling rumors. On the same page, the *Observer* printed a statement from Milton Thomson:

> To the Public—I do not expect to silence the clamor of those who devour character and fatten thereon; but I have a right to demand, and do demand, that all sensible people, and especially those who have professed to be my friends, withhold their judgment till they get the facts.
>
> MILTON H. THOMSON.[7]

But by now, the facts were public knowledge. The little boy and girl staying alone at the Butterfield Hotel while Josephine awaited trial in the Mohawk Street Jail were Milton Thomson's children, brought to Utica on their mother's murderous mission. "They are very bright, intelligent and winning children," the *Observer* reported, and "do not realize the extent of the terrible calamity which has befallen them."[8]

In addition to the prisoner's biography and updates on her children, the *Observer* offered its readers a little primer on the law. On the second page of Thursday's evening edition, a brief column simply headed "Murder and Homicide" provided readers with the precise legal definitions of murder in the first and second degree, as well as manslaughter in the first, second, third, and fourth degrees.[9] The column highlighted the problem of Josephine's case: the law had no specific rule defining the appropriate punishment for a person who, in the process of trying to murder one person, accidentally killed another. Should Josephine's crime be considered first-degree murder—"killing with premeditated design to effect the death of the person killed, or of any human being"? She had, after all, planned the death of one person, and she'd killed one person. Did the fact that they weren't the same person matter? Or should the court charge her with manslaughter in the fourth degree, defined as "the involuntary killing of another by any weapon . . . in the heat of passion"?

The difference was more than a technicality. If the jury convicted her of murder, Josephine would be sentenced to death. By contrast, if the court decided she was guilty of no more than fourth-degree man-slaughter, she could be sent to the penitentiary for a maximum of two years, or even walk off with no more than a fine. Either sentence, depending on one's perspective, might represent a grave miscarriage of justice. With the trial still weeks away and Henry Hall's body still await-ing burial, the *Observer* invited the people of Utica to conduct their own private deliberations.

The editors of the *Observer*, for their part, had already made up their minds: they were on Tom's side. "Assuming that this community wanted facts rather than theories bearing on the recent tragedy enacted here," read an editorial in the Saturday edition, "we have heretofore refrained from comment."[10] But the time for neutral objectivity had passed. Now, the editors of the *Observer* urged readers not to give too much credence to the rumors that Josephine had shot Thomson to avenge his mistreatment of her and the children:

> A shot is fired, a man is killed, the guilty party is arrested, and straightway a story is industriously circulated to the effect that the manslayer has suffered grievous wrongs, and has been ren-dered desperate thereby. The story may be true or it may be false. The breath of opinion created by its belief is not to be mistaken for the settled drift of public sentiment, which it resembles no more than a bellows-blast resembles the north wind.

As for Milton Thomson: "He has dwelt among us all his life, and his record is public property." The strength of the story against him rested on the character of "the person most interested in sustaining it." And Josephine, the editors claimed, was "a professional blackmailer." Alongside the editorial, they reprinted an article by William Cassidy, editor for the *Albany Argus*. "This case is not an exceptional one," he argued. "There is a large class of persons, principally women, who live by such threats of exposure."[11] After seducing a man, these blackmailing women would "work upon his fears and his shame when they have ceased to rely upon his love." Josephine was just another of these "social vampires."

"Now we neither deny nor affirm," the Saturday editorial concluded, "that Thomson, whom she attempted to kill, is responsible for her downfall."[12] Thomson himself hadn't tried to contradict the rumors outright. But Thomson's guilt was irrelevant, the editors insisted. Far more important was the fact that Josephine's life history spoke to a disregard for the rules, both written and unwritten, governing women's behavior in particular and morality in general. Not only that—but up till now, she had always gotten away with it: "Black as her career is, and dreadful as is the crime for which she is detained, this woman does not expect to be punished. She has always escaped. When she shot, she had calculated the chances. She expected to become a heroine and to escape after a brief detention the consequences of her crime."[13]

To some, she was already a heroine—or at least a victim. Whether she would escape this time was another matter. As the trial date approached, rumors began to circulate that Tom would use his considerable wealth to pay off the courts and get rid of Josephine once and for all. On January 29, Seth Wilbur Payne, editor of the *Utica Bee*, was arrested for "grossly reflecting on the character and judicial integrity" of Charles H. Doolittle, the judge expected to try Josephine's case. Payne had accused Judge Doolittle of taking money from Thomson and his associates in exchange for his promise to bring in a guilty verdict. Doolittle, the *Observer* reported, "appeared more amused than offended at the account given him of the silly and gratuitous attacks made upon his character" by Payne; he said he "never read the *Bee*."[14]

While editors and judges clashed over the relative guilt of the Utica murderess and her intended victim, Henry Hall's funeral took place at St. John's Episcopal Church in Ogdensburg. An estimated 1,500 people—over 10 percent of the city's population—attended the service, and "as many more," according to the *Ogdensburg Journal*, "were unable to gain entrance."[15] This large attendance and "solemn and impressive character" of the service "served to show the high esteem and respect entertained by all of his fellow citizens for the late Henry H. Hall."

In Utica, however, Henry Hall was all but forgotten. "Mrs. McCarty," the *Observer* announced at the end of January, was "comfortable in jail," despite the recent report of the grand jury that the conditions at the Mohawk Street Jail were "filthy" and "injurious to health."[16] Judge Doo-little was expected to hear her case in February, and in preparation she had hired a defense team, headed up by Robert O. Jones and his partner, Lewis H. Babcock. Henry J. Cookinham, in his *History of Oneida County*, calls Lewis H. Babcock "one of the most brilliant of Utica's lawyers" in his time.[17] Robert Jones, on the other hand, he describes as a member of the class of "all round practitioners" who were "well equipped in most branches of the law, and having a general practice they had no time, and perhaps no inclination, to devote enough energy to any particular branch to excel in it and thereby gain fame."[18] With Babcock's legal bril-liance and Jones's efficient breadth of practice, Josephine was prepared to mount a meaningful defense against Tom and his supporters.

The prosecution, meanwhile, was taking shape under the direction of the district attorney David C. Stoddard. It would not be the first time Babcock and Stoddard had found themselves in competition. Just the previous year, in fact, the two had been rival candidates for the post of district attorney, with Babcock running on the Democratic ticket against Stoddard on the Republican.[19] Now Stoddard sat in the D.A.'s seat while Babcock scrambled to construct a defense for a woman who had killed a man in the presence of a dozen witnesses.

On January 31, Babcock, Jones, and Stoddard met before Judge Doo-little for the first time to argue a motion by the defense for postpone-ment.[20] Babcock laid out his planned defense: "at the time it is alleged that the accused committed the offense the condition of her mind was such as she was not legally accountable for any act or acts committed." In other words, Babcock and Jones planned to use the insanity defense. But they weren't just going to argue that Josephine was insane—they planned to show *how* she'd lost her mind. "Among other things," Bab-cock said, "the conduct of Milton H. Thomson, to herself and her chil-dren, rendered her incapable of entertaining the intention to cause the death of Milton H. Thomson or the unfortunate Hall. Thomson's conduct so far unsettled the mind of the accused that at the time the offense was committed she was not legally accountable."[21]

In essence, Babcock and Jones planned to charge Milton Thomson, and not Josephine McCarty, as the guilty party in Henry Hall's killing. But in order to prove it, they would need to cast a wide evidential net:

> Every incident bearing on the question, from the time Thomson met Mrs. McCarty in her youth, when she was but 15 years of age,

a girl of unusual powers of fascination, in the town of Augusta, down to the time he occasioned her and her children to be turned out in the streets of Albany in mid-winter—everything in her life, down to this hour, must be considered at the proper time, in determining the question whether or not she was legally account-able for the act committed on the 17th of January, 1872.[22]

In light of such a vast burden of proof, Babcock concluded, it would be "utterly impossible to get the case ready for trial at this time." There were "a great many witnesses to be summoned, who cannot be secured on brief notice," and then there was the possibility that "a commission to determine in regard to the sanity of the accused" would need to be appointed. Josephine, Babcock reminded Doolittle, was a penniless single mother with no means of "defraying the heavy expense" of her own murder trial—and besides, she was still "laboring under great nervous excitement in reference to the welfare of her children."[23] In fact, she seemed to him "to be unable at this time to recall important incidents connected with the case." All this left Babcock and his colleague "wholly unprepared" to bring the case to trial at the moment, and he asked Doolittle to grant a postponement until the next term.

Stoddard was prepared to provide evidence to demonstrate that the postponement was unnecessary. Only yesterday, the prosecution had sent "two of the oldest, most respectable and skillful physicians of [the] City to the jail to examine into the physical and mental condition of the accused."[24] The doctors were D. G. Thomas and D. P. Bissell, the same physicians who had been called to the Butterfield Hotel to examine Henry Hall's body on the morning of January 17. Their examinations at the Mohawk Street Jail were conclusive: "THEY FOUND NO EVIDENCE OF INSANITY."[25] Not only was there "nothing in [Mrs. McCarty's] physical or mental condition to prevent her attendance at Court," but her currently acceptable condition "would not be improved by confinement," suggesting that a quick trial would be in her favor.

Doolittle took two days to make up his mind on the question of postponement. In the interim, the editors of the *Observer* accused the *Utica Herald* of "seek[ing] to force Doolittle into postponing the trial of Mrs. McCarty" with the dramatic claim that speedy trials were "as barbarous as lynch law."[26] "Bullying a judge into an opinion," the *Observer* wrote, "is a new and illegitimate branch of journalism, which our morning contemporary is welcome to monopolize . . . We have faith in Judge Doolittle's integrity, firmness, and fairness." Sure enough, the next day's *Observer* carried the full report of Doolittle's ruling: the McCarty case would not be postponed, but would be heard on schedule on the 12th of February. "The bullying demands of the Utica Herald," the *Observer* noted, had "failed to affect the Judge's mind."

But by mid-February, Stoddard had changed his mind. On February 8, four days before the trial was scheduled to begin, he appeared before Judge Doolittle along with Babcock to request a postponement for late March.[27] With another murder trial already on the docket and criminal cases threatening to overwhelm civil business, Doolittle granted the motion and set the new date for the McCarty trial for March 25.

Josephine, who had been driven from the jail to attend the hearing, "appeared care-worn and rather sad" as Doolittle read out his remarks. "Her costume," the *Observer*'s reporter noted, "was not put on as carefully as it was on the day of the murder." Two days later, the *Troy Weekly Times* reported that a commission of doctors had "determined that the prisoner is not in a fit condition, mentally or physically, to undertake her defense at present."[28] Although the *Times* was careful to add that "this decision does not affect the question of her sanity at the time of committing the murder, which must be determined at the trial," it lent ammunition to Babcock and Jones's insanity argument.

While the papers updated the public on Josephine's apparent mental and physical deterioration, the defense and prosecution began adding to their ranks in preparation for what was shaping up to be a complicated trial. Babcock and Jones, still busy gathering evidence and rounding up witnesses, had convinced Daniel C. Pomeroy of Rome, New York, to join the defense team. According to Henry Cookinham, Pomeroy "made no pretense of having a thorough knowledge of law; he trusted this part of the practice to others, but arousing the sympathies or prejudices of a jury he was ever effective."[29] Pomeroy's record as a persuasive orator would no doubt be essential to swaying the jury to Josephine's side, but Babcock and Jones also needed a lawyer with a proven track record of getting clients out of complicated murder charges through the use of an insanity plea.

They found him in the person of David J. Mitchell. Four years earlier, Mitchell had been a key member of the defense team who secured the acquittal of General George W. Cole on charges of first-degree murder. Cole had achieved high honors during the Civil War, but in June of 1867 he walked into the lobby of Stanwix Hall in Albany, pulled a pistol from his pocket, and shot the state assemblyman L. Harris Hiscock in the head at point-blank range.[30] Giving himself up immediately to the police, Cole declared that Hiscock had "ravished" his "pure, innocent and simple wife." David Mitchell and the other members of Cole's defense team invoked the insanity defense, arguing that the revelation of Hiscock's attack on his family and his honor had rendered Cole temporarily insane. Presenting Cole as a war hero and a respectable family man, the defense succeeded in getting an acquittal at Cole's second trial in December 1868, in what the *New York Times* called "probably . . . the most extraordinary verdict ever returned by a jury made up of men supposed to be sane themselves."[31] By hiring Mitchell to help defend Josephine, Babcock and Jones no doubt hoped to repeat the extraordinary precedent of the Cole verdict.

On the other side of the Cole trial in 1868 was a revered Central New York lawyer named Charles Baldwin Sedgwick. As Josephine McCarty's trial date approached in the spring of 1872, Stoddard brought Sedgwick on to assist in building the case against her. He also secured the services of Daniel B. Magone, an esteemed attorney from Henry Hall's home city of Ogdensburg. As the prosecution's ranks grew, critics of Thomson and Judge Doolittle continued to speculate that money had changed hands to ensure that the district attorney had the best assistance possible in pursuing a guilty verdict. On February 27, Seth Wilbur Payne's *Utica Bee* published a statement claiming that Doolittle "either has accepted, or has agreed to accept, money from Milton H. Thompson [*sic*], pending the result of the McCarty murder trial."[32] Thomson, of course, had every interest in "putting Josephine McCarty out of the way," as Payne put it, and he believed that Doolittle, for his part, was "self-seeking, tricky, cunning, and in every way a dishonorable man."[33] This time, Doolittle wasn't so quick to dismiss the allegations: he had Payne tried for libel. In mid-March, Payne was found guilty and sentenced to four months of hard labor in the Albany Penitentiary.[34] The McCarty trial hadn't even started, and already it had its first conviction.

"Trials," A. Cheree Carlson writes in her study of rhetoric in the trials of women in the nineteenth century, are "mirrors of attitudes in the public realm."[35]

Of course, not every trial has a lot to say about public attitudes. Plenty of crimes are prosecuted without saying very much about society or attracting any attention from the press or the public at large. But "sometimes a case becomes so compelling that it is reported, discussed, and dissected on a larger stage," and from those trials, Carlson says, we can learn "which legal issues are of genuine concern to citizens outside the courtroom."[36]

Josephine's trial was one of those popular trials. Before it had even started, the press coverage of the crime and its participants already reflected the issues that were of "genuine concern" to the citizens of New York. Was Josephine a bloodsucking blackmailer, deadened to her natural feminine empathy by an unnatural career as an abortionist? Or was she the honest victim of years of mistreatment by Milton Thomson, who stood in for all the abuses that white men with money could heap on marginalized women like her?

On February 12, just after Judge Doolittle announced the postponement of Josephine McCarty's trial, the *Observer* ran an article reprinted from the *New York World* on the front page titled "Why Laura Fair Is Not Yet Hung." "The privilege of a new trial," the paper announced, "has been granted to that pleasant person, Mrs. Laura Fair."[37] Readers would have been familiar with the name. Laura Fair, born in Mississippi in 1837, ran a hotel for silver miners in Virginia City, Nevada. Fair was her married name—her fourth, actually. First married at sixteen, she'd been widowed twice and divorced twice by the time she entered her mid-twenties. Like Josephine, Laura Fair had never found men to be a reliable source of support, financial or otherwise. In 1862, she opened the Tahoe House Hotel in Virginia City, and began paying her own bills.[38]

Not long after she opened the hotel, Laura began seeing a lawyer named Alexander Parker Crittenden. Crittenden, in his forties, was older than Laura; she didn't mind. Crittenden was also married, with a wife and three children in San Francisco; he promised Laura that he'd go to Indiana and get a divorce. Instead, the two carried on their affair publicly for seven years. For seven years, as Crittenden traveled back and forth between San Francisco and Virginia City and passionate trysts gave way to more and more frequent arguments, Laura waited for Crittenden to keep his promise and divorce his wife. He never did.

On November 3, 1870, Laura followed Crittenden onto a ferry bound from Oakland to San Francisco, pulled a pistol out of her pocket, and shot him in the heart. Arrested on the scene, she was tried in April 1871 for murder in the first degree. Her lawyers argued that she was not guilty by reason of temporary insanity—insanity induced by a painful menstrual period. But the argument was unconvincing to the twelve men assigned with Laura's fate. Laura Fair was sentenced to hang on July 28, 1871.[39]

Laura's life story mirrored Josephine's, and so did her crime. If her first trial was any indication, Josephine could expect an unsympathetic jury when she finally came to trial. But now, as Josephine waited in the Mohawk Street Jail for the trial to start, *Laura Fair was not yet hung*. In the months since her conviction, Laura had reached out to a number of women's rights activists, including Susan B. Anthony and Elizabeth Cady Stanton, who launched an appeal for a second trial. In the end, the court granted the appeal because Laura's attorney had not been allowed to make closing remarks, and because "evidence tending to sully her reputation was admitted at the original trial."[40] The former was nothing more than a technical quibble, the *World* stated, and "the latter purely preposterous."

The real reason Laura Fair had been granted a second trial, the *World* argued, was not because her first trial had failed to render justice but because Californian authorities were laboring under a "false chivalry" that caused them to "shrink from the unpleasant task of hanging a woman." In other words, the new trial reflected a crisis not of conscience but of the "aesthetic sense," which recoiled from the "ungraceful spectacle of a female figure" on the gallows.[41]

Here was the fundamental paradox that faced Josephine as she awaited trial. As a white woman on trial for murder in the United States in the nineteenth century, she was simultaneously privileged and disadvantaged by her own gender. Like Laura Fair, she was sensitive and weak—a painful period or a man's mistreatment could drive her insane. The trials of nineteenth-century women reveal, Carlson says, that "women were often being viewed as being closer to incompetence than men."[42] A jury of twelve men could dismiss her violence as more feminine incompetence—and the fact that she missed would probably help her case. Even if they weren't convinced by her argument, they might be reluctant to return a verdict that would lead to her execution. Womanhood, then, was a privilege that could protect even killers from punishment.

Or was it?

"The avaricious or revengeful woman," the *World's* commentary read, "is not as yet permitted the privilege of murder as a means of gaining a mercenary or malicious end."[43] If the jury concluded that Josephine was that kind of woman—a mercenary, gunning down her ex-lover out of greed or spite—it might overpower their chivalrous instincts.

It all came down to what kind of woman Josephine McCarty was. That was the question the trial would answer—not whether she was guilty of the crime she'd been charged with but whether she was the kind of woman who should be punished for it or the kind who should walk free. It was the same unspoken question that had underpinned the Campbell inquest just months before, and in deciding it, the lawyers and jury would have to answer another: could an abortionist be a good woman?

CHAPTER 10

Mrs. McCarty Takes the Stand

On May 1, 1872, the second page of the *Utica Daily Observer*, under the heading "Home Matters," printed the headline that all of Oneida County had been waiting for since January: "Begun! Josephine McCarty's Trial."[1]

The wait was over. The defense had already delayed the trial one last time in late March, claiming once again that they needed more time to secure key testimony.[2] A crucial witness, they claimed, was ill; Mrs. McCarty had no funds to pursue the most important leads; inconveniences and bad luck had conspired against them. But now, as May broke over central New York, the *Observer* announced that there would be "NO MORE POSTPONEMENT."[3] Judge Doolittle had summoned a panel of potential jurors, and now there was no going back.

On the morning of May 1, over a hundred men assembled before Doolittle to await jury selection. Between them and the audience that arrived to witness the start of the trial, the room was crowded. Two fires "burning fiercely" combined with "the accumulated breaths of hundreds of persons," and as a result "the atmosphere," as the *Observer* reported, "was not as agreeable as it should have been."[4]

In spite of these conditions, the trial began—much to the dismay of Josephine's lawyers. Before the first jury member could be selected, David Mitchell attempted to manufacture yet another delay, claiming that the court hadn't followed the proper procedure in summoning the jury panel. Judge Doolittle, who observed drily that he had "expected the counsel on both sides to raise numerous objections," rejected every legal challenge Mitchell threw at him. Even so, the debate over the legality of the panel occupied the court's time until noon, when Mitchell finally gave up and accepted the inevitable. At Doolittle's instruction, the clerk called forward Alonzo Nichols of Washington Mills, the first potential juror in the McCarty case.

The prosecution promptly rejected Nichols on the basis of conscientious scruples. The concern that newspapers raised about the Laura Fair trial—that respectable men would shrink at the prospect of condemning a woman to hang—seemed to be legitimate. Nichols stated to the court that he would not, even if he believed the defendant to be guilty, deliver a verdict that would result in the death penalty. There was another problem: Mr. Nichols had, by his own admission, formed an opinion on the case already. He wasn't alone. As the afternoon wore on, it became clear just how difficult it would prove to find twelve men in the whole county who, in the four months since the murder, hadn't read the newspapers, talked to their neighbors, and formed some opinion on the issue of Josephine's innocence or guilt. By the end of the day, out of the thirty-two men examined, only seven had been deemed competent to sit on the jury.[5]

The next day, things were different. "UNEXPECTED PROGRESS!" the *Observer* crowed. "A FULL JURY OBTAINED!"[6] Another development was surely equally welcome to those gathered in the courtroom: court officials had opened the windows and reduced the fires burning in the grates. "Pure air," the *Observer* reported, "is a priceless jewel."

In addition to this "wonderful improvement" in temperature, the trial's audience had another thing to celebrate on May 2: it seemed that Mitchell had put aside his determination to slow down the selection process. The first juror called on Thursday morning, a local mechanic and farmer, was sworn in without objections in spite of the fact that he openly stated that he had read about the case in the *Observer*, the *Herald*, and the *Rome Sentinel* and formed "impressions" of Mrs. McCarty's guilt or innocence. After two more men had been rejected, the defense, possibly afraid that the court would run out of potential jurors, withdrew their objections to a juror called the previous day and allowed Seth S. Penny to be sworn in. With nine men in the jury box, Stoddard began calling the roll of the People's witnesses, ready for the case to begin.[7]

At 12:10 p.m, the court swore in a farmer named Philip Sanford as the twelfth and final juror. Two hours later, after a recess for lunch, Stoddard stood up and opened the case for the People. "Gentlemen of the Jury," he began, "it devolves upon me to open this case . . . Your duties are serious and arduous. Your duties are to seek the truth." But, he reassured them, "the facts in this case are not complicated in their nature. There is but little if any circumstantial evidence. The facts transpired in a short space of time in the presence of witnesses, who will be called here."[8]

Stoddard gave a brief review of those facts. Mrs. McCarty had arrived in Utica on the Saturday before the shooting; she stayed at the Butterfield House; on January 17 she was seen standing over Milton Thomson in the streetcar with a pistol in her hand at the time of the shot that killed Henry Hall. For anyone who hadn't read the *Observer's* definitions of murder and manslaughter, Stoddard gave the jury a quick review of state law, reading aloud from a textbook. At 2:30 p.m., he called the first witness for the people: John S. Reed, the conductor who had followed Josephine off the streetcar on the morning of the killing.

Reed gave a measured and precise description of his memory of the events of the 17th, giving down to the last minute and foot the approximate times and locations at which it had all transpired. The strange lady had signaled to him "about 25 or 30 yards" after the car passed her at Oneida Square; the car stopped "about 100 feet" from where he had first seen her and she boarded at the left rear corner; and when he intercepted the lady after the shot was fired, she had traveled "about 100 feet" from the car. At only one point did Reed lapse into uncertainty. That was when the district attorney asked him to confirm the identity of the woman he had seen on the car. "I think," he allowed, "the accused is a lady of the same size as the one who got into my car; she resembles her very much." But on cross-examination by Mitchell, he admitted that he "did not notice her face particularly," and stated, "I never saw the lady before nor her face since until now, if that is the lady."[9]

The prosecution's second witness was Adolphus Schutz, a cigar maker from New York Mills who had been one of Thomson and McCarty's fellow passengers on the streetcar that morning. He remembered getting on the car, and remembered in great detail who had been sitting around him and where; he remembered the shot, and the smoke, and that in the moments after the gun went off the woman turned to him and said a few words—but what exactly those words were, he could not say for certain. Stoddard asked him to give his best recollection, but the defense objected; what point could there be in allowing into evidence an imprecise memory of something Schutz *thought* he had heard? But the court ruled that Schutz could, and should, give the words as closely as he could recall. So Schutz swore that the woman on the streetcar had said either "I kill," or "I murder."

Pomeroy, undertaking the cross-examination, tried to get Schutz to describe Mrs. McCarty's appearance upon leaving the streetcar. Was she, he suggested, "wild" or "haggard"?

"I do not know that I would call it a wild expression," Schutz said. "I do not know that she was haggard." The most he would agree to was that she had been "gasping for breath," and when she uttered the words he had repeated earlier "it was with difficulty that she spoke."[10] That evidence alone would not prove insanity, but it was a start.

Having gotten a thorough description of the crime from eyewitnesses, the prosecution turned to reconstructing the next chapter: Josephine's arrest and the hours and days that followed before her trial. William Supple, janitor of City Hall, remembered escorting Mrs. McCarty to the station house on the morning of the murder: "She looks better now," he noted, "than she did then." In cross-examination, he recalled the defendant's answer when he had asked her why she'd fired the gun: "If you knew what trouble that man had made." At this outburst, Isaac Tapping, the passenger who had helped to apprehend McCarty, had advised her not to say any more. "The conversation," Supple told the jury, "ended with me then."[11]

The chief of police, A. Charles Luce, corroborated Supple's testimony and produced the revolver he had taken off Josephine's person—a Smith and Wesson with four chambers loaded and one empty. The math there was fairly unambiguous. Cross-examined by Mitchell, Luce testified that "the accused was greatly excited at the Station House; she cried and wrung her hands; I noticed her pacing up and down the floor, wringing her hands."[12] On this note, court adjourned for the day, and the jury returned to their lodgings for the night with the image of Josephine McCarty pacing her cell in tears playing over and over in their minds.

On the third day of the trial, the prosecution continued to construct their picture of the events of January 17, picking up first with the autopsy of Henry H. Hall, the murder victim whose part in the story seemed so often to fade into insignificance. For a few hours on May 3, Henry Hall was at the forefront of everyone's mind, as Drs. Bissell and Woolcott and Lawton, the coroner, described the findings of their post-mortem exam. The bullet, Bissell explained, had "entered the left chest an inch below the clavicle bone" and then passed "from the left lung through the division between the lungs in which the aorta is situated, cutting the aorta and passing into the right lung."[13]

"We found the ball there," he concluded, and Lawton produced before the court the little lump of metal that had been pulled from Hall's body. After the inquest, he told the jury, he had compared the bullet to the gun taken from the prisoner: "The ball seemed to fit the empty chamber of the pistol," he found, and it was "apparently the same sized ball that would be used in such a pistol"; more than that he could not swear to with certainty. In Dr. Woolcott's opinion, however, it was certainly that ball that had caused Mr. Hall's death. Specifically, the cause of death had been massive hemorrhage following the dissection of the aorta—and to the relief of those listening he added, "I don't think this man lived any time; I think death resulted instantaneously."[14]

Having dealt with the body, the prosecution returned to the accused. How had Mrs. McCarty fared in her time of confinement between her arrest and the trial, and what evidence of her innocence or guilt had she let slip during that time? To answer those questions, the People called on Samuel J. Cole, keeper of the Mohawk Street Jail, where Josephine had been since three or four days following the shooting.

"Have you heard her talk about this shooting affair?" Stoddard asked Cole, but the defense objected immediately to the question, demanding to know what Stoddard hoped to prove by asking it. Judge Doolittle dismissed the objection—evidence like this had been heard before in his court, and he saw no reason to exclude it now. But the defense pressed the point. "Here [is] a woman charged with murder," Pomeroy pointed out. Any confession she might have made in the jail could have been made under promises or threat from her jailer, and thus couldn't be entered into evidence. Mitchell doubled down: any statement to a jailer was not voluntary; he had dealt with a similar case in Binghamton and was prepared to produce the precedent. To anyone watching, it became clear with each subsequent objection that whatever Samuel Cole might be about to say, the defense didn't want the jury to hear it. Despite all their objections, however, Doolittle insisted that Cole's testimony would be considered competent, and he motioned for Stoddard to proceed.[15]

Yes, Mr. Cole said, he had heard McCarty talk about the shooting. In fact, he had heard her make one statement in particular about "what she thought when she got to the front door after the shooting." And what had that thought been? She said, Cole told the jury, "it was her intention to shoot again, but she saw blood on Thomson's face, and, thinking the shot had the desired effect, she left the car."[16]

In a single sentence, Cole had introduced information that would prove more difficult for the defense to sweep from the jury's mind than all the evidence of the conductor, the passengers, the medical experts, and the police combined. This was unmistakable evidence of intent. "The desired effect" suggested motive; it suggested premeditation and cold calculation; above all, it suggested that the defendant still possessed a clear memory of the crime which the defense insisted she had almost no knowledge of whatsoever.

Mitchell immediately set out to break down Cole's testimony in cross-examination, demanding to know who else he had told this story to and how the district attorney had known to ask him about it in the first place. He inquired about Cole's relationship with the prisoner, suggesting that Cole had been "unfriendly" to her and that an article published in Seth Wilbur Payne's *Bee*, which alleged that the prisoner "did not have enough good food to eat, and had to use a billet of wood for a pillow," had its basis in truth. Cole denied it all, and also denied the allegation that he had entered the defendant's cell while drunk to "abuse her like a pick-pocket." On the contrary, he insisted, "I have tried to accommodate her in every way." While answering Mitchell's questions, Cole yawned. "Are you sleepy?" Mitchell demanded. "As wide awake as the counsel," replied Cole. If every man in Oneida County had formed their own opinions about the case by now, there could be no doubt as to which side Samuel Cole was on.[17]

When Mitchell finally exhausted his questions for Cole, the prosecution promptly called his wife Harriet, who repeated with confidence the same story that Cole had shared with the jury: Mrs. McCarty said she had intended to shoot Thomson again, but on seeing the blood had assumed that Thomson was dead and reconsidered. Unlike her husband, Harriet could remember when Josephine had made this remark: it was, she thought, about four or five weeks after the accused had come to stay at the jail.[18]

In cross-examination, though, the defense finally uncovered a promising friction between their client and the couple whose testimony worked so powerfully against her. Harriet Cole admitted to Pomeroy that she thought the prisoner felt "unfriendly" toward her, and that she had made complaints about Harriet and her husband's treatment of her. Though Mrs. Cole insisted, "I have not intended to let her know that I had any unkind feeling to her," those complaints "disturbed my feelings of course." This was a win for Pomeroy; he had established ill will between the defendant and the prosecution's best witness, and in a second round of cross-examination he would further establish that Mrs. McCarty had not yet paid her bill for board at the jail, evidently another sore spot between the jailer's wife and her prisoner. In fact, Pomeroy suggested, Mrs. Cole's husband had been so incensed by his prisoner's refusal to pay her bill that he had brought the bill to her cell while intoxicated and told her, "You cannot monkey with me any more."[19] Recalled to the stand, Cole flatly denied these allegations—again, he insisted that he had never entered her cell under the influence of alcohol; in fact, he had never taken her a bill at all. His denials didn't matter. The defense let Cole return to his seat, satisfied that the jury would remember the words "You cannot monkey with me" at least as well as they did Josephine's hope that her shot had "the desired effect."

Undeterred by the defense's badgering of their witness, the prosecution proceeded to call Robert Toberman, an Albany real estate agent and acquaintance of Josephine McCarty, who testified that seven days before the shooting Josephine had appeared in his office and told him that if she and her children were evicted, "she would go to Utica and take a terrible revenge."[20] Surprisingly, although this appeared to be a clear statement of premeditation and therefore disastrous to the defense, Mitchell and Pomeroy raised no immediate objections to having Toberman's testimony entered into the record. The reason quickly became apparent in cross-examination. Toberman, it transpired, was employed by a lawyer named Spriggs, the Thomson brothers' attorney, and had been involved in the sale of 62 Howard Street. Mrs. McCarty had provided no details about what her "terrible revenge" might look like, but Mitchell suggested that she might have meant nothing more than a demand for child support, and Toberman had no objection to that. Wrapping up his examination, Mitchell put one last question to Toberman: "Were you," he inquired, "one of [the Confederate commander] Moseby's guerillas against this Government?"[21] "I decline to answer," Toberman replied. "You decline to answer," Mitchell repeated. "That is enough." And he was right—the mere suggestion that the prosecution's witness had served with a notorious Confederate cavalry regiment was enough, in the eyes of a New York jury, to undermine his credibility.

Undeterred, Stoddard called the prosecution's next witness: Edward Leach, a dealer in fruit and oysters whose shop on Genesee Street gave him an excellent vantage point from which to view the drama of January 17. But Stoddard wasn't looking for another eyewitness. Instead, he asked Leach about an interaction that had taken place the day before the shooting. "A lady called at my store to make enquiries," Leach explained, but "I do not recognize the prisoner as the lady; I was busy."[22] Surprisingly, the defense came to Stoddard's aid, conceding freely that Mrs. McCarty was there. Continuing, Mr. Leach explained that the lady had asked him if he had seen Milton Thomson that evening, and what time he usually came into the office. Mr. Leach had said that he thought Thomson was out of town. Here was more evidence of premeditated murder: the day before the murder, Josephine was stalking Milton Thomson, looking for the right moment to strike.

By midday on May 3, the prosecution had finished calling their witnesses. Thus far, they'd established a compelling picture of a jealous woman who had planned the murder of her former lover—and then bungled it. The jury had heard Samuel Cole and his wife say that Josephine intended to fire a second shot until she saw that she'd hit Thomson. They'd heard Edward Leach talk about Josephine asking about Thomson's whereabouts less than twenty-four hours before she shot him. Even if the dead man wasn't the one she'd planned to kill, the evidence still fit the state's definition of premeditated murder. Now it was up to Lewis Babcock and his colleagues to convince the jury that none of that mattered and present an alternative reading of Josephine's story.

On the afternoon of May 3, with the courtroom packed and the jury waiting, Lewis Babcock rose to open the case for the defense. He had a daunting task before him. After all, multiple witnesses had already appeared in court to testify to seeing his client shooting Thomson and Hall in broad daylight. But despite all this, Babcock was on the offensive in his opening remarks.

"The prisoner," he proclaimed, "is met by an array of legal talent for the People which has never before been equaled at a trial in Central New York." He ran through their credentials: "the District Attorney is assisted by an eminent legal gentleman of the St. Lawrence county bar." He meant Daniel Magone, the lawyer from Henry Hall's hometown. "The Attorney General," Babcock went on, "is represented by a distinguished gentleman from Syracuse." That was Charles Sedgwick, who'd prosecuted General George Cole just a few years earlier. Why such a show of force in a case which could easily have been tried by the District Attorney alone? "We have been met," Babcock declared, "by the wealth of Milton H. Thomson, who is the real prosecutor in this case." "I think, gentlemen," he continued, "you are satisfied from the facts, as sworn to, that the killing of Mr. Hall was entirely accidental."[23] Josephine had never met Henry Hall, and he'd never done anything to harm her. Milton Thomson, on the other hand, had beaten her down over eighteen years, from the time she returned from Europe to the day he had her evicted. He'd promised her love. Instead, he gave her money, then a drunken seduction, then threats of violence and years of financial abuse, culminating in the final outrage that caused her, at long last, to snap.

"You must not be satisfied," Babcock instructed the jury, "that the accused discharged the pistol intending to take Thomson's life." He gestured to Josephine. "Here this woman is in court," he exclaimed, "sick, haggard, crushed in heart and body." Just as there was no particular mystery about whose hand had fired the pistol that killed Henry Hall, it was no mystery who had crushed Josephine's body and heart. "Milton Thomson," Babcock said, "may not be answerable to the law for this man's death, but the moral sentiment of the community will hold him guilty."[24] It was a bold move—accusing Milton Thomson, who wasn't even in the courtroom, of his own attempted murder. Even Babcock had to admit that there was no legal basis for his argument. But he was relying on something considerably stronger than state law: moral outrage at a man who'd tormented the mother of his children.

The legal historian Carolyn B. Ramsey has probably done more extensive research on the trials of nineteenth-century American women accused of murder than any other scholar.[25] A remarkably common feature of trials like Josephine's, she says, was the "degree of moral denunciation directed at the men," like Milton Thomson, "who allegedly drove these female defendants to kill."[26] These trials, Ramsey argues, were above all "a struggle to define American manhood."[27] A good man, according to the standards of the nineteenth-century middle class, was a defender of women. He showed restraint: didn't drink to excess, didn't lose his temper, didn't let his sexual appetites overpower him. "A man who beat, raped, or abandoned a woman," Ramsey writes, "failed in his duty to protect the so-called weaker sex; his actions thus justified or at least excused the woman's homicidal response."[28] As a result, men who killed their intimate partners—wives or mistresses—tended to receive harsh sentences from American juries, while women accused of the same crime enjoyed leniency.

It wasn't just squeamishness about hanging that let female defendants off the hook. While Ramsey's research confirms that male juries were reluctant to issue the death penalty in cases with a female defendant, she argues that they also sought justice for abused women through something akin to the modern "battered woman" defense.[29] "Intimate murder cases in the late 1800s and early 1900s," she writes, "not only policed ideals of civilized masculinity, but often tacitly recognized a factor similar to one emphasized by domestic-violence researchers today—past abuse that might lead a woman to kill her loved ones."[30]

There's no evidence that Tom ever hit Josephine, or that any of his alleged murder threats went farther than rumors and speculation. In fact, he barely had any opportunity to physically abuse her; he interacted with Josephine mostly by mail. But "the paternalistic understanding of social relations" prevalent in late nineteenth-century America, Ramsey points out, "tended to equate physical and emotional maltreatment of women."[31] Tom's false promises of marriage, the financial power he'd used to twist Josephine's home and office out of her hands, and even his cruelty to her on the streetcar all counted against him as evidence of unmanliness—and they would strengthen her defense. And Thomson wasn't the only man who'd abused her. "The law allows us," Babcock stated, "to prove any misfortunes, physical disease, infirmities, troubles, afflictions, &c., in fact, anything which could affect the condition of her mind, which transpired from the time of her birth to the present time."[32] Robert McCarty, R. K. Smith, and even the mysterious Mr. Thompson of Massachusetts with whom Josephine had a brief affair would all join the list of her abusers.

But Babcock needed to do more than prove that Milton Thomson and his fellow men had mistreated Josephine: he had to show that that mistreatment was worse than Josephine's own crimes. The leniency that nineteenth-century juries extended to female murderers, Ramsey finds, wasn't impartial. While women who had been "seduced, physically abused, or trapped in dire economic straits" could expect mercy from their male peers, women who "defied gender norms by drinking or engaging in illicit sex could expect harsher verdicts."[33] Good women with bad luck, in other words, got off while bad women faced punishment. Which kind of woman was Josephine McCarty?

The defense had one more intimidating task: in order to mount a successful insanity defense, they had to convince the jury that Josephine had no memory of the crime. "What occurred after Thomson told her and his offspring to 'go to hell'," Babcock told the jury, "is all a blank to her." She didn't remember the sound of the pistol; she couldn't recall the smell of smoke. "Whatever else may occur in this case," Babcock concluded, "thank God she will not have the memory of this tragedy to haunt her."[34]

At 3:45 p.m. on May 3, Babcock reached the end of his opening remarks. The speech, the *Observer* opined, "was probably the ablest effort of his life." Few in the courtroom, particularly those sympathetic to Josephine, heard it unaffected; a student of Babcock's, seated behind Josephine, "used his handkerchief very industriously" throughout the speech, to the point of causing a disturbance in the courtroom.[35] Since it was late, Judge Doolittle made the decision to adjourn for the night.

The following morning, Josephine McCarty would take the stand and tell the jury her life story. That narrative, stretching all the way back to her childhood in Augusta, would become the foundation of the defense's evidence. It would serve to implicate not only Milton Thomson but also almost every man in Josephine's life in a pattern of unmanly manipulation, seduction, and violence that had broken her down over the years until, faced with the ultimate shame and rejection, she resorted to the only remedy she had left against the battering of male cruelty.

On the morning of May 4, 1872, Josephine McCarty stepped into the witness box. She talked about her childhood in Richmond and Augusta and her school days at Cazenovia. She talked about her parents. "I was thirteen years of age," she told the jury, "when my father died," leaving her alone with her mother, "a very nervous, excitable woman." She talked about her children: "I have five children now living, as I suppose." And she talked about Milton Thomson, whom she'd met just after her father died, while she was at school under the care of her guardian. "He called upon me," Josephine remembered; "we were friends."[36]

Then she came to the subject of her first husband. Josephine told the jury about meeting Robert McCarty in Washington, about their engagement and hasty marriage, and about how he abandoned her and the children for the Great Exhibition, only to call her two years later to make the treacherous international journey to England. "I had difficulty there," Josephine said, explaining the circumstances of Robert's infidelity, his venereal disease, and his repeated kidnapping of their three children.[37] Altogether, Josephine's testimony regarding her first husband painted a picture of a man who failed to live up to any of the standards of nineteenth-century manliness. He had failed again and again to support his family, obliging Josephine to work outside the home and take refuge with her mother. He had abandoned her and the children, and his venereal disease suggested that he frequented brothels while married to Josephine. Finally, although Josephine struggled to remember the details, she stated that Robert had been physically violent, "knock[ing her] down" on at least one occasion.[38] Robert's adultery alone would have qualified Josephine for a divorce in New York State, and his cruelty further emphasized his betrayal of his duties as a man.

Mr. Mitchell then asked Josephine about her reunion with Milton Thomson. Josephine described the early days of their rekindled friendship: the shared dinners around her mother's table and occasional offers of money; the private rides in the countryside. But when she reached the story of the night they first slept together at the Globe Hotel in Syracuse, "the witness was affected to tears, and hesitated for some time." When she was able to recover her composure, she continued. Thomson had brought her wine, she said, and given her more than she was used to drinking. He had stayed with her for part of the night, made love to her for the first time, and told her "that he had loved me for so long." Racked by "tears and hysteric sobs" at the memory of that night, Josephine finally managed to choke out a single sentence: "He said he would be all to me that a husband could be."[39]

But he hadn't left his wife—and Josephine hadn't left him. Whether out of love, fear, or financial dependence, Josephine had stayed in Milton Thomson's life long after the incident at the Globe Hotel, and he spent the next decade trying to get rid of her. Josephine told the jury about the rumors that he had tried to have her killed during the war. When she'd come back from prison pregnant in 1862, Thomson tried to force her to get an abortion against her will.

But his threats didn't stop after the war. One night in 1867, Josephine remembered, Tom had showed up at her house in Albany. "I was complaining that I did not feel very well," she recalled, and so Thomson "took a little flask, which he called cordial, and said it was very good; he poured out a few spoonsful and I took it." Josephine did find the cordial "very agreeable," and Thomson urged her to take more, but rather than helping to relieve her symptoms, "in a short time I became very ill and was ill for more than a week; it affected my head and caused vomiting." Thomson "stayed pretty late" that night, and when he left, "he locked the door and threw the key through the window on to the parlor carpet." Josephine recovered, and at her next opportunity she'd asked Thomson what on earth was in the mysterious "cordial" that he gave her. "He said that it was Hostetter's Bitters, and he could not account for its singular effect on me; he acted so singular that I became suspicious."[40]

Around the same time, Josephine said, Thomson had taken to sending her letters written not in his own hand, but by cutting out text from newspapers and handbills and pasting it onto sheets of paper. Often, Josephine said, the letters simply contained dates on which Thomson wanted to meet, but the defense produced a letter, which she identified as one she'd received in Albany, consisting of four vague and increasingly ominous cut-and-paste lines:

"The *thorn* is *often* plucked for the rose."
"*Fools* and *obstinate* people make *lawyers* rich"
"Fools have liberty to say what they please"
"MUCH IS EXPECTED WHERE MUCH IS GIVEN."[41]

The behavior Josephine described fits the pattern observed by experts on battered woman syndrome: building tension, violence and threats of violence, followed by contrition and expressions of love. Tom wanted to see her; then he wanted her killed; then he was back again, taking her to hotels and buying her children ice cream.

But Tom wasn't the only man in her life in this period. "Did you ever," Mitchell asked, "have anything to do with any other man except Thomson after the child Juddie was born, and if so with whom?" The question, the *Observer* reported, "caused great agitation to the accused." As the jury watched, "her chin quivered and her whole frame shook convulsively. She burst into tears, and sobbed bitterly." The sobbing continued for several minutes; Mitchell repeated his question, but Josephine was crying too hard to hear him. Judge Doolittle was prepared to call a recess to allow the witness to compose herself, but Mitchell pressed on. "Mrs. McCarty," he said, "I want you to answer my question—please take your handkerchief down and answer my questions." When Josephine continued to sob, he changed his approach, asking simply, "Did you ever go to Massachusetts?" Josephine, still sobbing profusely, nodded. "Yes, sir—I went to North Adams, Great Barrington and Pittsfield." She'd gone to Massachusetts for the traveling sales job she had pursued in 1863 and early 1864, selling sewing machines and patent medicine. But there was another part to the story. With tears streaming down her face, she explained: "At Pittsfield I made the acquaintance of a person named Thompson [not *Thomson*]. That was more than a year after Juddie's birth. He was a furniture dealer," she finished, then put her handkerchief to her face again and continued to cry.[42]

After a pause, the story went on, still punctuated by Josephine's sobs. She had "had intercourse" with the Pittsfield Thompson, and not long after had found herself "in the family way" with her second daughter, little Josephine Cleopatra Seymour—the girl supposed to be the child of Milton Thomson.[43] The mysterious Mr. Thompson, Josephine told the jury, gave her $300 in child support and disappeared without a trace.

Then Josephine's testimony took an unexpected turn. She told the jury a strange story about her time in St. Louis following her expulsion from Philadelphia's Blockley Hospital. "In St. Louis," she said, "my sense of hearing became very much quickened and refined, to the extent that I could hear conversations that no one but myself could."[44] Mitchell asked his client to clarify—did she mean to say that she thought she developed superhuman hearing?

"I don't think it," Josephine replied. "I know it." She explained further: "My rooms were in a very large building, on the second floor; I could hear all that parties on the street said." On one occasion, she said, "I was sitting in my room with a lady friend and I heard a conversation in the second room from us." The "lady friend" heard nothing, but Josephine insisted, "I heard two gentlemen in that second room say they were going down the river . . . I heard the sound distinctly." Had she possessed this power of intensified hearing all her life, Mitchell asked? No, the power had come on "suddenly," and although "it went off more gradually than it came," it eventually subsided after about two months. Nonetheless, "there was a great deal of talk about it in St. Louis," in part because "one party claimed that I had done great injustice by reporting what I heard." "Do you really believe," Mitchell asked his client, "that you possessed any particular gift?" Sedgwick interrupted: "I object to her belief." "I have no doubt that it was a delusion," Mitchell clarified, and Judge Doolittle had to concede: "The witness says she knows it." The jury could make of that whatever they wished.[45]

Mitchell then turned to the topic of Josephine's physical health. It wasn't good, to put it bluntly; she had entered perimenopause, she explained, about four years ago, and ever since then had been consulting physicians and treating herself "almost constantly" for "uterine hemorrhage," "nervous headaches and neuralgia." These attacks were severe: "I have been confined to my bed about one-third of the time for the last three years." In addition to heavy bleeding, she had experienced significant psychological changes—in fact, she said, "my head has been more affected than any other part of my system," and her periods, sometimes lasting up to six weeks, were always "preceded by extreme nervousness." When was the last of these extended periods? "I had one of these hemorrhages two or three weeks before I was put out of the house," Josephine answered, and then another "two or three days after I came to Utica."[46] That is, the day before the murder. Just like Laura Fair on the San Francisco ferry, Josephine had been on her period the day she stepped onto the streetcar.

In addition to the difficulties of approaching menopause, Josephine's poor health had been complicated by an injury in the summer of 1871, when she visited a friend in Saratoga County, a Mrs. Henrietta Conley Cooper. One day, she rode out in a carriage along with Mrs. Cooper and her nephew, only for the carriage to crash and tip over. "My left shoulder was dislocated," she told Mitchell, and "the left clavicle was injured, and the scapular was injured," but "not broken." But the damage she sustained in the accident wasn't just physical: "My nervous system," she said, "was very much injured." She was confined to her bed for ten full days, and in the months following the incident, her "nerves [had] never recovered," and neither had the arm. Throughout the winter of 1871, she explained, she "suffered a great deal of nervous headache."[47]

Finally, Josephine described her arrival at Utica and the ensuing days at the Butterfield House, where she couldn't remember eating or sleeping or speaking to anyone. On Wednesday morning, wearing the same dress she had on when she left Albany four days earlier, she left the hotel determined to find Thomson and confront him. She waited for the Utica and New Hartford line to make its way down Genesee Street, and stopped the car when she saw Thomson emerge from his house. "Mr. Thomson came in with another gentleman and took a seat directly opposite me," she told Mitchell. "I did not speak immediately; I thought it was about a half hour after he got in when I spoke to him." This couldn't have been true. The testimony of eyewitnesses had already established that Josephine and Tom were on the streetcar together for no more than a few minutes. But Josephine carried on, describing their brief and hostile conversation; her confused memory of seeing her gun on the seat, stained with candy; and her recollection of the blood rolling down Tom's face and chest. [48]

But had she actually seen or heard the shooting, Mitchell asked? Josephine denied it, saying, "I have no knowledge of taking out the pistol or cocking it." In fact, she could not remember seeing it until she saw it lying on the seat, and "did not hear any report or see any smoke." Did she enter the car with the intent to shoot Thomson? "I did not have any intent of shooting Thomson or any one else when I entered that car," Josephine stated clearly. "I had never seen Mr. Hall before." Samuel Cole claimed that she'd told him she planned to fire another shot, but now Josephine said she "had no thought whatever of returning to shoot again." The gun had gone off—that much was obvious—but, Josephine insisted, "I have no knowledge how that shot was fired."[49]

Josephine's story, which took up nearly two full days, was compelling. But she wasn't done on the stand. Beginning on May 6, the prosecution took their cross-examination as an opportunity to grill Josephine on the long catalogue of scandals the local papers had published in the months leading up to the trial. Their goal was simple: to show that Josephine McCarty was just as bad as the men who'd abused her.

Forcing Josephine to admit to her past sins, however, proved more difficult than the prosecution had bargained for. At every turn, she evaded their questions, claimed ignorance of all types of criminal activity, and, when all else failed, simply insisted she had no memory of the events in question. Sedgwick asked her to comment on her relationship with Captain Isaiah Pratt of the *Margaret Evans*, the ship she'd taken to meet Robert in Europe. "I first knew Captain Pratt on the ship," Josephine said; Robert's agent had introduced them. "I occupied a stateroom on board the ship adjoining Captain Pratt's room; there was a door between our rooms," but "it was not open."

Getting straight to the point, Sedgwick demanded, "Did your husband and Captain Pratt have any difficulty?"

"I object," Mitchell intervened, "on the ground that it is immaterial."

But Doolittle disagreed: "The question is competent, as to the question of character." If the defense could dig into Josephine's history with men to bolster their theory of the crime, the prosecution could do the same. Sedgwick proceeded, repeating the question: had there been any conflict between Robert McCarty and Isaiah Pratt? Josephine hedged: they "had no personal collision or fight in which they used weapons," in part because Robert "was too cowardly to fight Captain Pratt." But yes, her husband had "abused" him, and they had "a controversy in a carriage," but it had never come to more than that.

"Did your husband complain of any intimacy with Captain Pratt?" Sedgwick asked.

"Wait a moment," Mitchell began, but Josephine answered before he could complete his objection.

"No, sir," she said. "He never made any complaint until after the first separation."

"You had better let your counsel try this case for you," Judge Doolittle warned her. "It will be better for you."

As Sedgwick continued to push, the outlines of the controversy emerged. "I had trouble with my husband about getting money from Captain Pratt," Josephine admitted finally, and "there was a collision" between the two men before her departure from Europe. In total, she believed that she had borrowed approximately ten pounds from Pratt to help pay her living expenses while separated from Robert. She insisted that money was the only kind of attention she got from Captain Pratt, but the money was bad enough. Josephine was accused in the press of being a heartless blackmailer, and now she'd told a story that illustrated her skill at getting money out of sympathetic men.[50]

Satisfied, Sedgwick moved on to grilling the defendant about her relationships with various Albany politicians, hoping to substantiate the recent rumors in the press that Josephine had been a "kept mistress" during her days as a lobbyist at the state capitol.[51] Josephine denied it, though she admitted that she'd worked there as a lobbyist. Although she pointed out that she failed to get the bill passed, this was another admission of her talents: lobbying, after all, employed the same skill set as blackmail.

Building on this point, Sedgwick jumped years forward in Josephine's biography, demanding, "Were you arrested in 1864?" The defense objected. Mrs. McCarty couldn't be made to incriminate herself. Judge Doolittle agreed, but Sedgwick persisted. He had reason to believe that Phebe Williams had made a complaint against her daughter, leading to Josephine's arrest, and he wanted to know about it. Mitchell continued to object, but Josephine didn't seem to share her attorneys' concerns. "If I could explain," she said, "I would answer, and the answer would not criminate me." She addressed Sedgwick: "I was arrested in 1863, I believe; the charge was made by my mother . . . who was partially insane."[52] Not long after their fight over Josephine's illicit pregnancy, Phebe had accused Josephine of stealing from the farm.

Had Josephine, Sedgwick asked, testified on August 16, 1862, that her mother had a "devilish temper" and had "pinched and tortured" her son Louis? Mitchell objected to the question, and Sedgwick agreed that if the defense would consent to strike out Josephine's statements about her mother's insanity, he would drop the question. But the defense refused: evidence of insanity in Josephine's family was worth more to them than striking out the record of her arrest. So the question and its answer remained on the record: Phebe had had her daughter arrested the summer before Juddie's birth; Josephine had accused her of insanity and child abuse; and the two had parted ways, never to meet again.

"Now," Sedgwick announced, "we will go back a little." He asked the prisoner about her time at Blockley Hospital and her relationship with R. K. Smith. Sedgwick asked if she had been studying "any particular branch of medicine" at Blockley. "I might," she acknowledged, "have given more attention to obstetrics." And what about Dr. Smith, the superintendent who'd been rumored to visit her at her landlady's house at night? "Dr. Smith was undoubtedly a visitor at my room," Josephine said, even admitting that "he may have visited my room alone," but she couldn't remember him ever visiting at night. Besides, she added, "that was not a charge against Dr. Smith, that he visited my room." After her departure from the hospital, she admitted that she had been arrested, but denied that Smith had paid her bail; "I forget who did," she claimed.[53]

Moving chronologically, Sedgwick came next to the issue of Josephine's movements during the Civil War. Ever since her arrest, the press had been exploding with stories about "Johnny McCarty," the cross-dressing blockade runner. Here Josephine became cagey, answering many questions with a simple "I do not remember." She did remember going to Washington, although she couldn't recall the date or the time of day. Once there, she confirmed that she went to stay at the Union club house, but denied the charge that she had spent the night in various officers' rooms. Instead, she had traveled to Port Tobacco, though at first she said she was "not positive" that she had gone there at all. "I had a bottle or two of quinine given me at Blockley Hospital," she said, and had been seen calling on families in Port Tobacco who, she admitted, "had sons in the rebel army and were all secessionists." The roads between Washington and Port Tobacco were tightly patrolled, and she remembered that she had been searched once—on the Anacostia Bridge, she thought. That February, she was arrested and sent to the Old Capitol Prison, but "I never heard of any charge," and she was released after "six or eight weeks." In particular, Josephine insisted, "I was not charged with being a spy."[54]

Finally, on May 7, Sedgwick came to the most scandalous rumor of all—the nature of the business "Dr. Burleigh" conducted in Albany. Sedgwick threw Josephine a copy of the Albany *Argus* from the previous December. He demanded to know if the printed ad was her own. "I think so, sir," she answered. Above the objections of the defense, Sedgwick read out Dr. Burleigh's advertisement for "a safe and effective remedy for all female irregularities and obstructions" in "a strictly private house."[55] At his urging, Josephine acknowledged that she had been indicted for abortion once in 1869, but nothing had come of the charge. Then Sedgwick asked about Maggie Campbell.

Josephine knew her. "She died in my house last fall."

"Was there a post-mortem examination held in your house?" Sedgwick asked. Mitchell objected, but Doolittle shook his head.

"Go on," he told Sedgwick, "if you expect to show that an offence was committed."

"They don't expect to show any such thing," Mitchell protested, but the question stood, and Josephine answered. There had been a post-mortem, but she wasn't present for it and knew nothing of the findings until she heard the doctors testify at the inquest.

"Did you employ the physicians to make the post-mortem?" Sedgwick asked. Again, the defense objected; again, Doolittle ruled in favor of the people.

"I employed Dr. Boulware to consult with me in the case of Maggie Campbell," Josephine said, and yes, "I told him that I wanted a post-mortem, and employed and paid him to make the post-mortem examination."

"Did you have instruments in your house which are commonly used for procuring abortions?" Sedgwick demanded.

Pomeroy objected: "The same question may be asked of any physician."

Mrs. McCarty seemed to agree that the question was a bad one. "I had an axe in my house," she said, "which might be used for procuring abortions." If there were specific medical tools designed for that purpose, she knew nothing of them: "I never saw an instrument being used for procuring abortions."

Sedgwick was not amused by the witness's evasions. "I want a plain answer," he said, "to a plain question."

"I think the answer is a full one," Pomeroy retorted.

Judge Doolittle stepped in to rule on the question: "She can answer yes or no." Sedgwick repeated his question: had Mrs. McCarty had in her house any instruments commonly used for procuring abortions?

"I have answered the question," Josephine replied. "I never saw an instrument used for an abortion in my life; I never knew of any instrument being used for forcing abortions." Certainly she had heard of it being done, but "an axe or blow or kick may procure an abortion."

What, Sedgwick asked, about medicine? "I never knew of an abortion produced by medicine," Josephine insisted. "Obstructions are removed by medicine and instructions; by obstructions, I mean retention or interruption of the menses."[56]

Josephine's feigned ignorance might have been a tactic to avoid incriminating herself, but it also happened to be a good argument against the rise of anti-abortion laws—and an excellent illustration of why it was so hard to convict an abortionist. As Josephine pointed out, the tools used for abortions could be used for other purposes, and vice versa; Sedgwick himself probably had tools in his home that could have been used for an abortion. And while physicians were pushing hard for strict legal definitions of abortion, most ordinary Americans still embraced a more fluid understanding of reproduction. Legally, removing an "obstruction to the menses" could be considered a felony under New York law, but without the medical technology to prove that the obstruction was an embryo, the regular practice of medication abortion remained untouchable.

Ignorance was a powerful weapon for Josephine. "The cultural values that helped spare women charged with homicide," Carolyn Ramsey writes, "underestimated female rationality, resourcefulness, and autonomy."[57] As long as she continued to deny any knowledge of abortion practices, she made it harder for Sedgwick and his colleagues to prove the thing they most needed to: that she was a bad woman.

At 4:20 p.m. on May 7, after three exhausting days of testimony, Josephine finally stepped down from the stand. After all that, the case stood more or less where it had started. The defense had shown—as they promised to—the lifelong pattern of abuse Josephine had endured from Milton Thomson and the rest of the men in her life. But the questions set by the prosecution had revealed an equally important thread: Josephine had a history of putting profit before propriety. Depending on how things played out over the coming days, this could play to the defense's advantage, or it could doom her case. On the one hand, it fit neatly into the prosecution's picture of a calculating blackmailer who knew how to get what she wanted out of men. On the other hand, the jury might take it as evidence of the desperate financial state that first Robert and then Tom had put her and her children in.

But the defense needed to do more than prove that Josephine was desperate. In order to win an acquittal, they would need to convince the jury that she was insane at the time of the murder. Over the next few days, a steady stream of witnesses took the stand to weigh in on the most pressing question of the trial: was Josephine McCarty sane or insane?

CHAPTER 11

The Unwritten Law

On May 8, the defense called Josephine's neighbor Timothy D. Strong to the stand. Strong, a printer working for an Albany newspaper, had first met the McCarty family a couple of months after moving into 54 Howard Street in April of 1871. In early June, Louis McCarty turned up at his door around dinnertime, asking him to come see his mother. Strong obliged and found Mrs. McCarty in a heightened emotional state.

"She told me about burglars from New York coming to go through her house," Strong said. "She said they were coming on the night boat," and even showed him a threatening letter postmarked "New York" and signed "A Friend." Strong was less than sympathetic. "[I] told her that it was all nonsense and spoke pretty rough," he admitted. But after returning home for a few hours, he came back around 10:30 p.m. "She gave me a revolver," he said. David Mitchell showed him the revolver Josephine McCarty had fired on the streetcar, and Strong identified it as the same gun she'd given him at her house last summer.[1]

"I stayed there until 3 or 4 o'clock," he stated, and then he went home. "If anyone came, I did not see them."[2] A few weeks later, Louis McCarty came to his house again—this time, crawling through the upstairs window in tears, begging Strong to come check for burglars in the yard and alleys. Strong complied, somewhat begrudgingly, and once again found no evidence of any would-be intruders.

"Did you form an opinion as to her condition at that time," Mitchell asked, "after talking with her and seeing her go on?"

"Yes, sir."

"What was it?"

Sedgwick objected. "The evidence," he said, "is incompetent. A printer is not an expert on such things."

So Mitchell changed course, asking Strong to describe Josephine's appearance instead. "She had on a loose gown," Strong remembered, and "her hair was loose; she appeared very much excited, wringing her hands." Was this unusual for his neighbor? Yes, Strong said: "ordinarily she was very neat." All in all, he concluded, "I thought her conduct at those times very irrational."[3]

James Brice, an attorney from Albany, took the stand immediately after Strong. Josephine had approached him shortly after Christmas 1870. "Through the instrumentality of certain parties from New York and Philadelphia," he explained, she'd told him that "persons of a rough character had come to Albany to enter her home and take her life."[4] She said that "she was a lone woman; she had no man." If Brice couldn't come himself, could he at least find her "one or two good, strong men" to sit up and watch the house for her?

Unlike Strong, Brice disregarded the request entirely the first time he heard it, but a few months later Josephine came to him with proof: an anonymous note threatening to send burglars to her house. She asked him "to get a black coat, black pants and a trusty revolver, and send to her house before 7 P.M., as there was going to be trouble."[5] Again, he ignored her. For months, Josephine repeated the burglar story to Brice, describing her plans for fighting off the attack: "she said she would have her assistance down stairs; they would drive the burglars upstairs, and she would stand at the head of the stairs with a club and defend herself."

"I told her several times that she was crazy," Brice stated, "and positively refused to have anything to do with her. Her acts impressed me as being very irrational at that time." The last time Josephine came to his office, he recalled, it was to tell him her fear of being thrown out of 62 Howard Street. "Her eyes glistened," he said, and "her voice was like that of revenge." While Brice gave his testimony, Josephine held her handkerchief to her face, apparently overcome with emotion.

After Brice stepped down, the defense called on Nancy Scrivens, the friend Josephine and her children had stayed with just before coming to Utica. Unlike the rest of the witnesses, Nancy had been in court all week, listening to Josephine's testimony and the arguments of both the defense and the prosecution.[6] Now, on the stand, Nancy told the jury about Josephine's brief stay with her in January: about Josephine's headaches and uncontrollable weeping, about the wild look in her eyes. "I did not like the way she appeared," Mrs. Scrivens said. "I did not like to leave her alone."[7]

Finally, at the end of the day, the jury heard from Henrietta Conley Cooper, the friend from Saratoga County who had been in a carriage accident with Josephine the previous August. She described the accident for the jury, making note of the "excruciating agony" Josephine had suffered. "I can't conceive how she submitted to it," Mrs. Cooper said. Before she left for Albany, Mrs. Cooper remembered, "she told me some extravagant stories; I thought her delirium was not over."[8]

Months later, when she heard the news that Josephine and her children had been evicted from their home in Albany, Mrs. Cooper had come down from Charlton to help out. While they packed all their belongings to leave the property, she recalled, "Mrs. McCarty acted strangely. I don't know how to describe it."

"Do the best you can," Doolittle told her.

Obliging, Mrs. Cooper tried. "She was tired and had an automatic appearance," she said; "she had on an old straw hat and looked like 'Ophelia.'" The audience laughed at the image, but Mrs. Cooper went on. "She was pale and still," moving like an automaton and "throwing things about in a heterogenous manner." She couldn't find her keys, then discovered that they were in her pocket. Then she lost her pocketbook. On Wednesday morning, as the two women stood outside 62 Howard Street watching passersby pick through the family's scattered belongings, Mrs. Cooper reported, "She said to me, 'See the sharks?'" "Her acts were irrational," she concluded. "I have seen her often before; there was a decided and marked change."

Then Daniel Magone stood up to cross-examine the witness. He didn't care about any changes Mrs. Cooper had observed in Josephine's behavior; he wanted to know how they'd met. "Did you call on Mrs. McCarty," he asked, "to have an abortion performed?"

"Is that material?" Mrs. Cooper asked. The defense had evidently prepared her for this question.

"It is," Magone insisted. "I want an answer."

"I did not," Mrs. Cooper said—but she had called on someone else's behalf. "I do not wish to give the lady's name," she explained. But Doolittle ordered her to give up the name, and Mrs. Cooper reluctantly agreed. "It was a Miss Sarah Walton," she said, "a school mate" who went by her married name, Mrs. Guy. The two of them had gone to Josephine together—just for "a short call," she said.[9] But again, Mrs. Cooper asked, "Is this matter material?"

"Of as much importance as Ophelia," Magone replied.[10]

On May 9, the defense called twelve-year-old Louis McCarty to the stand. He'd been sick for the past two weeks, which prevented him from testifying sooner, but on the morning of the 9th he stood beside his mother in court, "looking very pale."[11]

Louis remembered sneaking through Timothy Strong's roof to call him to defend against his mother's imaginary burglars. He remembered "the day our things were put out of doors," and he remembered his mother packing a bag for him to take to the boys' home in Niagara Falls.[12] And he remembered the three tense, miserable days his family had spent at the Butterfield House before the tragedy. "Mother did not eat on Monday, Tuesday, or Wednesday," he said. "She was out to the lawyers." Then, on Wednesday morning, while Louis and his siblings were sitting in the parlor of the hotel, "I heard someone holler out that a man was killed."[13] Shortly afterwards, he said, "I saw Uncle Tom in the front office," covered in blood.

Stoddard handled Louis's cross-examination himself. Instead of questioning him about his mother or the morning of the murder, he started by asking Louis if he carried a pistol. "I never carried a pistol," Louis said. Stoddard pushed: maybe not, but did he *own* one? Yes, Louis said, but "I don't carry it loaded." Stoddard asked when Louis had purchased the gun. Thinking back, he said he thought he'd bought it a few weeks ago, around March 25. "I earned the money to buy the pistol by selling pictures and newspapers," Louis said. "I got it to play with." But when Josephine found out about the gun, she confiscated it, and he hadn't seen it since. Before that happened, he said, "I showed the pistol to the boys," but he hadn't told them—as Stoddard suggested—that he'd use the gun to shoot Thomson. He also denied any knowledge of his mother's profession. "I remember lady patients," he said—"quite a number of them," but he couldn't explain what his mother had done for them. With that, Louis was allowed to return to his seat by his mother's side.[14]

Everyone who had known Josephine in the months leading up to 1872, from her friends and neighbors to her own son, agreed that she'd been anxious, irrational, and paranoid. Some were sympathetic to her situation; others were just annoyed. But, taken together, their testimony painted a picture of a woman on the verge of a mental breakdown. There was just one problem: none of the defense's witnesses were doctors. Without expert witnesses, Josephine's insanity defense would fall flat.

Medical evidence didn't always play a major role in murder trials. At the beginning of the nineteenth century, lawyers rarely, if ever, called on physicians to testify in court. But that changed over the course of the century: professional doctors wanted to prove their scientific and moral authority, and what better place to do it than the witness stand? "Leading American physicians," the historian James Mohr explains, "believed that the future of their profession lay in civic-minded interaction with the nation's courts, legislatures, and lawyers."[15]

In 1823, an Albany physician named Theodric Romeyn Beck published *Elements of Medical Jurisprudence*, the first major American text on the subject of forensic medicine. As American medical schools standardized their training in the following decades, Beck's *Jurisprudence* became a staple of the curriculum, and for a short period most allopathic doctors received some training in how to relate their medical findings to a legal audience.[16]

But by mid-century, medical jurisprudence was falling out of vogue. In 1851, Horatio Storer's father, David Humphreys Storer, delivered an annual address to the Massachusetts Medical Society bemoaning doctors' treatment in court.[17] "The medical witness," he lamented, "is subject to have his whole testimony reviewed, ridiculed, doubted."

> Often asked questions which cannot be answered, and which frequently have no bearing upon the subject at issue, cross-questioned in such a manner by a subtle advocate as to make his replies appear inconsistent with his previous statements, the physician is compelled to stand in the witness-box, to have his feelings wounded by insolent interrogatories and unkind insinuations, long after every end of justice has been answered by his testimony.[18]

To make matters worse, sometimes doctors undermined each other's authority in the courtroom. Doctors who took the stand as medical witnesses swore to tell the truth, the whole truth, and nothing but the truth—but scientific truth was (and still is) a surprisingly slippery notion. The medical experts at Maggie Campbell's inquest had disagreed—maybe for selfish reasons and maybe not—about the correct interpretation of the evidence they'd found in her body. And when it came to the all-important question of Josephine McCarty's insanity, finding any type of medical consensus would be all but impossible.

For one thing, the definition of *insanity* itself was a subject of controversy. The study of mental health (and illness) was still an emerging field in the mid-nineteenth century, and recent years had seen a sharp division between two main schools of thought. In one camp were psychiatrists, who insisted that all mental illness has a physical cause; they looked for "lesions" in the brain that could explain a patient's unusual behavior or emotional disturbance. On the other side of the schism were alienists, who believed that insanity could have emotional causes, not just physical ones.[19] Over the middle decades of the nineteenth century, these debates leaked from the pages of medical journals into courtrooms across the country, stirring up controversy and muddying the waters of medical jurisprudence.

Because doctors disagreed on what constituted scientific truth, juries were often left with conflicting evidence—sometimes, as David Storer pointed out, from a single "expert" witness. As a result, medical evidence often served a purpose that was anything but scientific: it created a legal foothold for arguments that really rested on juries' empathy with the participants in a case. In the case of the insanity defense, lawyers often used medical evidence to build a narrative that had very little to do with medicine and everything to do with notions of gender, honor, and family that mattered much more to juries than the definition of insanity. In doing so, they invoked what legal historians call the "unwritten law." This unique form of the insanity defense can be traced back to a specific case: the 1859 murder trial of Daniel E. Sickles.

Daniel Sickles was a New York politician and diplomat. The son of a wealthy patent lawyer, he'd served as a member of the New York State Assembly, corporation counsel of the city of New York, secretary of the US legation to London, and a member of the New York State Senate before being elected, at age thirty-seven, to the US House of Representatives as the Democratic representative of the 3rd congressional district on Long Island, a position he would hold for the next five years.

Then, in 1859, Sickles learned that his wife Teresa had been sleeping with Philip Barton Key II, the US Attorney for the District of Columbia.

Sickles, twice Teresa's age and a serial adulterer himself, took the news badly, to say the least. On February 27, 1859, he found Key in Lafayette Square and shot him to death in full view of the White House. At trial, Sickles and his lawyers claimed that he fired the fatal shots in the grip of temporary insanity. Neither the defense nor the prosecution called a single doctor to testify to Sickles's mental state: instead, the key witness to his insanity was a close friend and fellow Democrat, Robert J. Walker.[20] Walker told the jury how Sickles had sobbed to him after receiving the anonymous letter that disclosed Teresa's infidelity. The jury called for an acquittal, and Sickles went on to become a decorated general in the Civil War.

Nobody really believed that Sickles was medically insane—or, at least, that he was unaware of his actions and their consequences. It took at least three shots to kill Key; by the end, he was cowering behind a tree as Sickles advanced on him and fired directly at his prostrate body, ranting about the dishonor Key had brought on his house.[21] The jury knew all of this, but they shared Sickles's outrage at being cuckolded by Key, and the insanity defense offered an unusually clean out.

In his book *Crime Without Punishment*, the legal historian Lawrence Friedman writes about crimes like Sickles's: killings that fit the legal definition of murder, but that nonetheless consistently saw acquittals in the mid-nineteenth century. In trials like these, he argues, the written text of the law was overridden by the "unwritten law," under which the killing of romantic rivals or abusers could be justified. The unwritten law circumvented the actual law to deliver a kind of social justice that assigned blame to the victim of the crime and allowed the defendant, more often than not, to walk free without even a fine to his name. In many of these trials, the insanity plea functioned as a kind of "legal fig leaf."[22] Defense attorneys borrowed the notion of "temporary insanity" caused by emotional disturbance from ongoing debates in psychiatric medicine in order to pursue what was in fact a social argument—not a medical or legal one—condemning men who transgressed the boundaries of appropriate male behavior and threatened the sanctity of family and the marriage bond. In other words, the unwritten law didn't just pardon killers; it implicitly sanctioned their actions as punishment for criminals the law couldn't reach: dishonorable men.

In 1859, Sickles's lawyers invoked this unwritten law without calling a single expert witness to back up their insanity argument. But subsequent trials, like the 1868 George Cole trial in Albany, saw increasing use of medical evidence—including contradictory medical evidence.

And as debates over the definition of insanity intensified, the burden of proof on defense attorneys grew heavier, and lawyers turned to physicians for more specialized diagnoses that would serve the purposes of the unwritten law.

The 1871 trial of Aratus Piece in Lockport, New York, illustrates the changes in the unwritten law in just twelve years since Daniel Sickles's acquittal. Unlike Sickles, Aratus Pierce wasn't a wealthy politician or a war hero. He was an ordinary clerk from Lockport, New York—but he had one thing, according to his defense attorneys, that made him unique: "He seemed to have a strong attachment to his sister that was almost beyond human conception."[23]

When he learned that William Bullock had gotten his sister pregnant and refused to marry her, he was outraged. "He could scarcely stand up under a condition that he had never dreamed of could happen to his family," Pierce's attorney said, "because of his manly confidence in man's honor." Distraught, Pierce tracked Bullock down and tried to reason with him: "You owe it to yourself," he told him, and "you owe it to your manhood, not to perpetrate such a cruel and infamous act!" Bullock was unmoved. "He said," Pierce told the jury, "that he would see me in hell."[24]

At this, the defense attorneys claimed, "the mind of Mr. Pierce was racked by agony and reflection." Bullock's callous reply "completely shocked and upset his whole mental system, and what followed to him is now a blank."[25] It wasn't a blank to the eyewitnesses. Pierce had pulled out a pistol and fired several shots into Bullock's abdomen, chasing him down the street as Bullock yelled "murder!" Bullock lingered in agony for just over a month and died on April 29.

Legally, Pierce was guilty of murder. But at his trial in September, Drs. William McCollum and Simeon T. Clark diagnosed Pierce with a condition they called "transitory mania," a condition they claimed could cause a brief spurt of violent insanity followed by a return to sanity. McCollum and Clark spent hours on the stand, reviewing the medical literature on insanity for the benefit of the jury. Since Pierce had been, in their judgment, incapable of reason at the time of the murder, he could not be held legally responsible. To bolster their evidence, the defense called witnesses to testify to the long history of insanity in the Pierce family. His uncle had spent years in the New York State Lunatic Asylum at Utica and died there; his aunt had passed away at age twenty-five from similar causes.

The medical evidence wasn't unanimous, though. Dr. George Cook of the State Lunatic Asylum, testifying for the prosecution, disagreed with McCollum and Clark's diagnosis. "I do not believe a person can be sane all his life," he stated, "and then insane five minutes, and then sane immediately after it and continue."[26] And, like McCollum and Clark, he backed his statements up with a demonstrated familiarity with the latest scientific research on insanity. With doctors disagreeing on the stand, the jury were left to draw their own conclusions about Pierce's sanity–and his guilt.

They did so without hesitation. Although the judge declared a ninety-minute recess upon the conclusion of closing arguments, the jury took just a few minutes to agree that Aratus Pierce was not guilty of the murder of William Bullock. According to the official report of the trial published weeks later, "The scene that followed beggars description. Men and women wept for joy. Men shouted and cheered. Women rushed forward over railings and chairs and embraced and shook hands with the prisoner."[27]

McCollum and Clark's testimony was convincing to the jury, Friedman's research suggests, not because they'd done a better job than Cook of proving the scientific basis of their evidence. They'd simply told a better story. The medical concept of "temporary insanity" resonated with juries because it described an extreme emotional state to which all decent men had access.[28]

Without expert witnesses, the evidence of Josephine's neighbors and friends only established that she'd been in a heightened emotional state. In order to sway the jury, Josephine's defense team would need to call expert witnesses who could demonstrate that any decent woman would act the same way if subjected to the torment Milton Thomson had put her through.

On May 9, after Louis McCarty stepped down, the defense called Dr. Charles Corey to the stand. Corey, a resident of Brooklyn, testified that he had been practicing medicine for more than fourteen years, ten of which he'd spent as the First Assistant Physician at New York's prestigious Bloomingdale Asylum. In that time, he'd devoted most of his time to the study of insanity and its possible causes. Physical disease, he said, could cause insanity, but so could "intense grief" and "religious excitement." In the case of women, he stated, "the uterine organs react on the nervous system so as to make a person more liable to insanity," particularly at the critical period of menopause.[29]

"How does domestic affliction rank among the causes of insanity?" Mitchell asked him.

Corey was cautious. "I am not able to say how large a proportion of the cases are so caused," he said; he continued, "I know it is not an infrequent cause of insanity."[30]

Next, Mitchell asked Corey to define the term "mania transitoria." Transitory mania, Corey stated, "is the form of insanity which occurs suddenly in persons not previously known to be of unsound mind, generally of short duration and generally subsiding more or less completely."[31] What evidence, Mitchell asked, might indicate someone's susceptibility to this form of short-lived madness?

"Delusions are unfailing evidences of insanity," Corey said. Previous episodes of insanity, "extreme nervousness," or "hallucinations causing persons to believe that they can see in the dark or hear through thick walls" could also be evidence of insanity, he added.[32] Just two days ago, Josephine had testified to all four of those symptoms, including a confident delusion that she'd been able to hear through walls.

Thus far, Corey's description of transitory mania seemed to fit perfectly with the defense's evidence. To underscore the point, Mitchell excused Corey briefly to recall Louis McCarty, asking him about his mother's recent periods of illness. While they lived at Howard Street, Louis recalled, his mother "was sick, every two or three weeks," with headaches and total prostration. These bouts of illness were severe and lasted about a week every time; all in all, Louis estimated, "she was in bed about half the time she lived in the Howard Street house."[33]

Mitchell called Corey back and asked him what he made of that evidence. "If a woman was in her climactic [menopausal] period and confined to her bed," Corey said, "with hemorrhages occurring every two or three weeks, I should expect a very troubled and nervous system." If subject to a "sudden mental shock," he thought, such a patient might even have "homicidal paroxysms."[34]

Having gotten through all of his medical questions, Mitchell began to tell Corey a story. It was a story the jury had already heard: the story "of a young girl born in Virginia" whose life had been ruined by dishonorable men.[35] Mitchell told Corey about the "unquestioned virtue" of her youth and about her tumultuous first marriage; he touched on her seduction by Thomson, her "delusions of supernatural hearing," the interminable financial struggle between her and "her seducer," and finally her "failing health" and the head injury in the summer of 1871.

At last, after nearly an hour, he came to the exchange on the streetcar on January 17.

> She finally sees her seducer; desires an interview with him, steps on the car; the revolver was loaded, and had been for months; soon after she got in her suitor steps in with a friend, whom she never knew, and takes a seat opposite her; she reaches over and speaks in a plain voice in the presence of passengers, saying, "Tom, I have brought your children to you, which you have turned out into the streets to starve. I cannot support them any longer." Some reply was made. He replied instantly, "Go to hell with them." In an instant, so quick that no one saw what occurred, the pistol is discharged, striking her seducer in the face, wounding him, but unfortunately, striking, too, another person, and causing his death. She is seen standing on the floor, she sees her revolver on the seat open, she closes it; sees in it four more charges; makes no other effort to shoot; gasps for breath; shows much excitement on the way to the Station House; expresses no regrets; makes no concealment; hands the pistol to the officers of the law and is soon thereafter committed to jail; after she reaches the Station House, becomes calm and remains so.[36]

This long question, the *Observer* noted, "occupied a full hour in its asking," but Mitchell was building to a point. "In your judgment," he asked Corey, "was she sane or insane when that act was committed?"

"I would say," Dr. Corey replied, "that she was insane."[37]

"Wait a moment," Sedgwick interjected, "don't be in such a hurry." The question, he argued, was based on facts the defense hadn't proved; it wasn't a fair question. Mitchell should drop the embellishments and confine himself to the facts.

Mitchell complied. Corey could ignore all the other evidence, he said, and stick to a few facts: that Josephine "was deprived of her children in Europe, and was seduced by Thomson"; that there were mortgages on her house and her mother's farm; that she was going through menopause; that she'd been evicted and came to Utica to see the father of her illegitimate children; that she entered the streetcar on January 17 "in failing health and an extreme nervous condition"; that she'd been injured in a carriage accident the previous summer; and that she'd had hallucinations while living in St. Louis years ago. Taking those facts together, he asked Corey, "is there any doubt about her insanity at that moment?"

"I think," Corey said, "the facts will still justify me in saying that she was insane."[38] And with that, Mitchell concluded his examination.

Sedgwick launched into cross-examination determined to undermine Corey's authority as an expert witness. Under his questioning, Corey admitted that it was "nearly six years" since he had worked at a hospital for the insane. Then Sedgwick asked about the causes of insanity. This time, Corey said that "insanity is always the result of diseases of the brain," which seemed like a clear contradiction of his previous testimony. "Heavy shocks," he added, "do not always tend to insanity." Moreover, "if a person is in unquestionably sound mind I do not believe they can become suddenly insane and then have their mind restored."[39] Only someone who had previously suffered from insanity and whose mental condition was already fragile could have their self-control diminished by a sudden shock—and that person would still be insane afterwards.

Finally, Sedgwick pressed Corey to define how long an episode of so-called "transitory mania" could last. "The shortest time in which transitory mania could develop and pass away," Corey stated, "is within half an hour."[40] He would also consider half an hour "the least time for an utter suppression of the recollection."[41] This, clearly, posed a serious problem for the defense. At most, Josephine had been on the streetcar for ten or fifteen minutes, and the only part of that day she claimed not to remember was the moment that the gun went off. Suddenly, Josephine's apparently impossible claim that she'd been on the streetcar for what seemed like half an hour took on new significance.

But then Corey said something else that put Josephine's defense in danger: "In transitory mania, there is always an absence of motive for killing."[42] If there was one thing that wasn't ambiguous in Josephine's case, it was her motive to kill Milton Thomson.

Sedgwick posed one last question to Dr. Corey: what effect, he asked, could a person's character have on his evaluation of their sanity? At first, Corey said that the previous character of a patient would probably have "but very little weight." But Sedgwick clarified: would a person of bad character be more likely to feign insanity? Yes, Corey said; knowing that someone's character was bad "would make a difference in my estimate of the case."[43] Satisfied with that answer, Sedgwick concluded his cross-examination.

Mitchell returned to question Dr. Corey one last time—but the question he asked had nothing to do with medicine or insanity. "Does not a mother love an illegitimate child," he asked, "as much as a mother does a legitimate child?"[44]

Sedgwick objected. "That is not a question of science."

Mitchell changed his question. "Would you call it a domestic affliction," he asked, "if a mother saw an illegitimate child starving?"

Dr. Corey thought about it. "I do not think that would come under the head of domestic affliction," he decided, but he acknowledged that it would still be a great affliction. What about "coming into the presence of a party who had done one great wrong," Mitchell asked—like the case of a man who stumbled on his wife's seducer? That would also fall under the category of a shock, Corey agreed. In fact, it might be enough to cause insanity, especially if the person had had their mind and body broken down, and had no support network.

And what about "the case of a woman who has shown great affection for her illegitimate children," Mitchell asked—a woman "who had always shown a great love for children, and her seducer told her to go to hell with the children. Would that have a great effect on the mother's mind?"

"I think it would have a decided effect," Corey said.

After Mitchell finished questioning Corey, the defense called three more medical experts to testify to Josephine's alleged insanity at the time of the murder. One was C. B. Coventry, a Utica physician who had "urged the American Medical Association to distance itself from the controversies over insanity in the late 1850s." Another was Simeon T. Clark, one of the two expert witnesses from the previous year's Pierce-Bullock trial; Josephine had been seen chatting with him throughout Charles Corey's testimony. Now Josephine's defense attorney asked each of the three doctors to refer to the "long question" that Mitchell had asked Corey, and every doctor agreed: they believed Josephine to have been insane at the time of the shooting. "My impression," Coventry stated, "is that she has been more or less insane from the time she was turned out of the house up to the present time."[45] Clark concurred, saying, "I think she was laboring under a hallucination; I have had a conversation with her in that direction."[46]

Just as Clark finished his testimony, Josephine stood up from her seat and "walked out crying." "Let some Sheriff take charge of that person," Judge Doolittle exclaimed. "She should not be allowed to go out alone."[47] For several minutes, the trial stalled as Josephine refused to come back. Eventually Babcock persuaded her to return to the courtroom, where she "sat with her fan to her face and her eyes shut." Afterwards, Clark explained to the *Observer*'s reporter that "Mrs. McCarty was very angry with him for saying that she was still crazy." She wouldn't speak to him now, and "he also said that he would not be surprised if she had all of the doctors arrested after the trial was over."[48] Carolyn Ramsey was right: to successfully win an insanity plea, women in the nineteenth century had to give up their claim to rationality and autonomy. Listening to her colleagues swear confidently to her total loss of reason, Josephine was experiencing the other side of that double-edged sword.

Despite Josephine's objections, the trial proceeded. The defense was still awaiting the arrival of one final medical expert: William Hammond, former surgeon general of the United States Army and a leading authority on insanity who favored an inclusive view of its causes. Hammond was a big deal: his testimony, and his credentials, would have given the defense a major advantage. But by 4:50 p.m., Hammond's train still hadn't arrived. Mitchell made the call. As the hands of the clock crept toward 5, he addressed the court: "As the trial has been long already, we rest the case for the defence."[49]

Immediately, Stoddard began to summon character witnesses who could undermine Josephine's insanity plea by convincing the jury that she was not a good enough woman to save. The prosecution's first rebutting witness was Aaron D. Pratt, an Albany lawyer who'd represented one of Josephine's neighbors in a civil lawsuit she brought against him. Josephine had lied on the stand, he said, claiming to be married to a man named Seymour who had never existed. "From the speech of the people," he added, "her character is bad." Police officers John B. Conkling and Francis E. Bailey agreed, though both acknowledged on cross-examination that they'd never heard anyone talk about "her character for truth and veracity." Helen Gow and Edgar P. Dennison, both neighbors of Josephine's on Howard Street, testified that her character in their city was known to be "very bad," but both admitted to Mitchell in cross-examination that they had been involved in various petty disputes with the accused.[50] John O'Donnell, late of Washington, DC, remembered Josephine from Barney Donnelly's Club House in 1862. He was happy to testify that she had arrived at the club house in men's clothes and in the company of a Union officer, with whom she shared a bed for several days. On cross-examination, Mitchell forced O'Donnell to admit that he was a gambler and that his subpoena had been personally served by Milton Thomson himself. Stephen Franklin, a detective from Philadelphia who had worked at the Blockley Almshouse in 1859, remembered the defendant from the insane department and told the jury that "from the speech of people her character was bad."[51] Casting farther back, the prosecution called Seth Mayo and Lyman Warren of Augusta, both of whom testified that the defendant's reputation in that area had been bad as early as the 1840s.[52]

Finally, the district attorney called a woman named Hattie Baker to the stand. Baker, a thirty-three-year-old domestic servant, testified that she lived in Albany and had known the defendant since March 1871.[53] For a few months the previous spring, she had lived and worked at 62 Howard Street as Josephine McCarty's servant. She remembered her former employer's paranoia about burglars. She remembered Mrs. McCarty's lie to Aaron Pratt about the fictional Mr. Seymour, and she remembered that Mrs. McCarty had "induced [her] to make complaints against the Dennisons" next door, even going so far as to ask Baker to "provoke" Edgar Dennison. Multiple witnesses already testified to Josephine's ailing health during this period, but Baker said, "her general health during that time was very good."[54]

And "what," Magone asked, "was Mrs. McCarty's business when you lived with her?"

"I object to it," Mitchell interjected instantly. "It is entirely immaterial what the business was." Doolittle pointed out that the jury had already heard evidence concerning the defendant's business, but Babcock insisted, "We cannot see how in any possible aspect this evidence can bear on that question."[55]

"If your Honor pleases," Magone said, "this woman is charged with a homicide." Given the magnitude of the crime, the whole of the prisoner's life could be considered evidence, if not of the crime itself, of the moral weaknesses that had led her to commit it. "If she was engaged in unlawful business," Magone said, "we propose to show it." But it wasn't just her past crimes that mattered to the prosecution. "We also propose to show," Magone added, "that this woman's affections and feelings were not so delicate that she would be easily excited or shocked over the alleged expression in the case."[56] Critics had argued for decades that studying medicine would dull the natural sensitivity that allowed women to be such good mothers. A woman who'd practiced abortion for years couldn't be shocked by something as simple as a curse word.

"The more I think of this evidence," Mitchell remarked, "the more I think it is inadmissible."[57] The argument went on for several more minutes, until Judge Doolittle finally gave his ruling: he would record the defense's objection, but the question was admissible and the witness could have to answer.

"Now," Magone addressed Baker triumphantly, "answer it."

Hattie Baker didn't have to think. "She was an abortionist."[58]

Pomeroy immediately jumped in to remind the jury that "physicians of the highest standing may be called upon to produce abortions." "It seems to be a covert plan and it seems to be a wicked plan to give this answer," Pomeroy declared, and Mitchell proposed to "send to Albany and get a cloud of witnesses from the best families" to testify to Josephine's high professional standards.[59] But it was too late for that. Hattie Baker had said what everyone already knew: Josephine McCarty had been an abortionist in Albany. Although Judge Doolittle eventually relented and allowed the answer to be struck out of the official transcript, he declined to give the jury a special instruction not to let it influence their ruling.

All that remained for the prosecution was to show the jury that it was really Josephine, and not Thomson, who had been the aggressor in their troubled relationship. After dismissing Hattie Baker, the district attorney called the Honorable J. Thomas Spriggs to the stand.

"I have resided in Utica about fourteen years," Spriggs stated, during which time he worked as an attorney for Milton H. Thomson.[60] At Stoddard's prompting, he recalled the first time he had met Josephine McCarty. It was the spring of 1862, at Bagg's Hotel in Utica; Thomson had sent him there to meet with Josephine in a room on the second floor. When he arrived, Spriggs found that his boss's mistress was pregnant.

"She said she was without means and in a condition which required that she should be provided for, and she wanted a suitable provision," Spriggs remembered. "She said $150 would be necessary."[61] The following morning, he brought her the money, and Mrs. McCarty made a remark about going to California. Spriggs had imagined that that would be the end of the affair, but later that summer, Thomson called on him again to negotiate with Josephine.

This time, Mrs. McCarty's demands were steeper, and so was the price she was willing to pay: if Tom agreed to her demands, she would release him from all claims of paternity. Thomson and McCarty had finally agreed on the sum of $1,500, and accordingly, Spriggs said, "the papers were drawn and the money was paid" in "three five hundred dollar packages."[62] Since 1862, he had seen her only five or six more times, never outside of a certain set of circumstances.

As Spriggs put it to Stoddard, "I can say that she never asked for money without my paying it, and she never came to me without asking for money."[63] In the summer of 1871, Josephine had appeared at

Spriggs's office in Utica accompanied by her middle child, Ernest Judson. "Mr. Spriggs," she said, "I have come to Utica to introduce Milton H. Thomson's son to the citizens of Utica, and I take pleasure in introducing him to you first."[64] In spite of her promise years ago to release Thomson from any paternity claims, Josephine would not be dissuaded from her plans: she took Juddie to visit Thomson's mother, his neighbors, and the rector at his church."[65] Returning to Spriggs's office, she demanded $5,000, the deed to the Howard Street house in Juddie's name, and payment for the mortgage on her mother's farm. "I told her," Spriggs said, "that the terms were unreasonable, but I would submit them." In response, he continued, "she told me she was in the condition she always was when she saw me—without money."[66] He gave her $30 for her expenses in Utica, and she went away. That was the last time, Spriggs explained, that he had seen her before the homicide.

Sprigg's evidence threatened to turn the defense's argument on its head. For Thomson's mistreatment to drive Josephine insane, he would have to hold all the cards—and if Spriggs's story was true, Josephine had held more than her share. Was she a victim of "domestic afflictions," as the defense wanted the jury to believe—or was she really their author?

As Spriggs's examination drew to a close on May 11, reporters noticed the entrance into the courtroom of a person who had not been present through any of the previous testimony, and who now said nothing and took no action other than to listen, apparently intently, to the testimony of his lawyer. It was Milton Thomson.[67] He sat through the last of the day's testimony, and when court adjourned just after four o'clock, he disappeared as suddenly as he had arrived. He would not return to the courtroom for the remainder of the trial.

CHAPTER 12

The Smoking Pistol

The trial of Josephine McCarty entered its final week on May 13, 1872. Josephine arrived early that morning, sitting beside Babcock in silence as they waited for Judge Doolittle to call the court to order. The whole room was quiet. Two weeks of repetitive testimony had ground down the public's enthusiasm, or maybe nobody cared to get up early on a Monday morning to watch the proceedings grind on. Whatever the reason, the reporter covering the trial for the *Observer* noted that "attendance at the Court House this morning was quite small."[1]

By now, the twelve members of the jury had been sequestered together for nearly two full weeks. Mainly middle-aged farmers and carpenters from small towns surrounding Utica, they were "remarkably quiet looking men in general," the *Observer* reported, but over the past thirteen days reporters had had the opportunity to glean a sense of their individual characters. Seth Penny and Philip Sanford were "the funny men of the jury," who "[kept] their associates supplied with plenty of fun" in between screeds of medical testimony and lengthy cross-examinations. An elderly carpenter from Utica named Jacob W. Schuyler, on the other hand, had distinguished himself as "the first one to discover when it is 11 A.M. and 4 P.M., the hours for recess." The foreman of this unremarkable crew—"and, by the way, the best looking man," noted the *Observer*—was twenty-eight-year-old James H. Spencer of Camden, a farmer's son who aspired to a career in law himself.[2]

Despite the lull in public interest, Monday morning would see the prosecution's star witness on the stand. His name was John Perdue Gray, the superintendent of the New York State Lunatic Asylum in Utica and a former president of the state medical society. It was John P. Gray who, in 1868, had called for stricter laws on abortion and the sale of abortifacients. He had also been the editor of the *American Journal of Insanity* since 1850.[3] If anyone was qualified as an expert witness in the trial of Josephine McCarty, it was John Perdue Gray.

In his previous writings and public appearances, Gray had made his perspective on the question of insanity clear: in his view, insanity could not be caused by emotional shocks, bad character, or indeed anything other than purely organic disease.[4] For Gray, the problem with diagnoses like "transitory mania" was that they "conflated moral causes of human actions with physical."[5] Gray believed so strongly in the idea that mental illness could only be caused by physical disease or damage to the brain that he had appointed a pathologist to the staff of the state asylum two years earlier, making Utica's institution the first American asylum to do so.[6] A "short, broad man" who was a "distinguished and commanding" expert to his supporters and "a powerful, manipulative enduring hater" in the eyes of his opponents, Gray came to court on May 13 to encourage the jury to reject the notion that anything less than brain damage could have driven Josephine insane.[7]

On the last day of January that year, Gray had visited Josephine at the Mohawk Street Jail along with several of his colleagues, a few of whom would also testify on Monday and the following day. Gray began his testimony by giving an account of that visit. Before he could even answer Sedgwick's first question, the defense had already objected. The evidence, Pomeroy claimed, was "incompetent," because Josephine had not freely consented to Gray's examination. "The law forced those jail doors open," Mitchell claimed, and Gray had questioned her without his attorneys present.[8]

"I stated," Gray explained, "that we were sent by the Court and she could decline to answer any questions." When Josephine did not, in fact, decline, he asked her about "her girlhood, of her early health when she first menstruated, her occupation and health in that occupation." From Josephine's answers, he concluded that she was "in ordinary health."[9]

In spite of this, he acknowledged that Josephine had described significant health issues to him. "She said she thought she was passing through the period of change of life," he explained, "as her menstruation was irregular; that she had been confined to her bed at times, and suffered from headache and nervousness; that at times she suffered from noise and light." Following her accident in Saratoga County, she had headaches, difficulty raising her arm, and a sense that "her system was generally jarred." She'd told Gray that she carried a pistol for protection and that she couldn't remember what happened on the streetcar—only the sight of her pistol on the seat, the blood on Thomson's face, and the smoke. But, Gray finished, "in my opinion she was sane at that time."[10]

Had Gray, Sedgwick asked, read Mitchell's "hypothetical" account of Josephine's life, complete with all of her traumas and all Thomson's wrongdoings? Gray had. "Assuming that to be a true statement," Sedgwick said, "was she laboring under transitory mania in your judgment?" "No, sir," Gray replied.[11]

It was a well-informed opinion. A few years earlier, Gray had observed the case of a woman claiming temporary insanity following the murder of an ex-lover. In 1866, American psychiatry was absorbed in debates over the trial of Mary Harris, who in January 1865 entered the US Treasury Building in Washington, DC, and shot her former lover, a clerk named Adoniram J. Burroughs, as he emerged from his office. Unlike Josephine, Mary immediately expressed regret. "Why did I do it?" she wailed on the scene. "I would give my life to save him."[12] But there was no saving Adoniram; she had shot him in the head. Unlike Josephine, Mary didn't miss.

On the way to jail, Mary told police that Burroughs had "ruined her." She was only twelve when she met him at her job in a millinery store in Burlington, Iowa. Although he was twenty-three years her senior, Adoniram took an immediate interest in Mary. "She seems to have been a bright and pretty child," one account said, "and he was so much pleased with her as to fondle and caress her, take charge of her education, and finally to introduce her into the society in which he moved." As Mary approached adulthood, Adoniram's letters to her showed "the closest intimacy of the parties, as lovers, and the subject of marriage [was] freely alluded to."[13] The wedding was planned for June of 1863: Mary would be twenty, and Adoniram forty-three. She moved to Chicago that spring in preparation.

But the wedding never happened. As suddenly as Adoniram had appeared in Mary's life, he disappeared. He moved to Washington for a job at the Treasury and stopped writing to her. In September 1863, three months after they were meant to be married, Mary opened the newspaper and read the announcement of the marriage of Adoniram J. Burroughs to Amelia Louise Boggs. It was after this, witnesses later recalled, that her attacks began.

Nobody could quite explain the fits that Mary had in the fall of 1863. She slept on the bare floor, went out in her nightclothes in the dead of the Chicago winter, threw objects and ripped her clothing. On one occasion, she attacked her friends with a knife at the mention of Burroughs's name. At the same time, she began complaining of painful periods. By December 1864, her condition was unbearable, both for herself and for those around her. The women who ran the Chicago boarding house where Mary had been living encouraged her to go to Washington to have it out with Burroughs, and she took their advice. On January 30, 1865, Mary made her way to the Treasury Building, asked around until she found Adoniram's office, and waited patiently until he emerged. There was no attempt at conversation; she shot him in the head at point-blank range and began to cry.

Gray didn't testify at Mary's trial. In fact, the only physician examined as an expert witness in the summer of 1865 was Charles H. Nichols, a defender of exactly the kind of "moral insanity" theory that Gray despised.[14] Nichols testified that Mary's actions were caused by an "insane impulse" triggered by severe menstrual pains along with her emotional distress at Burroughs's betrayal. Nichols's expert evidence helped to win her an acquittal.

In January 1866, the *American Journal of Insanity* published an article on "The Trial of Mary Harris." No author was listed, suggesting that it was written by the journal's editor—that is, by John Gray. The article certainly squared with his views on the insanity defense. Mary's acquittal, the author stated, was "extraordinary," for, contrary to Nichols's testimony, "there was nothing in her history, or the circumstances of the homicide, to suggest insanity to the ordinary observer."[15] Mary's attack of madness, he argued, was instead indicative of "a girl *voluntarily* yielding herself to the control of her wayward feelings."[16] The defense's argument for insanity displayed "the greatest inconsistency and seeming ignorance," and the public's apparent sympathy could only be explained by Mary's youth, beauty, and "irresistible appeal" to chivalry.

"They do these things infinitely better in New York," the anonymous author wrote.[17]

Nichols had been called as an expert witness in the Harris trial, but in Gray's estimation, his testimony failed to meet scientific standards. In order to qualify as temporary moral insanity, the article argued, an act "must consist of two elements": first, there must be no way to account for the act except for insanity, and second, "some efficient pre-disposing cause of mental disease" must exist. Possible causes of insanity might include "heredity, previous attacks of insanity, wounds of the head, brain fever, the sudden suppression of a discharge, the puerperal state, and some others"—but not menstrual pain or emotional trauma. In cases that failed to meet these essential criteria, he wrote, "moral insanity . . . has not a single symptom to distinguish it from moral depravity."[18]

Not only was the author critical of juries and so-called experts who claimed that Mary's emotional trauma alone could drive her insane; he ended his article by casting doubt on her love for Adoniram in the first place. "The evidence," he wrote, "does not show any deep-rooted, serious attachment between the parties. He was nearly twice as old as she, a foolish, trifling fellow, and quite incompetent to feel or excite anything worth the name of love." What Mary felt for him, Gray concluded, wasn't really love, but "flattered vanity and excited ambition."[19]

Now, faced with the case of Josephine McCarty, Gray weighed up the same evidence. In his judgment, Josephine's defense had met neither of the criteria for temporary insanity: her attack had a clear motive easily explained by something other than madness, and none of the emotional blows and health problems she'd described amounted to an "efficient predisposing case" of insanity.

What, Sedgwick asked, about her alleged ability to hear through walls in St. Louis? Should the jury take that testimony as evidence of a history of mental illness—hallucinations, maybe, or delusions? Or, Sedgwick suggested, "does it describe a trick?"

Mitchell objected. That, he argued, was "not a question of skill or science," and Gray couldn't be expected to give an expert opinion on it. "We shall have to get an expert here on the subject of tricks," he said.

"They can be easily procured," Sedgwick returned, "if some of the counsel are sworn."[20]

Seeing the question ready to devolve into petty bickering between the two attorneys, Doolittle dismissed it altogether, but the suggestion was already planted in the jury's minds. If Josephine didn't meet the scientific criteria for insanity, maybe the stories she'd told about her own delusions were deliberately designed to convince the jury that she'd been insane for years. After all, the defense hadn't called any other witnesses to corroborate her story.

On cross-examination, Mitchell tried to push Gray to loosen his definition of insanity to admit that madness could be caused by emotional shocks. But Gray was stubborn: emotional causes, he insisted, could only be "predisposing to insanity; physical causes are direct."[21] Diseases of the uterus, he acknowledged, were "often the preceding cause" of an attack of insanity, but only if they affected the brain directly.

Would this, Mitchell wondered, be more likely to happen to a woman entering menopause? "The climacteric period," Gray stated, "is recognized as one most critical in a woman's life, as one of the particular periods which predispose her to insanity."[22] This was not an original notion; for decades, medical men had passed along variations on the belief that any kind of "female complaint" could lead to insanity. Horatio Storer had even argued that the mere thought of abortion could render a woman clinically insane.[23] In Josephine's case, Gray was willing to acknowledge that her frequent hemorrhages might have caused "great nervousness," but that wouldn't rise to the level of unseating her capacity for rational thought. Neither would the loss of her children, her "domestic affliction," or anything else. All of these, though they might predispose her to insanity, could not actually cause it—not even when put together.

"Will you state the case," Mitchell asked in apparent frustration, "of a woman who would be more liable to be insane than that of a woman who had been separated from her children, had bastard children, was in the climacteric state, was turned into the street with her bastard children without means of support; if these are not calculated to produce insanity, in Heaven's name what will?"[24]

Sedgwick objected. Doolittle agreed; Gray didn't need to answer the question. Mitchell concluded his cross-examination with a series of rapid-fire questions that he read directly from a medical textbook too quickly for the *Observer*'s reporter to write them down.[25] Finally, as evening approached, he elicited one crucial statement from Gray that seemed to open a tiny crack in the wall of medical confidence he'd erected over the previous several hours.

"This woman," Gray stated in answer to one of Mitchell's many questions, "may have fired that pistol without knowing the fact when it occurred."[26]

This was a crucial point. Since the start of the trial, Josephine and her attorneys had insisted that she had no memory of the actual gunshot that had killed Hall. She remembered getting onto the car; she remembered what Thomson had said to her; she remembered getting off and walking toward downtown. But the actual moment of crime was a blank in her memory. Now John P. Gray, perhaps the nation's greatest opponent of the theory of transitory mania, had admitted that it was possible that Josephine had fired the gun without knowledge of doing so.

On the evening of May 13, after six or seven hours on the stand, Gray concluded his testimony. The prosecution called three more doctors to back up his evidence. First, James B. Boyd testified that he had examined Josephine in Albany after her injury last summer and "saw no nervousness then," adding that "her reputation is not very good from the speech of people" in Albany. Dr. Albert Vanderveer, who had participated in the inquest following the death of Maggie Campbell the previous September, remembered Josephine. She had exhibited "no apparent nervousness" at the inquest, he recalled; in fact, she was "remarkably cool." Finally, Dr. Alonzo Churchill of Utica testified regarding his visit to the Mohawk Street Jail with Gray in January. "I think she was sane," he said, although some doubt lingered in his mind around "the reference to supernatural hearing in St. Louis, and the idea in reference to the burglars at Albany." But, in the end, it was "not very much doubt." Josephine was sane, he thought, and the painful events of her life story didn't change that fact.[27]

Before the day was out, the jury had heard from four of the prosecution's medical experts.[28] The following morning, with just thirteen people watching in the audience, the prosecution called Judson Andrews of the State Lunatic Asylum to the stand. Like his colleague Gray, he denied that Josephine's case could be considered one of transitory mania; she was, in his view, definitely sane.

"Transitory mania," he explained, "rarely occurs in women, most invariably among men; it is noted particularly among soldiers." During an attack, a patient could be expected to display a complete loss of memory and either "great violence" or "complete incoherence," all of which Josephine seemed to show. But, Andrews cautioned, attacks of transitory mania also usually ended either in sleep, or in "unusual calmness and quiet." Josephine, by all accounts, had been wide awake after the murder, suggesting that her case did not fit the diagnostic criteria after all.

"If you were called on to determine as to a real or feigned case of transitory mania," Sedgwick asked, "would you look for any predisposing evidence?"

"Yes, sir," Andrews answered. "I should look for evidences [sic] of congestion of the brain." In a real case, a patient suffering from transitory mania would be compelled by those "cerebral disturbances" and would exhibit the symptoms already described: blind fury, confusion, a total loss of memory, and unconsciousness following the attack. But above all, he said, "in a real case of transitory mania the act would be without motive."[29]

And what about a feigned case? The first step in identifying fraud, Andrews said, would be to determine how much the person really remembered. "There might drop out from the person feigning transitory mania something apparently trivial connected with the act," he said, "which those who did not understand the symptoms might expect would be passed unnoticed."[30] Had Josephine let anything slip?

At 11:30 a.m. on May 14, Stoddard informed Doolittle that the People had issued a subpoena to Milton H. Thomson. For days, they had looked for an opportunity to put him on the stand to give his version of the story, but the previous night doctors had informed them that Thomson was not fit to be examined. Now, as the evidence drew to a close, Stoddard had dispatched "two of our best physicians to see Mr. Thomson to decide if he is in a condition to be examined or not."[31] Doolittle granted a brief recess while the prosecution waited for news.

At noon, the doctors returned. The last witness for the prosecution was Dr. Edward Hutchinson, who stated that he had practiced in Utica for some years and knew Milton Thomson. Stoddard asked him about Thomson's condition—would he be well enough to appear in court?—but Mitchell objected and Stoddard didn't fight it. He released Hutchinson and answered the unspoken question himself by resting the case for the People.[32]

Mitchell lost no time in calling rebutting witnesses. In steady succession Sidney Pulnam, William F. Warren, Albert Newell, Calvin Bently, and Menzo Cole testified to Josephine's good character in her hometown of Augusta. Warren said that "up to her marriage" he had thought her character was good—though he admitted to the district attorney that that was at least in part "because [he] did not hear very much said about her" one way or another."[33] The others agreed: none of them had had very much to do with the Fagan family, but their general impression of Josephine before she moved away and married Robert was positive.

At 1 p.m., Doolittle called a two-hour recess, which ran over when Mitchell and Sedgwick both arrived fifteen minutes late to court. By this time, the *Observer* noted, "there was a larger attendance . . . than has been present for two or three days past."[34] The testimony was drawing to a close, and people knew it; everyone wanted to be there for the conclusion.

At 3:30 p.m., Mitchell called his final witness. Josephine McCarty returned to the stand one last time to offer clarifications and corrections to a number of suggestions dropped by the prosecution over the previous week. She rejected the rumors that she had slept with Union officers during the war, and stated that she'd never been married to any man but Robert McCarty. When Mitchell asked her about Hattie Baker, the servant who had told the court she was an abortionist, Josephine dismissed it, saying, "I discharged her from my employ." Before she fired Hattie, Josephine said, they'd had "a quarrel," but contrary to Baker's testimony, she never forced her to call the neighbors names to incite a dispute.[35]

Mitchell had just one more question for Josephine. "When Dr. Gray came to your room in jail," he said, "did you intend to say that you saw the smoke of the pistol?"

And there it was, the very thing Dr. Andrews had said would prove a feigned case of transitory mania: an apparently trivial detail that revealed the defendant remembered a little too much about the moment of the crime.

"I did not say so to Dr. Gray," Josephine replied. "He must have been mistaken."

The People declined to cross-examine, and Josephine took her seat, looking "more serious than usual."[36]

The evidence was complete. The witnesses had all been called, and the experts had made their cases. Now, the attorneys for the prosecution and defense had the opportunity to sum up the case for the jury in closing arguments.

Pomeroy, the defense team's best orator, stood first to address the jury. "The investigation of a question of life and death under any circumstance, no matter who the person may be, is an awful thing," he told them. "But, gentlemen, I submit that in this case it is peculiarly solemn and impressive."[37]

"It has not been proved," Pomeroy went on, "that money has been raised to suborn witnesses; to bring them here from East, West, North, and South; it has not been proved that Milton H. Thomson and his brothers have been on the trail of the officers sent for our witnesses."[38] He paused for effect and added, "It may not have been true, but you have your opinion."

As a young girl growing up in their own county, Pomeroy told his audience, Josephine McCarty "believed she had the world before her where she might do good, where she might be useful." Chasing that dream of usefulness, she traveled first to the Hudson River, and then south to Washington, DC—"the great centre of vice," Pomeroy called it. There she met Robert McCarty, a man twice her age—"I will assume," Pomeroy added, "a captivating man, who held out inducements to her. Thus," he declared, "the first misstep in her life, the step that tended downwards was taken."[39]

Robert had wronged her, taken her children, and abandoned her— but her maternal instinct remained intact. "What is the closing scene on that side of the ocean?" Pomeroy asked. "She found one of her children by the instincts of a mother." And then, in her most vulnerable moment, lamenting the loss of her children, "a deceitful, disguising, lecherous man, in the shape of Milton H. Thomson, overtook her . . . professing to call on her mother, but intent upon possessing her." Thomson had stalked her, following her from city to city: "He left money; he knew she needed it. He came again, and again, and again, holding out all the allurements possible." The prosecution wanted the jury to believe that Josephine was the blackmailer in the relationship, but Thomson had his share of things to hold over her: "Wealth and power took advantage of her distress."[40]

But despite all of the trouble she'd endured, Josephine had preserved one quality above all others: she loved her children. "No woman," Pomeroy said, "has ever evinced greater love for her children than she." Louis McCarty was proof enough of that: "Her love for her own children was such that she adopted the child of another, and has cared for it as her own." In the end, it was Josephine's unshakable love for her children that had driven her insane. "Has she not been the victim of circumstances which many women might give way to?" Pomeroy asked. "Think of your daughters; they may come to that. Think of your sisters; they may be placed there. Think of your wives, for you know not how long you will be their protectors."[41]

Pomeroy continued at length, calling on Shakespeare and the Bible to lend weight to his arguments. As he approached the close of his remarks, Babcock leaned forward and interrupted a soulful oratory on the nature of justice to whisper in his colleague's ear. Pomeroy paused, took his bearings, and straightened up. "As it is suggested by my associates," he remarked, "how came the pistol discharged[?] Was it accidental or otherwise? No man has told you."[42] Only Thomson and Josephine had actually witnessed the crime; she had forgotten, and he didn't dare take the stand. "With his wife at home," Pomeroy said, "I don't wonder that his health would not let him come to this Court House. I wonder that God in his justice would permit such things."[43] There could be only one conclusion. "I charge him," Pomeroy proclaimed, "as the author of this woman's wrongs, and morally responsible for the murder of Hall."[44]

Josephine was sobbing in her seat; even Robert Jones and David Mitchell had been moved to tears by their colleague's words. But lunch was approaching, and though "the closest attention was paid" to Pomeroy's remarks by all in the room, some people were beginning to flag under the onslaught of rhetoric; Jacob Schuyler's eye was no doubt on the clock.[45] "Gentlemen," Pomeroy said, "this has been a long tedious case for you and for me," and perhaps, he acknowledged, "I have said more than I should." He concluded:

> Gentlemen, I leave this case with you. I leave Mrs. McCarty with you. I leave the children with you. In the name of justice save this little girl's mother. I leave the boy with you and charge you as you love your homes and families and your daughters, I ask that you see that injustice is not done to this woman. I know that justice will govern you, I know that you will act justly; I ask you to render such a verdict that when you return to your children and homes you will not see the vision of a woman led out from her cell, haggard and tottering. I hope, on the other hand, that the spirit of Him whose attribute is mercy will govern you. Let justice have his part, but let mercy be there also.[46]

At 12:30 p.m., amid sobs and clamor, Pomeroy took his seat. Judge Doolittle called a recess, and the courtroom emptied as audience and jurors alike hurried to find lunch before the prosecution began their first closing speech.

But Daniel Magone wasted no time in breaking down the case. ("He spoke with a rapidity that defied the reporter's pencil," the *Observer* reported, by way of apology for the lack of detail in their account.) "The homicide is admitted," Magone reminded the jury; "that is, it is admitted that she did the shooting as charged in the indictment." The defense had argued that she should be excused because Thomson had driven her to murder, but Magone found their evidence of Thomson's wrong-doing unconvincing. Take, for instance, "her intimacy with Thomson at Syracuse," which the defense called seduction. "Who ever heard of such an act being called a seduction?" Magone demanded.[47] Josephine knew what she was doing that night, and she knew what she was doing on the morning of January 17.

Magone brought the jury back to Josephine's testimony about the morning of the crime. She'd described leaning down to listen to Thomson, turning her face and body away from him so she could hear better. "Does this seem probable," Magone asked, "that the woman whose hearing was so acute that she formerly heard through stone walls, in St. Louis, would have to put her ear to Thomson's mouth to hear his remarks?" "That was not the cause of that movement," he concluded. "She turned her face to the back of the car to conceal the pistol from Thomson."[48]

"This woman," Magone went on, "is described as one of remarkable affection toward children. Does it seem probable that she who claims to have fought for her children in England, would voluntarily give up her two children to a man whom she has followed, dogged, and despised?" The case was simple, and so was the jury's duty. They had been called "to protect the interests of the community at large, and to stem the tide of blood which is flowing in this land," and in that duty there could be no room for sympathy. They were not to worry about Josephine's children—in fact, "it would be better if they were laid in their graves than be subjected to such influences."[49]

David Mitchell was the last person to speak in defense of Josephine McCarty, and he took full advantage of the opportunity. He began his speech at 3 p.m. on May 16, but it would take six full hours, stretched across two days, for him to say his piece.

First, Mitchell urged the jury not to let the prosecution's attempts to paint Josephine as a woman of low morals influence their verdict. "If this woman had been an inmate of a house of prostitution," he reminded them, "you should examine her rights. It makes no difference if she was a fallen woman." In fact, they might owe more to a "fallen woman" than to one who enjoyed the protections of society. "You know, gentlemen, as well as I," Mitchell said, "that when a woman falls she never gets on her feet again to go about. A man may sin, but can go about in society afterwards as he will, especially if he has as much money as this man Thomson. A poor woman who falls is not received into society again."[50]

But Josephine had not always been "fallen." "I doubt," Mitchell stated boldly, "if this county ever raised a purer, more beautiful woman than this same Josephine Fagan."[51] In fact, "she was so pure and beautiful that such bad men, adulterers as Thomson, went on her track." There was "no proof," Mitchell claimed, "that this woman was bad up to the time Thomson became acquainted with her, and by means of wine and promises lodged with her in the Globe Hotel in Syracuse."[52]

But Tom wasn't the first man to shake Josephine's innocence. "Tell me," Mitchell demanded, "if the treatment she received in Europe would not give her a terrible shock." Robert had terrorized her, and maybe hit her, but worst of all, he'd taken her children away. "A woman will love something," Mitchell reminded the jury. "If she has no child, she will love a dog."[53] When Thomson came calling with promises of friendship and support, how could Josephine do anything but love him? "Her mind was unhinged," Mitchell insisted, "when she lost her children in Europe. She has been a wanderer since and the victim of unprincipled men."[54]

In light of that, he demanded, "Will you punish her?"[55] No one had proven, he insisted, that Josephine consciously fired the shot that killed Henry Hall. "The shot was fired unconsciously," he told the jury, "as Dr. Gray describes it could have occurred."[56] And so, who was really responsible for Hall's death? "I deny that it was Josephine McCarty," Mitchell concluded. "It was Milton Thomson who fired that pistol, or caused it to be fired. He is responsible for the death of poor Hall."

Mitchell's speech ended at 12:45 p.m. on May 17, after nearly six cumulative hours of desperate oratory. "It was," the *Observer* acknowledged, "a brilliant effort, and it commanded the closest attention of all."[57]

After a brief recess, Charles Sedgwick rose to give the final closing argument for the prosecution. He acknowledged the disadvantages that Josephine and her defense faced, but applauded Mitchell, Pomeroy, Babcock, and Jones for their efforts. "I never have heard more able efforts in behalf of any prisoner than has been made for this woman," he said. "Their labors are concluded by the most eloquent and powerful appeals, which have challenged the admiration of all who heard them. No one," he concluded, "can say that her legal rights have not been ably defended and protected."[58]

But the facts, as Magone had said, were so simple as to be inescapable. "On the morning of the 17th of January," Sedgwick said, "a respectable, well disposed stranger in this city, Henry H. Hall, of the city of Ogdensburg, while riding in a street car was instantly killed by a ball from a pistol in the hands of the prisoner at the bar." Given such a straightforward case of homicide, he asked, "Is it possible that this case should be passed over quickly by the people of this county?" The murder "took place in a public conveyance, in a public street, in the presence of several persons, in broad daylight, and so patent are the facts that the prisoner's counsel cannot pretend to deny them."[59]

Sedgwick took his time in working through every detail of the killing—the exact position of each participant in the streetcar; the precise phrasing of every remark recalled by the various witnesses; and above all, Josephine's own avowed memories of the event. She "says she found herself standing in the middle of the car; says that she saw the pistol unhinged on the seat near the murdered man; saw that it was hers by candy or gum on the barrel; she closed the pistol and while standing there saw the wound on Thomson's face and saw him raising his hand to his face." And "in January," he said, "she stated to [Gray] that she saw the smoke."[60] Her last-ditch attempt to take that comment back couldn't cover up the facts: Josephine remembered the murder all too well.

Josephine had known what she was doing all along, Sedgwick told the jury—from the moment she left her mother's house up to the present. Mitchell had blamed Josephine's marriage to Robert for the first major blow to her sanity, but "if this marriage was an unhappy one, has she any right to complain? It was one of her own choosing."[61] Likewise, Sedgwick dismissed the idea that losing her children had driven Josephine to insanity. "Don't tell me of a mother's love that ceases," he scoffed. "She has never inquired for them since. There is no maternal love there." And, after all, how could there be? Josephine McCarty was an abortionist; Hattie Baker's evidence made clear what everyone in Central New York knew within days of the shooting. "A woman who has led the life she has led," Sedgwick claimed, "can not have the maternal affection claimed by the counsel."[62] As for the idea that Thomson telling her to "go to hell" had snapped the final thread of Josephine's sanity, Sedgwick found the argument laughable. "In such a life as she has led, this language would not even raise a blush to her cheek. She has been accustomed to such language." No, Sedgwick said, "this is a clear case of premeditated murder."[63]

As for the claim that Josephine was insane, Sedgwick dismissed it. "This woman has not exhibited the slightest form of insanity," he said: "no matter how you look at this case." There was "no hereditary taint" to prove the presence of insanity, and though the defense had demonstrated that their client's health was failing, "a person may have nearly all bodily disease and not be insane." Since the Sickles trial in 1859, Sedgwick argued, any defense attorney could find a medical expert ready to "swear to the insanity of the accused. They may not be corrupt, but they are easily swayed." The defense, he said, had failed to prove that Josephine was insane, but "we have proved that she was a person who could commit personal violence."[64] The conclusion was clear.

And Josephine's case, he argued, was different from Sickles's case, or George Cole's, Aratus Pierce's, or even Mary Harris's. "In such cases," Sedgwick said, "juries have winked hard at acts of violence for the protection of the family altar." Sickles, Cole, and Pierce had killed to punish a case of seduction; Mary Harris had taken vengeance against her own seducer.

"But, gentlemen," Sedgwick said, "there is no seduction here or violation of the family altar."[65] Instead, this was the story Sedgwick found in the evidence:

> A prostitute, living a life of criminal indulgence with several men, and who had gone into a business incompatible with female virtue or modesty, who, failing to blackmail her victim any longer, seek him with threats of vengeance; who had become so abandoned in character, so violent that she was determined to wreak vengeance on the man who had broken off intimacy with her—that is the case of this woman.[66]

The time for chivalry had passed. "Discharge your duties as men," Sedgwick told the jury, and find Josephine McCarty guilty of murder.[67]

At 10:30 a.m., Sedgwick concluded his remarks and returned to his seat under the eyes of a crowd of eager spectators. Over the course of the past three days, as closing arguments wound down, more and more people had crowded into the audience to watch the trial of Josephine McCarty come to an end. But at 11 a.m., as Judge Doolittle stood to address the jury, "the most absolute silence prevailed."[68]

CHAPTER 13

The Representative Bad Woman

On May 18, the day Judge Charles Doolittle issued his final address to the jury, the front page of the *Utica Daily Observer* proclaimed in block capitals "THE END" of Josephine McCarty's murder trial.[1]

It was, after all, a murder trial. "The statute provides," Doolittle explained to the jury, "that the killing, 'when perpetrated with a premeditated design to effect the death of the person killed, or of *any human being*,' shall be murder in the first degree." It made no difference that, in this case, the person killed was not the person the defendant was aiming for. "The wicked and criminal intent to kill is there," Doolittle said, "and the death of a human being is effected."[2] That was all the jury needed to worry about.

And worry they should. "The government is organized," Doolittle said, and "the laws providing for the punishment of crime are made and enforced, to shield the citizens from personal violence." If a jury of twelve respectable men failed to allow the authorities to enforce the law, Doolittle argued, "a peaceable and orderly appeal to the law . . . will give way to a reign of violence." If they voted to acquit Josephine, "do you not practically say she can kill Thomson whenever she meets him with impunity[?]" Verdicts that rejected the rule of law, Doolittle warned, "are revolutionary, are calculated to destroy all the safeguards the law throws around the citizen." The jury box, he cautioned, was not a place for revolution.[3]

In case any members of the jury were harboring any uncomfortable feelings about ordering the execution of a woman, Doolittle told them, "You have nothing to do with the consequences of your verdict."[4] Murder by a woman, after all, was still murder. To drive the point home, Doolittle read directly from the laws of New York State on murder and manslaughter, laying out for the jury the three major questions they would have to consider when rendering their verdict. The first was simple: Was Henry H. Hall killed? That was easy enough: countless people had seen Hall bleeding out in the streetcar and laid out at the Butterfield Hotel. There'd been a funeral. If there was one fact that everyone involved agreed on, it was that Henry Hall was killed on the 17th of January.

The second question offered more difficulty: Did Josephine kill him? The defense had carefully generated ambiguity around this question. On the one hand, they insisted that Josephine had no memory of the event and couldn't be held responsible. But both Pomeroy and Mitchell had also accused Thomson, not Josephine, of bringing about Henry Hall's death. Still, Doolittle pointed out, on the day of the crime "the report of a revolver at the place where she stood was heard and smoke seen." Seen by Josephine, by her own admission to Dr. Gray, in spite of her claims of amnesia. Immediately afterward, Thomson was wounded and Hall was killed. Putting aside the bigger philosophical and psychiatric questions of responsibility, it seemed hard to deny that Josephine McCarty had fired the gun that killed Henry Hall. After all, Doolittle said, "there is no evidence implicating any other person in the shooting."[5]

This brought Doolittle to the final question, the most crucial question in the whole trial: Did Josephine commit the act that killed Henry H. Hall with a premeditated design to kill Milton H. Thomson? This, Doolittle said, made all the difference, for "there can be no murder without the existence of this premeditated design to kill. It is the very essence of the crime." If Josephine did, in fact, fire the gun, that would show premeditation, since "the law presumes that in such a case a man intends that which is the natural result of the act he commits."[6] What other natural result could be expected to come from firing a gun aimed at Milton Thomson's face?

Besides, Josephine had shown not just hostility but an active desire for revenge on Thomson long before she stepped on the streetcar.

Doolittle read out Josephine's threatening letter to Spriggs from the summer before the eviction, in which she dropped such incriminating sentences as "The *revenge* is worth more to me than the money" and "The next step will be forever irretrievable."[7] All of this seemed to suggest premeditation, if not explicitly of murder then of some form of permanent revenge against Milton Thomson.

Josephine, of course, had denied any suggestion of a plot to kill Thomson. But how much faith could the jury really place in her testimony? "Until within a few years," Doolittle told them, "a person on trial for crime could not be sworn in his own behalf." Josephine, Doolittle said, "is testifying in a case that involves her life, and is therefore as deeply interested in the case as she can be."[8] Given the new rules surrounding defendant testimony, Doolittle couldn't reject Josephine's evidence out of hand; it was, after all, legally admissible. But he encouraged the jury to consider the implications of Josephine's position when deciding how much weight to give to her testimony.

Coming finally to the question of insanity, Doolittle told the jury that, just as they should proceed from the assumption that Josephine was innocent until proven guilty, they should also assume that she was sane unless given sufficient evidence to believe otherwise. And what evidence was there? The hallucinations in St. Louis, the obsessive delusions about burglars, her delirium following the injury in Saratoga County—all of this, Doolittle argued, was irrelevant to the killing of Henry Hall. The question the jury needed to answer was not whether Josephine McCarty had been insane at various points in the past but whether she'd been criminally insane at the moment she pulled the trigger. Drs. Gray, Churchill, and Bissell, Doolittle said, had shown "that the accused, at the time the homicide was committed, was not disabled by any disease of the mind from knowing it was wrong to shoot a man." Doolittle knew that medical evidence could be controversial, but thought that it carried extra weight if obtained "from persons of great experience, and persons in whose correctness and sobriety of judgment just confidence can be had."[9] There could be nobody more experienced or correct than John Perdue Gray.

If the jury was satisfied with the defense's argument that Josephine was insane at the time of the shooting, Doolittle concluded, then they must render a verdict of not guilty.

If, on the other hand, you are satisfied by the evidence in this case beyond a reasonable doubt, not beyond a possibility, that Hall was killed; that he was killed by the accused; that she fired the pistol by which he was killed, with a premeditated design to kill Thomson, and that, at the time the pistol was fired, she was in such a state of mind as to know the nature and quality of the act complained of, and that it was unlawful and morally wrong, your duty is equally plain, no matter how painful it may be, to render a verdict of guilty.[10]

"But," Doolittle went on, there was a third ruling available. "If, on a careful review of the whole case, you are satisfied that the accused fired the pistol without entertaining a premeditated design to effect the death of Thomson, and was sane the time the act was committed, then it will be your duty to render a verdict of manslaughter in the third degree." "If you shall approach their final decision without passion, without prejudice, and after a patient and careful consideration of the whole case," Doolittle told the twelve men in the jury box, "your verdict shall reflect the honest and deliberate conclusions of your own judgment, your whole duty will be discharged."[11]

The judge finished, and the courtroom took a moment to breathe. The *Observer* noted that throughout Doolittle's speech, Josephine appeared "careworn and anxious," sitting beside Mitchell with her head in her hands and lifting her eyes only occasionally when she heard something particularly interesting. Beside her sat Jones, with his arms folded across his chest; Mitchell and Babcock, taking furious notes throughout; and Pomeroy, apparently transfixed by the judge's words. In the audience, the reporter noticed two women listening intently: Mrs. Conley Cooper, the friend from Saratoga County, who was "said to be an authoress of some celebrity" and spent the entire charge taking notes nearly as diligently as the defense counsel; and Mrs. Scrivens, "the tall, honest-looking and evidently kind-hearted lady" who had given the McCarty family a home in the days between their eviction and the murder.[12] She sat in the front row and did not take notes as she listened to Judge Doolittle reviewing the evidence in her friend's case.

Before the jury could retire, Mitchell, obstinate to the last, rose and entered forty-two separate propositions that he wanted the judge to incorporate into his charge. The jury must be instructed that "the will of the accused must have joined the act;" that "if there was doubt whether or not the pistol was accidentally discharged, the prisoner must have the benefit of such doubt;" that indeed "the accused was entitled to the benefit of all doubts;" that "the omission by the Prosecution to call

Thomson might be taken into consideration by the jury;" and thirty-eight other propositions.[13] Doolittle insisted that his charge already addressed most of these issues, and declined to revise his language. Mitchell objected; Sedgwick pushed back; an exception was entered and after a full hour of debate the case was left in the hands of the jury, substantially unchanged by Mitchell's final effort in his client's defense.

The jury were led out just before 5 p.m.; many audience members left, too, but others kept their seats, waiting to see how long the deliberations would last. The courthouse swarmed with murmuring spectators, all asking "that unanswerable question": What would the verdict be?[14] After an hour, Judge Doolittle announced that the court would disperse for supper and return at 7 p.m. If, in that time, the jury concluded their deliberation, they could send for the court. Samuel Cole arrived and took Josephine back to the Mohawk Street Jail for her supper.

The reporter for the *Observer* noticed Lewis Babcock, who two weeks ago had opened the case with such an "able and exhaustive argument," now sitting "with an anxious face, awaiting the result of the twelve men's deliberations, who had Mrs. McCarty's fate in their hands." The reporter approached; the two engaged in conversation. Babcock commented that "if his client was acquitted (and he confidently expected that she would be) he would take his fishing rod and tackle and start over the Deerfield hills, early Saturday morning, for an extended vacation. No man," the reporter wrote, "deserves it more than he."[15]

At 6:30 p.m., rumors began to circulate around the building that the jury had sent for members of the court; their verdict was ready. People began spilling back into the courtroom. Mitchell and Pomeroy, both out for a well-earned supper, hurried back to hear the final verdict. Shortly afterward, Doolittle reappeared at the head of the court, followed "by quite a crowd."[16] The room was nearly half-full by now. Five minutes later, Josephine walked into the room along with Babcock. As they took their seats, the courtroom was nearly full.

At 7:10, the jury filed in. "The prisoner," seated with her counsel, "scanned the faces of the jurors with the deepest anxiety depicted on her countenance," no doubt trying to discern her fate from their expressions. Next to her, Mitchell sat with his face in his hands, then put it down on the table.

The clerk called the roll. "Gentlemen of the Jury," he asked, "have you agreed upon your verdict? Who shall say for you?"

James Spencer, the young law student from Camden, answered: "We have."

"How say you, gentlemen? Do you find the prisoner at the bar guilty of the murder and felony whereof she stands indicted, or not guilty?"

Spencer took a breath, looked at Josephine, and addressed the court. "We find the prisoner of the bar—NOT GUILTY."

A "perfect storm of applause" interrupted the clerk's attempts to confirm the verdict, and for a few seconds pandemonium reigned in the courtroom. Josephine burst into tears. "The officers of the Court," the *Observer* reported, "labored to preserve order."

"Jurors," the clerk managed above the hubbub, "harken to your verdict as the Court hath reported it. You say you find the prisoner at the bar, "Not Guilty," and so say you all?"

The jurors replied, "We do."[17]

Court adjourned. Mrs. McCarty, temporarily swarmed with friends and counselors, was arrested again in the courtroom on an indictment for assault against Thomson, but it barely seemed to matter. Babcock, Mitchell, and Pomeroy paid her $2,000 bail, Judge Doolittle signed the paperwork, and Josephine headed back to the jail where her children were waiting, accompanied by three loud cheers from the crowds surrounding the courthouse. As she departed, Judge Doolittle "remarked to her that in his opinion she was smarter than any of her counsel. Mrs. McCarty smiled, bowed, and responded good naturedly."[18]

The chaos continued well into the night, as the people of Utica cheered for the verdict and for "the counsel who had defended the prisoner so ably." A rumor started running around town that the jury hadn't even used the full hour and forty minutes that they'd been out. They'd taken a silent vote upon entering the jury room, and after some discussion of the evidence opened the ballots to discover that every man had voted to acquit. They remained the rest of the time, according to one juror, because "they hesitated about returning to the courtroom too soon."[19] The *Observer* reported,

> Thus closes one of the most remarkable criminal trials ever recorded in this country. Its conclusion is a great relief to the accused, the Court and its officers, county officials generally, the able counsel for the People and the prisoner, the jurors, reporters for the press and the public generally. Probably none will regret that it is over except the little news boys.
>
> Mrs. McCarty announces her intention of going to live on the Augusta farm. Counselor Babcock and Justice Sherman are going to the woods fishing. Counselors Mitchell and Sedgwick have

gone to Auburn to attend to the Fralick, Bennet and Briggs Syracuse arson case, where they will be arrayed against one another. The ways of the law are peculiar.[20]

Within days of the McCarty verdict in May 1872, the 95th New York State Legislature passed a new abortion statute. Under the old 1869 law, abortion at any stage of pregnancy was punishable as second-degree manslaughter and carried a maximum sentence of seven years in state prison if either mother or child died. The same law also punished patients who got abortions and the pharmacists who advertised and sold them abortifacients with misdemeanor charges good for no more than a year in a county jail. It was under this law that Josephine McCarty narrowly avoided being charged in 1871 after the death of Maggie Campbell.

Under the 1872 law, practicing abortion in New York State became more dangerous than ever. The new statute made abortion at any stage of pregnancy a felony crime of its own, punishable by four to twenty years in the state penitentiary for doctors and patients alike. Milder punishments were still available for druggists and advertisers, but they too could go to state prison for between one and three years if convicted. It was the strictest abortion law in state history, and it would remain on the books essentially unchanged until the 1960s.

For Jacob Rosenzweig, the Jewish abortionist arrested in New York just weeks before the Campbell inquest, the 1872 law was a piece of ironic good luck. While Josephine stood trial for the murder of Henry Hall, Rosenzweig was still awaiting trial in New York City. In February 1873, a rumor circulated in the press that a grand jury had reindicted Rosenzweig on charges of first-degree murder, but by March newspapers reported that the new charge had been abandoned.[21] The notorious abortionist now lingered in a legal limbo: he had already been tried once under the 1869 law, and the new law had passed well after his original crime. "There are good many [sic] people," the Indianapolis Sentinel reported, who sincerely believe that the Legislature has bungled the matter and that Rosenzweig can never be legally tried."[22] Meanwhile, the Paterson Daily Press remarked, "Rosenzweig is growing fat" in the Tombs.[23] In November 1873, with no law to hold him, Jacob Rosenzweig was finally released from prison.[24]

In early 1873, as lawyers argued over what to do with Rosenzweig, a young man named Anthony Comstock traveled from New York City to Washington, DC, on a mission to establish a new federal law outlawing the vast and thorny category of "vice."[25] Comstock, raised in a strict Congregationalist community in New Canaan, Connecticut, was primarily concerned with "obscenity"—pornography, vulgar books, and contraceptive devices. For years, he'd been visiting New York bookstores, buying books he considered obscene, and then showing the books to police and convincing them to arrest the offending booksellers. This routine was effective on a small scale, but it was clear to Comstock that he was, at best, chipping away grain by grain at the vast edifice of American obscenity.

Abortion was on Comstock's radar, too, but not for the same reasons as earlier reformers. The historian Clifford Browder argues that Comstock, whose mother had died when Comstock himself was only ten after having given birth to ten children, opposed abortionists "not so much out of a concern to preserve the life of the fetus, or to protect the life and health of the mother, nor even because (as he stoutly maintained) they abetted lewdness by striving to conceal its results, but because their ads were inherently indecent."[26] To Comstock, abortion advertisements were no different, morally, from pornography, and the key to restricting both was stiffer mail laws. In February of 1873, Comstock spent weeks lobbying members of the national legislature in support of a bill to impose harsh restrictions on the postal service to prevent the transmission of obscene material by mail.

On March 3, 1873, the "Comstock Act" was signed into law. Under the new bill, it was a federal misdemeanor to sell or advertise any obscene materials by mail, and that category included medicines and devices for contraception and abortion. Never one to sit back and let the law work passively for him, Comstock set out to personally ensure that his new law was enforced. In April 1873, while Jacob Rosenzweig fattened in the Tombs, Comstock served as the principal witness in a sweep on abortionists in New York City and Albany that resulted in seventeen arrests.[27] By June, he had lobbied successfully in the New York legislature for the passage of a bill that made the sale, advertisement, or possession of any obscene matter punishable by a fine of up to $5,000 and three months to two years of hard labor. By the summer of 1873, not only could abortionists be legally tried for murder but merely owning the necessary tools or substances to produce an abortion could land a doctor in legal trouble. Finally, in 1875, a new law making the dying declarations of female patients legally admissible in court gave prosecutors the ultimate evidential edge in abortion trials.[28]

The age of the abortionists was at an end—at least, in theory. In reality, abortionists continued to practice in New York with a high degree of impunity. The late 1870s and 1880s ushered in what the historian Leslie J. Reagan has called the era of "continuity" in abortion history. Despite the passage of strict anti-abortion statutes in virtually every state by the end of the 1880s, physicians continued to give abortions, and women continued to need them.[29] Although the law now theoretically had the power to charge any doctor performing abortions with murder, abortion trials remained rare—the exception, not the rule—well into the twentieth century. Of the ninety-seven people Comstock arrested between 1872 and 1880 for advertising abortifacients or contraceptives, most returned to practice after they were released.[30] "By the end of the nineteenth century," writes the historian Rickie Solinger, "abortion rates may have been even higher than before the Comstock Law."[31]

On January 28, 1878, Anthony Comstock knocked on the door of Ann Lohman, alias Madame Restell, in lower Manhattan.[32] Following the passage of the 1872 and 1873 state laws on abortion and obscenity, Restell had continued to advertise her services, modifying the language of the ads to remove any specific references to abortion. For her, out of all the nation's abortionists, there was no need to spell it out: her name had been synonymous with the practice for decades. Between Restell's ads and her longstanding notoriety, Comstock had no trouble finding her office.

He was disguised as a client, asking on behalf of a girlfriend for medicine capable of producing abortion. Restell gave him what he needed. On February 7, he called again, this time asking for contraceptives. Again, Madame Restell provided the goods. Finally, on February 11, Comstock appeared at her door a third time, accompanied this time by four policemen and two reporters. He introduced himself to Madame Restell, and had her arrested on the spot. Visibly shaken but determined to maintain her composure, the "Wickedest Woman in New York" insisted on taking her own carriage to the police court and on having a lunch of oysters before she left.[33]

No one wanted to pay her bail. To do so now, with the law so rigidly set against everything she stood for, would be professional suicide. On March 29, Madame Restell was called before the court for arraignment; her trial would begin the following morning. April 1 would be the culmination not only of Comstock's one-man war on obscenity but of decades of lobbying by physicians and moral reformers: after years of evading the law, the nation's most famous abortionist was finally going to stand trial.

That evening, Madame Restell, who had finally found bondsmen willing to pay her bail, went home to her mansion. It was a lonely house; her husband had died the year before. Her daughter Caroline, spending the night with her mother before the commencement of her historic trial, recalled that she went to bed nervous.

On the morning of April 1, 1878, Madame Restell was found dead in her bathtub.[34] She had slit her own throat. When the news was announced in court later that day, most people, including Comstock—who was there, of course, waiting to observe the results of his diligent work—thought it was an April Fool's joke.[35] Later, when the death had been confirmed and the trial dissolved, Comstock noted the occurrence with a single line in his diary: "A bloody ending to a bloody life."[36]

What became of Josephine McCarty after her trial? While Anthony Comstock crusaded against obscenity and Madame Restell approached the bitter end of her career and life, Josephine didn't return to her Albany abortion practice. In late May, the *Albany Evening Journal* reported that Josephine had declined a number of "urgent" lecture requests in favor of seeking peace and quiet on her mother's farm.[37] But by July 12, she was back in Albany, where she applied to the county's Superintendent of the Poor for child support.[38] The superintendent denied her request, but told her that she could sue Milton Thomson for child support. Josephine took his advice, but the case never reached a settlement.

Just a few days later, the *Schenectady Evening Star* reported that "a stout built woman named Mrs. McCarty, living on Arch street, yesterday, in consequence of domestic troubles, ran and jumped out of the window."[39] Because the window was on the first story, the paper assured readers, "she was not much hurt and only made a ludicrous exhibition of herself." The *Star* didn't specify the nature of the "domestic troubles" that sent Josephine jumping out the window, but given the timing, it's not hard to imagine that the dispute had something to do with the Thomsons. On the same page, the *Star* announced that "Mrs. Dr. Burleigh, alias McCarty, alias Seymour, will Friday next commence the publication, at Albany, of 'Woman's Truth Teller,' a weekly journal in the interest of women."[40]

The first and only issue of *The Woman's Truth Teller* was published on July 19, 1872, for ten cents a copy. On the third page, Josephine described the paper as "a semi-monthly paper,

> devoted to the interests of all women; women in gilded boudoirs—women at sewing machines—women behind counters—women over cook stoves—betrayed women, commonly called harlots, to whom society permits no home and no vocation—women who follow highest art, painters, sculptors, musicians, and authors—shall each and all be fairly represented.[41]

If one looked closely at the paper's columns, however, it became clear that the paper was published in the interest of just one woman: Josephine herself. The *Truth Teller* had a little of everything: poetry, short stories, and editorials on the recent McCarty trial. There were news bulletins on other high-profile trials, and brief snippets of gossip: "It is current in fast circles that the 'brilliant editor' of the Albany *Argus*, who prides himself on his Harry-the-Eighth proportions, is solicitous of the honor of hob-nobbing with Milton Thomson."[42] There was a section on page 5 labeled "Thomsonania," which consisted entirely of jokes at Milton Thomson's expense: "A GENTLEMAN riding in a Genesee Street car was accosted jocosely by Milton Thomson with—'You are not afraid of being shot in the street car?' reply: 'Oh no, not if I keep at a distance from you.'" And on the last page were ads for S. Sweet, Real Estate and General Broker; Gardner Scrivens, Family Grocer; and R.O. Jones and Lewis Babcock, Attorneys at Law.

Most of the *Truth Teller*'s content reads as an attempt to tie up loose ends from the trial and get in one last word. In one column, for instance, Josephine excoriated one of the prosecution's witnesses, saying, "Probably there was not a person in the Court Room, unless it might have been the prosecuting Judge, who believed a word of his testimony." Elsewhere, she praised the jury who had acquitted her, writing that they "struck a heavier blow to rich men's monopoly of hunting down women and immolating helpless childhood than all the pulpits in christendom. Let every woman in every land hold warm in her prayers the name of these twelve men."[43]

But on the fourth page was an article, signed by Josephine McCarty, Editor and Proprietor, which summed up the mission of the *Truth Teller*. "Today we launch upon the tide of events," it began, "a newspaper devoted to the interests of woman." Josephine went on: "The women of

Oneida county have laid upon us a debt of obligation which we can only repay by life-long service." It was the local women, after all, who had cared for Josephine's children, including her sick son Louis, throughout her months of imprisonment. "During the past five months," Josephine wrote, "the women of Oneida county have fed and clothed a rich, bad man's children."[44]

A bad man's—and a bad woman's. "We are proud that we are a woman," Josephine wrote. "We have been called a 'bad woman,' we accept the issue, and henceforth take rank among those women who, honorable themselves, have trusted in men's honor and proven it full of black lies, perjuries and cruelties." She had made mistakes, she acknowledged—what woman hadn't? "We hope," she wrote, "that we are the representative 'bad woman'; that we are the wickedest woman in this great Empire State, but we have a very weak belief in the badness of women."[45] Bad or not, Josephine had done what she could to save her children, which was more than Thomson had ever done.

"Many women have asked us," Josephine wrote at the end of the article, "was there no legal redress for your wrongs?" She continued,

> We propose now to answer with facts. We have no faith in law as administered by libertines and perjurers. We do not know of an instance where a woman received justice through the law from a rich man. But if the further sacrifice of ourself shall awaken women and men to the great fact that one-half the human race may trample unchecked upon the most sacred nature of the other half, we shall be content. Through all the future we labor for women, not for ourself. This paper is established to that end.[46]

On the last page of the *Woman's Truth Teller*, Josephine printed a long advertisement, addressed "TO LADIES," for the obstetrical services of Mrs. Burleigh, M.D.: "Female Diseases a Specialty."

Josephine advertised the *Truth Teller* for ten cents a copy, or two dollars for an annual subscription. It's unlikely she got many $2 subscriptions; the July issue was the only one ever published. By August, she was embroiled once again in legal struggles with Tom. The court refused to accept proof of her divorce from Robert in the child support case, and evidently she never received any more money from Tom.[47] In October, Josephine visited a Shaker settlement in Watervliet, just north of Albany. After spending an evening with them under an assumed name and a claim of being a reformer, she asked the Shakers to care for Juddie and Josie, her youngest children. The Shakers agreed, but soon after

Josephine left, they learned her true identity from the children's "prattle" and demanded that she return and reclaim them.[48]

On January 11, 1873, the *Trenton State Gazette* reported that Josephine had moved to Bayonne, New Jersey.[49] After that, Josephine McCarty, Emma Burleigh, and Virginia Seymour all but vanish completely from the historical record. The 1885 New Jersey State Census found her in Shrewsbury Township in Monmouth County, living in a boarding house.[50] Ten years later, Josephine McCarty was boarding in the home of William Walker in Bayonne.[51]

In December of 1898, just a year before the turn of the twentieth century, Josephine McCarty died in Neptune Township, New Jersey. The one member of Josephine's family who remained nearby was her youngest son, the older of her two children with Milton Thomson. Ernest J. Seymour is buried alongside his mother in Neptune Township's Mount Prospect Cemetery.

When I visited Mount Prospect Cemetery in 2017, I found that the graveyard, like much of the greater New York City area, had not yet recovered from the damage wreaked by Hurricane Sandy in 2012. Gravestones were thrown askew, sunken sideways in loamy soil, eroded by both the catastrophic blasts of the hurricane and by more than a century of erosion. Many of the graves dated back to the 1800s or early 1900s, but one corner of the cemetery was full of freshly dug graves marked only with metal placards and temporary paper labels, each sponsored by a local Muslim burial society. Walking between the displaced rows of headstones, my wife and I didn't encounter any visitors tending to the graves—only a large black-and-white cat who rushed across the path in front of us and vanished into the overgrown woods encroaching on the cemetery's border.

We followed the cat to Virginia S. Seymour's gravestone. When I found it under a leaning evergreen, the marker had been half-swallowed by the earth, so that I had to scrape tufts of grass and dirt away from the "V." The stone was unremarkable: a flat rectangle of granite, with the wrong birthdate and the wrong name, inscribed with a middle initial she never used in life. It seems fitting, in a way, that the stone under which Josephine McCarty rests for eternity is itself a fabrication, a lie without a readily apparent motive. In death, she keeps her secrets.

Epilogue

Milton Thomson never fully recovered from the wound he received on the Genesee streetcar on January 17, 1872. But despite the dismal predictions of his doctors, he survived for over twenty years after the incident, dying suddenly on the morning of March 6, 1893. His obituary in the *Utica Daily Press* made no mention of Josephine or of how he became an invalid. "He never complained," the obituary read, "but bore his illness with the greatest of patience and fortitude . . . He was a man of great energy and determination, and generally succeeded in whatever he undertook."[1]

After his celebratory fishing trip, Lewis Babcock returned to practice in Utica, entering an advertisement in the sole issue of the *Woman's Truth Teller*.[2] Whatever blush of celebrity might have buoyed his career after the McCarty victory didn't last long. On April 21, 1883, Lewis H. Babcock was admitted to the Oneida County Poorhouse.[3] His admission record noted that he had already served two terms in the Albany Penitentiary for vagrancy and drunkenness. Now, the form stated, he was "Homeless & Intemperate." Under the line asking what kind of labor the patient was "able to pursue, and to what extent," someone wrote "first class Lawyer when Sober." Babcock passed away on March 1, 1905, at the age of sixty-seven.[4]

In May 1874, Judge Charles Doolittle boarded the steamer *Abyssinia*, bound for Europe to seek a better climate for his failing health. On the 21st of the month, the judge was lost overboard.[5] One of the two witnesses to Doolittle's last will and testament was none other than John Perdue Gray, who after his testimony in the McCarty trial went on to act as a key witness in the trial of Charles Guiteau in 1882 for the shooting of President James A. Garfield.[6] Guiteau, a disgruntled office-seeker, advanced a defense of insanity, but Gray stayed true to his principles, testifying that no insanity could exist without organic disease, and he could find no evidence of such disorder in the accused. Guiteau was convicted and hanged on the 30th of June, 1882. An autopsy after the execution revealed that Guiteau's brain did in fact exhibit certain abnormalities consistent with neurosyphilis. But Gray was in no position to wring his hands over the challenge to his diagnosis. Upon his return to Utica, Gray was shot in the face by a man named Henry Remshaw, a bath attendant apparently upset with the result of the Guiteau case. John Gray seems to have enjoyed some of the same good luck that had graced Milton Thomson, because the bullet passed under his left eye and out his right cheek without killing him. Still, like Tom, he never recovered from the injury. John P. Gray passed away in 1886 at the age of 61 as a result of the gunshot wound.[7]

On February 27, 1872, Emily Elvira Storer, Horatio Storer's second wife, died after years of mental and physical illness.[8] It was Horatio's forty-second birthday. After Emily's death, he became ill himself, contracting a painful bacterial blood infection in the first few days of the McCarty trial. On May 7, he was forced to miss the meeting of the Gynaecological Society of Boston, of which he was the secretary.[9] He resigned that spring, marking his effective retirement from medicine.

In October of 1872, Horatio and his family, including a new wife, sailed to Europe, where he spent the following five years bouncing between France, Germany, and southern Italy as he recovered his health.[10] Upon his return to New England in 1877, he settled in Newport, Rhode Island, turning his attention away from medical practice to medical numismatics; in his later years, the "father of gynecology" became an expert on collecting medical medals and commemorative coins.

But he had not fully given up the abortion cause: On August 12, 1897, the year before Josephine's death, Horatio addressed the Rhode Island Medico-Legal Society on the topic of "Criminal Abortion: Its Prevalence, Its Prevention, and Its Relation to the Medical Examiner."[11] After giving a brief history of the movement against abortion that devoted considerable time to his and his father's own contributions to the cause, Horatio bemoaned what historians like Leslie Reagan have demonstrated about the AMA's vigorous anti-abortion efforts in the mid-1800s: they didn't really work. Abortion was still a common practice, despite state laws that formally out-lawed it; convictions were all but impossible to obtain. Despite these frustrations, Horatio believed that the solutions remained the same: doctors should work together with "friendly lawyers" to overhaul the existing statutes and pass better ones. Above all, he insisted, doctors must educate the public about the physical risks and moral wrongs of abortion. "If the belief of [judges and juries], who are but repre-sentatives of the true character of the crime, rests upon popular igno-rance of the true character of the crime," Horatio told his audience, "and if prevention of abortion is better than attempts at conviction of foetal murder after it has been committed, and if it can be pre-vented only through awakening women's consciences, arousing her maternal instinct, and exciting her fear of physical peril to herself, then your course is clear."[12]

But the course was not so clear, or maybe Horatio overestimated other doctors' agreement with his views. Doctors continued to per-form abortions regularly through the end of the nineteenth century and into the twentieth. Only in the 1930s, as medical practice began to move increasingly out of private offices and into public spaces like clinics and hospitals, did the practice begin to come under meaningful public scrutiny, and it wasn't until the post-WWII period that serious legal crackdowns began.[13] In the end, Horatio Storer's work did more to develop a way of thinking about abortion by marrying medicine and morality than it did to curtail the actual practice of abortion. When he died on September 18, 1922, Storer's greatest claim to fame was that he was Harvard University's oldest living graduate.[14]

In the late 1870s, Louis Napoleon Seymour and his brother Ernest moved to Philadelphia. In 1880, seventeen-year-old Juddie was work-ing as a store clerk and living in a boarding house on Green Street, while Louis, twenty-one, lived on 11th Street and worked as a dentist.[15] In 1884, Louis graduated from the Philadelphia Dental College, and in 1886 he married Minnehaha Ferris.[16] On April 23, 1888, Minnie Seymour gave birth to a daughter—Josephine's first grandchild. They named her Marion Josephine.

Minnehaha died one year after her daughter's birth. Louis, a wid-ower at 30, stayed in the country long enough to graduate as part of the University of Michigan School of Dentistry's Class of 1893.[17] Two years later, he departed to begin his dentistry practice in England, where he remained until the outbreak of war in 1914. Louis spent World War I in British East Africa, then moved north from Nairobi to Cairo, where he spent the remainder of his career.[18]

While his half-brother was busy pulling teeth and filling cavities in Egypt, Juddie settled down in New Jersey. He and his wife Emma were married in 1887 and had five children over the following eighteen years: Bruce, Cleo, Milton, Norma, and Virginia.[19] Juddie passed away in 1925 and was buried, alongside his wife and his mother, in Mount Prospect Cemetery in Neptune Township, New Jersey.

Josephine Cleopatra, the youngest of Josephine's children, grew up and went west—to Wisconsin, where, in 1897, she married an Irishman named Dillon Heath in an Episcopal ceremony.[20] On the marriage certificate, Josie listed her father's name as Robert Seymour and her mother's as Josephine Ingram—possibly another pseudonym that Josephine took on after her trial. Josie and Dillon had one child, a boy named Phillip born in 1899. But the 1905 Wisconsin state census recorded four people in their household: Dillon, Josie, Phillip, and his seventeen-year old cousin, Marion Josephine—Louis's daughter.

As a young woman, Marion J. Seymour followed in her father's footsteps. In 1907, she left Wisconsin and traveled first to Switzerland, then to Germany, and from there to Austria, where, in 1914, she was forced to apply for an emergency passport to get out of the country following the assassination of Archduke Franz Ferdinand.[21] But unlike Louis, she settled down eventually: on February 17, 1921, Marion married Phillip Heath, her first cousin, eleven years her junior.[22] They hyphenated their surname; in middle age, she became Marion Josephine Seymour-Heath. She passed away in 1974 in Los Angeles, California.

As for Josephine's oldest children—Eugene, Ella, and Terrence—they're harder to find. The biggest clue pointing in their direction is a series of notices posted in Albany newspapers in 1870 following the death of Robert McCarty, summoning his living children to appear before his lawyers in New York to attend the probate of his last will and testament.[23] According to the *Argus*, Ella McCarty was living in Brooklyn in 1870, and Eugene was living in San Francisco. The notice makes no mention of Terrence. Robert named three children in his will: Eugene, Ella, and "Robert." Either Robert renamed Terrence after taking him from Josephine—he was, after all, named after *her* father—or Terrence passed away and Robert had another child with his mistress, Kate Susannah Cooper, to whom he left the fourth share of his estate and profits from his steam gun. Either way, the historical record shows no trace of a Terrence McCarty after 1850.

Maggie Campbell is buried in an unmarked grave in Section 98 of the Albany Rural Cemetery. The cemetery, renowned as one of the country's first and most beautiful rural cemeteries, advertises "dignity for all" on its website.[24] But Section 98, a tiny triangle of earth in the heart of the cemetery just past the intersection of Josephine Avenue and North Ridge Road, is not a particularly dignified resting place. Most of the graves are unmarked; the lot's few headstones are mainly shattered, sunken into the earth, or swallowed by weeds. When I visited Section 98 in the summer of 2016, I had to count off paces through the uncut grass to approximate the spot where Maggie's body, laid out in 1871 for public scrutiny in an inquest that led nowhere, was eventually laid to rest. It's an unremarkable patch of grass, scattered with pink clover and buttercups. But it's quiet. Far from the road, a few long paces from the shade of a white ash tree, all that touches her grave is wind, and sun, and silence.

NOTES

Preface

1. When I emailed the Oneida County clerk to locate the original trial records, I was told that they were destroyed by weather in the 1990s. The records of Josephine's trial were housed in an off-site facility; vandals broke the windows, and rain, wind, and snow drifted in, wiping out the original record of the trial of Josephine McCarty along with many, many other precious sources. The *Utica Daily Observer*, scanned and uploaded to fultonhistory.com by Thomas M. Tryniski, remains the best source available on the trial.

1. Mother and Daughter

1. "Woman's Revenge," *New York Herald*, January 19, 1872.

2. "Woman's Revenge."

3. The land the Fagans settled on, just north of the village of Oriskany Falls, was part of a 60,000-acre tract that the surveyor Peter Smith "leased" in 1794 from the Oneida Nation. The lease was a convenient legal fiction: under the 1790 Trade and Intercourse Act, no individual could purchase land from Indigenous nations without federal involvement. But Peter Smith, undeterred, insisted that he had signed a lease for the land for 999 years and began subletting parcels to white settlers. It might be illegal to *purchase* land from the Oneida without their agreement, but the law said nothing about leasing. In his *Annals and Recollections of Oneida County*, Pomroy Jones reports that the Oneida Nation was "opposed to the leasing to Mr. Smith, and at one time they proceeded so far as to drive the surveyor off from the tract." Pomroy Jones, *Annals and Recollections of Oneida County* (Rome, NY, 1851), 85–86; Oneida Indian Nation, "Historical Timeline of the Oneida Indian Nation," Oneida Indian Nation website, accessed April 21, 2021, https://www.oneidaindiannation.com/wp-content/uploads/2019/03/Historical-Timeline-2019.pdf.

4. "The Great Trial," *Utica Daily Observer*, May 7, 1872.

5. Jones, *Annals*, 99.

6. Rickie Solinger, *Pregnancy and Power: A History of Reproductive Politics in the United States* (New York University Press, 2019), 63; Janet Farrell Brodie, *Contraception and Abortion in Nineteenth-Century America* (Ithaca, NY: Cornell University Press, 1994), 2.

7. Susan E. Klepp, *Revolutionary Conceptions: Women, Fertility, and Family Limitation in America, 1760–1820* (University of North Carolina Press, 2009), 4.

8. Klepp, *Revolutionary Conceptions*, 70.

9. John Riddle, *Eve's Herbs: A History of Contraception and Abortion in the West* (Harvard University Press, 1997).

10. Klepp, *Revolutionary Conceptions*, 58; 57.

11. Klepp, *Revolutionary Conceptions*, 66; 126–27.

12. Klepp, *Revolutionary Conceptions*, 6; 110.

13. Historian Linda Kerber calls this new idealized role, in which it was the quality and not the quantity of a woman's children that mattered, "republican motherhood." Linda Kerber, "The Republican Mother: Women and the Enlightenment—An American Perspective," *American Quarterly* 28 no. 2 (1976): 187–205; Klepp, *Revolutionary Conceptions*, 127.

14. Judith Walzer Leavitt, "Under the Shadow of Maternity: American Women's Responses to Death and Debility Fears in Nineteenth-Century Childbirth," *Feminist Studies* 12 (1986): 129–54.

15. *Chambers Dictionary of Etymology* (1988), s.v. "abortion."

16. Lindsay Tigar, "Baby Size by Week According to Millennials, Not Fruit," *Parents*.com, updated November 8, 2022, https://www.parents.com/pregnancy/week-by-week/baby-size-by-week-not-fruit/.

17. For a historian's personal discussion of this phenomenon, see Catherine J. Denial, "How I Met My Mother: The Story of an Unexpected Pregnancy," *Nursing Clio*, June 5, 2019, https://nursingclio.org/2019/06/05/how-i-met-my-mother-the-story-of-an-unexpected-pregnancy/.

18. Klepp, *Revolutionary Conceptions*, 182.

19. Klepp, *Revolutionary Conceptions*, 186; 184.

20. "CDC Abortion Surveillance System FAQs," Centers for Disease Control and Prevention website, 2019, https://www.cdc.gov/reproductivehealth/data_stats/abortion.htm.

21. James C. Mohr, *Abortion in America: The Origins and Evolution of National Policy* (Oxford University Press, 1978), 3.

22. Mohr, *Abortion in America*, 3.

23. These sections of the 1829 Revised Statutes were not the first anti-abortion laws in US history—that distinction belongs to an 1821 Connecticut bill that made it a crime to administer poison to a woman "quick with child," either for the purpose of murdering that woman or to produce a miscarriage. Technically, this was the first US abortion law, but James Mohr points out that the purpose of the law had far more to do with poison than with abortion: "Section 14 [of the crime bill] did not proscribe abortion per se; it declared illegal one particular method of attempting to induce abortion because that method was considered prohibitively unsafe owing to the threat of death by poisoning."

24. Mohr, *Abortion in America*, 18.

25. Solinger, *Pregnancy and Power*, 61.

26. Christine Stansell, *City of Women: Sex and Class in New York, 1789–1860* (Urbana: University of Illinois Press, 1986); Patricia Cline Cohen, *The Murder of Helen Jewett: The Life and Death of a Prostitute in Nineteenth-Century New York* (Alfred A. Knopf, 1998).

27. Mary Kelley, *Learning to Stand and Speak: Women, Education, and Public Life in America's Republic* (Omohundro Institute and University of North Carolina Press, 2008), 5; 10; 82.

28. Kelley, *Learning to Stand*, 81.

29. John Robert Greene, *Generations of Excellence: An Illustrated History of Cazenovia Seminary and Cazenovia College, 1824 to the Present* (Syracuse Litho, 2007), 36.

30. Kelley, *Learning to Stand*, 32; 67.

31. *Catalogue and Circular of Oneida Conference Seminary, Cazenovia, N.Y.* (R.L. Myrick, 1842), 19.

32. "The Great Trial," *Utica Daily Observer*, May 4, 1872, 2.

33. "The Great Trial," May 4. Josephine refers to her employer only as "Judge Barnes," but Port Tobacco was a small town, and Richard Barnes seems the most likely candidate for that title. Barnes and his wife were known for taking in orphans in addition to their three biological children, and census records from 1850 show a teacher, John R. J. Reeves, living with the family, indicating that they were in the practice of employing a live-in teacher.

34. Kelley, *Learning to Stand*, 34.

35. Emma Willard, *An Address to the Public: Particularly to the Members of the Legislature of New York, Proposing a Plan for Improving Female Education* (J. W. Copeland, 1819), 20.

2. A Cigar Girl and a Wicked Woman

1. *Proceedings of the Board of Aldermen of the City of New York* 82 (1861): 455.

2. The only period in New York City's two-hundred-plus-year history that saw more rapid population growth was 1771 to 1790, when the city's population grew by 126%.

3. Janet Farrell Brodie, *Abortion and Contraception in Nineteenth-Century America* (Cornell University Press, 1994), 204–241.

4. Amy Gilman Srebnick, *The Mysterious Death of Mary Rogers: Sex and Culture in Nineteenth-Century New York* (Oxford University Press, 1995), 38–43.

5. Srebnick *Mysterious Death*, 60.

6. The Elysian Fields, four years later, would become the site of the first organized baseball game in US history.

7. Srebnick, *Mysterious Death*, 18.

8. Srebnick, *Mysterious Death*, 29.

9. Srebnick, *Mysterious Death*, 29.

10. Clifford Browder, *The Wickedest Woman in New York: Madame Restell, The Abortionist* (Archon Books, 1988), 32.

11. Browder, *Wickedest Woman*, 42.

12. Srebnick, *Mysterious Death*, 11.

13. Browder, *Wickedest Woman*, 57.

14. Browder, *Wickedest Woman*, 66; "The Female Abortionist," *National Police Gazette*, March 13, 1847, 209.

15. *Laws of the State of New York*, United States: State of New York., 1845, 285–86.

16. In 1846, the legislature amended the first section of the act to specify that abortion after quickening was only manslaughter if either the mother or the child died. John Canfield Spencer, John Duer, Benjamin Franklin Butler,

Statutes at Large of the State of New York: Comprising the Revised Statutes, as They Existed on the 1st Day of January, 1867, and All the General Public Statutes Then in Force, with References to Judicial Decisions, and the Material Notes of the Revisers in Their Report to the Legislature. Weed, Parsons, 1869, 146.

17. "The Great Trial," *Utica Daily Observer*, May 4, 1872.

18. Browder, *Wickedest Woman*, 76; 91.

19. "The Great Trial," May 4.

20. Owen Whooley, *Knowledge in the Time of Cholera: The Struggle Over American Medicine in the Nineteenth Century* (University of Chicago Press, 2013), 74.

21. "The Great Trial," May 4.

22. "The Great Trial," *Utica Daily Observer*, May 4 and 6, 1872.

23. "The Great Trial," May 6.

24. Tony Bennett, "The Exhibitionary Complex," *New Formations* 4 (1988): 73–102.

25. Wolfgang Schivelbusch, *The Railway Journey: The Industrialization of Time and Space in the Nineteenth Century* (University of California Press, 1986), 46; 49.

26. *Official Catalog of the Great Exhibition of the Works of Industry of All Nations* (London, Spicer Brothers, 1851).

27. Michael Leapman, *The World for a Shilling: How the Great Exhibition of 1851 Shaped a Nation* (Headline, 2002), 95.

28. Great Exhibition, *Reports by the Juries on the Subjects in the Thirty Classes into which the Exhibition was Divided* (Spicer Brothers, 1852).

29. *Reports by the Juries*, 1852.

30. "The Great Trial," May 4 and 6.

31. "The Great Trial," May 4.

32. Class: *HO 2*; Piece: *235*; Certificate Number: *3385*, Ancestry.com, *England, Alien Arrivals, 1810–1811, 1826–1869* [database on-line], Provo, UT, USA: Ancestry.com Operations, Inc., 2010.

33. Mary Ann Mason, *From Father's Property to Children's Rights: The History of Child Custody in the United States* (Columbia University Press, 1994).

34. Mason, *From Father's Property to Children's Rights*, 163.

35. The fact that two years following the original Mercein decision the court removed the child, described by some accounts as infirm, from his mother's home to his father's indicates how strong the factors of gender and age were in influencing judicial custody decisions.

36. "The Great Trial," May 6.

37. Sybil Wolfram, "Divorce in England 1700–1857," *Oxford Journal of Legal Studies* 5 (1985): 157; 186.

38. "The Great Trial," May 6.

39. John R. Brooks, "A History of Cholera Epidemics in New York City, 1849 and 1854" (PhD diss., University of Nebraska at Omaha, 1973), 58–59.

40. Brooks, "History of Cholera," 86.

3. "Bent on Making Quick Money"

1. "The Great Trial," *Utica Daily Observer*, May 4, 1872, 2.

2. Henry C. Rogers, *History of the Town of Paris, and the Valley of the Sauquoit* (White & Floyd, 1881), 38.

3. Rogers, *History of the Town of Paris*, 37.

4. "Married," *Oneida Weekly Herald*, June 15, 1852, 3.

5. *Utica City Directory* (Utica, 1868), 345–46.

6. "The Great Trial," May 4, 2.

7. "The Great Trial," May 4, 2.

8. "The Great Trial," May 4, 2.

9. "The Great Trial," May 4, 2.

10. Susan Ingalls Lewis, "More Than Just Penny Capitalists: The Range of Female Entrepreneurship in Mid-Nineteenth-Century US Cities," in J. Aston and C. Bishop, eds., *Female Entrepreneurs in the Long Nineteenth Century* (Palgrave, 2020), 244.

11. Lewis, "Penny Capitalists," 248; Susan Ingalls Lewis, *Unexceptional Women: Female Proprietors in Mid-Nineteenth-Century Albany, New York, 1830–1885* (The Ohio State University Press, 2009).

12. Lewis, *Unexceptional Women*, 65.

13. Adolphus Ranney's story is a fascinating story of entrepreneurial highs and lows. Born in 1824 to Oliver and Sally Reynolds Ranney, Adolphus was one of only three of the Ranney children to live to adulthood. Along with Root's *Medical Lighthouse*, Ranney published a book called *Woman and Her Diseases: From the Cradle to the Grave* by the New York physician Edward H. Dixon. Evidently his sales were good, because when Adolphus was arrested for fraud in 1860, he was able to hire James T. Brady, one of New York's leading lawyers, for his defense. But even Brady couldn't get Adolphus off; he went to jail and fourteen years later died suddenly in Philadelphia. "Gift-Book Ranney," *New York Tribune*, February 24, 1860, 7; "Swindling Punished," *Manufacturers and Farmers Journal*, Providence, June 18, 1860; "Court of Appeals," *The World*, February 13, 1861, 7; "Ranney," *New York Herald*, April 20, 1874, 5.

14. "The Great Trial," May 4, 2.

15. "Teachers! Attention!," *Frank Leslie's Illustrated Newspaper*, December 15, 1855.

16. "Gift-Book Ranney," *New York Tribune*, February 24, 1860, 7; "Police Intelligence," *New York Herald*, February 24, 1860; "Swindling Punished," *Manufacturers and Farmers Journal*, Providence, June 18, 1860.

17. "The Great Trial," May 4, 2.

18. "Teachers! Attention!," 1855.

19. Douglas E. Bowers, "From Logrolling to Corruption: The Development of Lobbying in Pennsylvania, 1815–1861," *Journal of the Early Republic* 3 (Winter 1983): 440.

20. Bowers, "From Logrolling to Corruption," 444.

21. Bowers, "From Logrolling to Corruption," 448.

22. Bowers, "From Logrolling to Corruption," 447; 450; 461.

23. Bowers, "From Logrolling to Corruption," 466.

24. "The Great Trial," *Utica Daily Observer*, May 6, 1872, 3. On Delavan House, see Jennifer Mele, "Gone and Forgotten: Victims of the Delavan House Fire; December, 1894," *Albany Diocesan Cemeteries: A Tradition of Faith*, December 1, 2019, https://blog.capitaldistrictcemeteries.org/gone-and-forgotten-victims-of-the-delavan-house-fire-december-1894/; Carl Johnson, "The Delavan House," *Hoxsie!*, November 9, 2015, https://hoxsie.org/2015/11/09/the-delavan-house/.

25. "The Great Trial," *Utica Daily Observer*, May 7, 1872, 3. Josephine claimed that Ranney had promised her thirty thousand dollars, but this seems high. However, given his later proven tendency to promise money he had no means or intention of paying, it's possible that he did in fact quote her thirty thousand dollars for the curriculum bill.

26. Harmon Knox Root, *The People's Medical Lighthouse: A Series of Popular and Scientific Essays* (A. Ranney, 1856), v.

27. Regina Morantz-Sanchez, *Sympathy and Science: Women Physicians in American Medicine* (University of North Carolina Press, 2000), 65; Thomas Neville Bonner, *To The Ends of the Earth: Women's Search for Education in Medicine* (Harvard University Press, 1992), 18; Steven J. Peitzman, *A New and Untried Course: Woman's Medical College and Medical College of Pennsylvania, 1850–1998* (Alumnae and Alumni Association of MCP Hahnemann School of Medicine, 2000), 9–11.

28. Morantz-Sanchez, *Sympathy and Science*, 58; "The Great Trial," May 4, 2.

29. "The Great Trial," May 4, 2.

30. "The Great Trial," May 4, 2.

31. "Gift-Book Ranney," *New York Tribune*, February 24, 1860, 7.

32. Paul Starr, *The Social Transformation of American Medicine: The Rise Of A Sovereign Profession and the Making of a Vast Industry* (Basic Books, 1982), 4.

33. William G. Rothstein, *American Physicians in the Nineteenth Century: From Sects to Science* (Johns Hopkins University Press, 1972), 34; Starr, *Social Transformation of American Medicine*, 39.

34. Starr, *Social Transformation of American Medicine*, 40.

35. Rothstein, *From Sects to Science*, 77.

36. Owen Whooley, *Knowledge in the Time of Cholera: The Struggle Over American Medicine in the Nineteenth Century* (University of Chicago Press, 2013), 38–39.

37. Whooley, *Knowledge in the Time of Cholera*, 40–42; Starr, *Social Transformation of American Medicine*, 42.

38. Rothstein, *From Sects to Science*, 51.

39. Rothstein, *From Sects to Science*, 130.

40. Rothstein, *From Sects to Science*, 130.

41. Rothstein, *From Sects to Science*, 131.

42. Whooley, *Knowledge in the Time of Cholera*, 50.

43. Rothstein, *From Sects to Science*, 140.

44. Whooley, *Knowledge in the Time of Cholera*, 55.

45. John S. Haller, *The History of American Homeopathy: From Rational Medicine to Holistic Health Care* (Rutgers University Press, 2009), 7.

46. The group of physicians to whose knowledge systems Thomsonian and homeopathic medicine get compared by medical historians are variously called "regular" doctors, "allopathic" doctors, and "mineral" doctors. The latter was a largely pejorative name applied to allopaths by their nineteenth-century rivals. "Allopathic" acts as a direct antonym to "homeopathic"; *allo,* meaning opposite, and *pathy,* meaning illness, come together to indicate a system of medicine where medicines are meant to produce effects opposite to the symptoms being treated. "Regular" is another term often applied to physicians who followed that system and formed professional organizations and educational

institutions to preserve and promote that form of medical knowledge. The problem with calling these doctors "regulars" is the danger of adopting the assumption—already easy to slip into, since their professional organizations did eventually "win out" and develop into the system of medicine we rely on today—that these doctors were the "regular" ones in the sense of "standard," "familiar," or "proper." For that reason, I use the words "allopathic" and "organized" to refer to this group—though both of those words have their own misleading connotations.

47. Whooley, *Knowledge in the Time of Cholera,* 55.

48. Whooley, *Knowledge in the Time of Cholera,* 33; 31.

49. Rothstein, *From Sects to Science,* 56.

50. Whooley, *Knowledge in the Time of Cholera,* 57; 7.

51. Whooley, *Knowledge in the Time of Cholera,* 39.

52. Morantz-Sanchez, *Sympathy and Science,* 29.

53. On the history of patent medicines in the United States, see James Harvey Young, *The Toadstool Millionaires: A Social History of Patent Medicines in America Before Federal Regulation* (Princeton University Press, 1972); John Parascandola, *Patent Medicines in Nineteenth-Century America* (Dept. of Medical Humanities, Southern Illinois University, School of Medicine, 1985); and Sarah Stage, *Female Complaints: Lydia Pinkham and the Business of Women's Medicine* (Norton, 1979).

54. Morantz-Sanchez, *Sympathy and Science,* 12. One of the classic texts of women's medical history is Laurel Thatcher Ulrich's *A Midwife's Tale: The Life of Martha Ballard, Based on Her Diary, 1785–1812* (Random House, 1990), which provides an intimate study of the daily life of Martha Ballard, a midwife working in a small town in Maine in the late eighteenth and early nineteenth centuries.

55. Morantz-Sanchez, *Sympathy and Science,* 12; 15.

56. Morantz-Sanchez, *Sympathy and Science,* 47–49.

57. Peitzman, *A New and Untried Course,* 9–13.

58. Peitzman, *A New and Untried Course,* 14; Bonner, *To the Ends of the Earth,* 18.

59. Peitzman, *A New and Untried Course,* 5.

60. WMC/MCP Medical Students, Records, [1850–1981] (ACC-072),), Legacy Center Archives & Special Collections, Drexel University College of Medicine.

61. Peitzman, *A New and Untried Course,* 13; 6.

62. Morantz-Sanchez, *Sympathy and Science,* 52.

63. Morantz-Sanchez, *Sympathy and Science,* 8; 76.

64. Morantz-Sanchez, *Sympathy and Science,* 69; Peitzman, *A New and Untried Course,* 15.

65. Peitzman, *A New and Untried Course,* 16–18; "Seventh Annual Announcement of the Female Medical College of Pennsylvania, Located in Philadelphia, at No. 229 Arch Street, for the Session 1856–57," Female Medical College of Pennsylvania, Woman's Medical College / Medical College of Pennsylvania publications (ACC-076), Legacy Center Archives & Special Collections, Drexel University College of Medicine, http://hdl.handle.net/1860/lca:1147.

66. Morantz-Sanchez, *Sympathy and Science*, 61; 60; 52.

67. Bonner, *To the Ends of the Earth*, 14.

68. Morantz-Sanchez, *Sympathy and Science*, 60.

69. Peitzman, *A New and Untried Course*, 8.

70. WMC/MCP Medical Students, Records, [1850–1981] (ACC-072), Legacy Center Archives & Special Collections, Drexel University College of Medicine.

71. Peitzman, *A New and Untried Course*, 14.

72. "Penn Medical University," *Liberator* (Boston, MA), July 17, 1857.

73. "The Great Trial," May 4, 2; Peitzman, *A New and Untried Course*, 19.

74. "The Great Trial," May 4, 2.

4. "A Woman's Remedy"

1. "The Great Trial," *Utica Daily Observer*, May 4, 1872, 2.

2. Norma Basch, *Framing American Divorce: From the Revolutionary Generation to the Victorians* (University of California Press, 1999).

3. Basch, *Framing American Divorce*, 4; 20.

4. Basch, *Framing American Divorce*, 25.

5. Basch, *Framing American Divorce*, 40; 102; 110; 114–15.

6. *History of Jackson County, Indiana: From the Earliest Time to the Present, with Biographical Sketches, Notes, Etc., Together with an Extended History of the Northwest, The Indiana Territory, and the State of Indiana*, (Chicago: Brant & Fuller, 1886), 193.

7. Val Nolan, Jr., "Indiana: Birthplace of Migratory Divorce," *Indiana Law Journal* 26.4 (Summer 1951): 521.

8. "Divorce," *Putnam's Monthly Magazine of American Science, Literature, and Art* 8 (December 1858), 633.

9. Basch, *Framing American Divorce*, 48; 49.

10. Basch, *Framing American Divorce*, 107.

11. "The Great Trial," May 4, 2.

12. James Mohr, *Abortion in America: The Origins and Evolution of National Policy* (Oxford University Press, 1978), 47.

13. Mohr, *Abortion in America*, 46–47.

14. Janet Farrell Brodie, *Contraception and Abortion in Nineteenth-Century America* (Cornell University Press, 1994), 224–227.

15. Brodie, *Contraception and Abortion*, 160.

16. Sara Dubow, *Ourselves Unborn: A History of the Fetus in Modern America* (Oxford University Press, 2011), 20.

17. Rickie Solinger, *Pregnancy and Power: A History of Reproductive Politics in the United States* (New York University Press, 2019), 62.

18. Frederick N. Dyer, *Champion of Women and the Unborn: Horatio Robinson Storer, M.D.* (Science History Publications/USA, 1999), 9–10.

19. James C. White, "David Humphreys Storer; a Commemorative Sketch," in *The Proceedings of the Boston Society of Natural History* (1891), 348; Dyer, *Champion of Women*, 17–40.

20. Dyer, *Champion of Women*, 78.

21. Dubow, *Ourselves Unborn*, 11–12; John Riddle, *Eve's Herbs: A History of Contraception and Abortion in the West* (Cambridge: Harvard University Press, 1997), 78.

22. Dubow, *Ourselves Unborn*, 12–13.

23. Dyer, *Champion of Women*, 81; 82.

24. Dyer, *Champion of Women*, 82; 83–84.

25. Brodie, *Contraception and Abortion*, 154.

26. Dyer, *Champion of Women*, 85.

27. Mohr, *Abortion in America*, 152.

28. Dyer, *Champion of Women*, 106; 109.

29. Dyer, *Champion of Women*, 103.

30. "The Great Trial," May 4, 2.

31. Brodie, *Contraception and Abortion*, 107.

32. "Varieties," *Water-Cure Journal* 10 (September 1850): 131

33. "The Great Trial," *UDO*, May 4, 1872, 2.

34. Estelle B. Freedman, *Redefining Rape: Sexual Violence in the Era of Suffrage and Segregation* (Harvard University Press, 2013).

35. Freedman, *Redefining Rape*, 22.

36. Freedman, *Redefining Rape*, 12–13; 14.

37. Freedman, *Redefining Rape*, 1.

38. Freedman, *Redefining Rape*, 38.

39. Freedman, *Redefining Rape*, 35.

40. Freedman, *Redefining Rape*, 36.

41. Freedman, *Redefining Rape*, 40.

42. Freedman, *Redefining Rape*, 45; 42; 51.

43. *The Revised Statutes of the State of New-York, 1829, Vol 2.* (Albany, 1829), 663.

44. Thomas Neville Bonner, *To The Ends of the Earth: Women's Search for Education in Medicine* (Harvard University Press, 1992), 12.

5. "I Went There to Perfect Myself"

1. Regina Morantz-Sanchez, *Sympathy and Science: Women Physicians in American Medicine* (University of North Carolina Press, 2000), 69–78; Thomas Neville Bonner, *To The Ends of the Earth: Women's Search for Education in Medicine* (Harvard University Press, 1992), 25–27.

2. The American neurologist Charles K. Mills gives a detailed description of the Blockley complex in *The Philadelphia Almshouse and the Philadelphia Hospital from 1854 to 1908* (Philadelphia: 1909), 1–4.

3. "The Great Trial," *Utica Daily Observer*, May 4, 1872, 2.

4. Charles Rosenberg, *The Care of Strangers: The Rise of America's Hospital System* (Basic Books, 1987), 4.

5. Rosenberg, *Care of Strangers*, 18.

6. Charles Rosenberg, "From Almshouse to Hospital: The Shaping of the Philadelphia General Hospital," *Milbank Memorial Fund Quarterly Health and Society* 60 (1982): 110.

7. Robert John Hunter, *The Origin of the Philadelphia General Hospital, Blockley Division* (Philadelphia: n.p., 1955), 6.

8. Hunter, *Origin of the Philadelphia General Hospital*, 14.

9. Mills, *Philadelphia Almshouse*, 2.

10. Rosenberg, "From Almshouse to Hospital," 120; 120–22.

11. Monique Bourque, "Women and Work in the Philadelphia Almshouse, 1790–1840," *Journal of the Early Republic* 32 (2012): 385; 388; 387.

12. Bourque, "Women and Work," 402.

13. Charles Lawrence, *History of the Philadelphia Almshouses and Hospitals* (Charles Lawrence, 1905), 162; 163.

14. Lawrence, *History of the Philadelphia Almshouses*, 162–163.

15. Lawrence, *History of the Philadelphia Almshouses*, 161–62; 195–97.

16. Mills, *Philadelphia Almshouse*, 11.

17. Rosenberg, "From Almshouse to Hospital," 125.

18. Mills, *Philadelphia Almshouse*, 44; Morantz-Sanchez, *Sympathy and Science*, 8; 78.

19. Lawrence, *History of the Philadelphia Almshouses*, 178; Mills, *Philadelphia Almshouse*, 43.

20. Josephine stated that she went to Blockley "before the winter [of 1857–58] expired" and stayed there "all of the summer" ("The Great Trial," May 4, 2). By contrast, a board member by the name of William Hoops testified that she was assigned as night watch on the mental ward "sometime during the summer of 1858" and left that September, while the chief resident Dr. Smith stated that she was "appointed to a position on the 5th or 6th of September" ("Court Proceedings—Hearing of the Writ of Habeas Corpus, and Mrs. Fagan Discharged," *Philadelphia Inquirer*, April 4, 1859). Smith's estimate is most exact, suggesting that he may be right about the timing of Josephine's formal appointment, but Josephine's memory as well as the testimony of William Hoops indicate that she was probably at Blockley in some capacity by the beginning of the summer.

21. "Almshouse Disclosures," *Dollar Newspaper*, January 26, 1859.

22. "Almshouse Disclosures."

23. "Court Proceedings."

24. "The Guardians of the Poor Again—Hearing of an Extraordinary Case at the Office of Alderman Freeman," *Daily Pennsylvanian*, January 22, 1859, 3.

25. "The Guardians of the Poor Again."

26. "The Fagan Case," *Press*, February 7, 1859.

27. "In Memoriam: F. Carroll Brewster (Philadelphia: Press of Allen, Lane & Scott, 1899), 9.

28. "The Fagan Case," *Press*, February 14, 1859.

29. Lawrence, *History of the Philadelphia Almshouses*, 192.

30. J. W. Croskey, *History of Blockley: A History of the Philadelphia General Hospital from its Inception* (Philadelphia: F. A. Davis, 1929), 560.

31. "Guardians of the Poor," *Press*, March 15, 1859.

32. "Guardians of the Poor."

33. "Court Proceedings."

34. "Court Proceedings."

35. "Court Proceedings."

36. Application for registration (native citizen) for Louis Napoleon Seymour, March 5, 1918, Ancestry.com. *U.S., Consular Registration Applications, 1916–1925* [database on-line]. Provo, UT, USA: Ancestry.com Operations, Inc.,

2012. Passport application for Louis Napoleon Seymour, January 29, 1919, National Archives and Records Administration (NARA); Washington DC; *Roll #: 730; Volume #: Roll 0730–Certificates: 71000–71249, 21 Mar 1919–22 Mar 1919.* While Josephine's testimony suggests that he could have been born as late as 1860 or 1861, in his testimony at her 1872 trial Louis very clearly states that he turned twelve the previous November, meaning he would have been born in November 1859 ("The Great Trial," May 9, 2).

37. *Register of Births, 1855–1864*, Guardians of the Poor, Alms House Hospital, Philadelphia City Archives.

38. R.E. Fulton, "Pictures of an Institution: Birth Records at Old Blockley," *Nursing Clio*, August 30, 2016, https://nursingclio.org/2016/08/30/pictures-of-an-institution-birth-records-at-old-blockley/.

39. Dr. John W. Lodge, in the margin of the register, noted that Samuel, at eleven pounds, was the "largest & heaviest child for many years."

40. Clifford Browder, *The Wickedest Woman in New York: Madame Restell, the Abortionist* (Archon Books, 1988), 57–66; "Mrs. Fagan's Card," *National Police Gazette*, July 16, 1859.

41. "Mrs. Fagan's Card."

42. "Mrs. Fagan's Card."

43. "Mrs. Fagan's Card."

44. "Mrs. Fagan's Card."

45. Horatio R. Storer, "No. I—Criminal Abortion," *North American Medico-Chirurgical Review* (1859), 69; 68.

46. Storer, "Criminal Abortion," 69.

47. Storer, "Criminal Abortion," 69; 67.

48. Historians have found that a modern pro-life movement focused on the rights of the fetus didn't take form until the mid-twentieth century. For more on this, see Daniel K. Williams, *Defenders of the Unborn: The Pro-Life Movement Before* Roe v. Wade (Oxford University Press, 2016); Karissa Haugeberg, *Women Against Abortion: Inside the Largest Moral Reform Movement of the Twentieth Century* (University of Illinois Press, 2017); Jennifer L. Holland, *Tiny You: A Western History of the Anti-Abortion Movement* (University of California Press, 2020); Sara Dubow, *Ourselves Unborn: A History of the Fetus in Modern America* (Oxford University Press, 2011).

49. Horatio R. Storer, "Its Frequency, and the Causes Thereof," *North American Medico-Chirurgical Review* (1859): 269.

50. Horatio R. Storer, "Its Victims," *North American Medico-Chirurgical Review* 3 (1859): 449.

51. Storer, "Its Frequency," 276.

52. Nicola Beisel and Tamara Kay, "Abortion, Race, and Gender in Nineteenth-Century America," *American Sociological Review* 69 (2004): 501.

53. Storer, "Its Victims," 453; 454.

54. Storer, "Its Victims," 455, emphasis mine.

55. Storer, "Its Victims," 454.

56. Horatio R. Storer, "Its Perpetrators," *North American Medico-Chirurgical Review* 3 (1859): 469.

57. Storer, "Its Perpetrators," 467–68.

58. Storer, "Its Perpetrators," 466.

59. Storer, "Its Perpetrators," 466.

60. Storer, "Its Perpetrators," 465.

61. Horatio R. Storer, "Its Obstacles to Conviction," *North American Medico-Chirurgical Review* 3 (1859): 847–48.

62. Horatio R. Storer, "The Duty of the Profession," *North American Medico-Chirurgical Review* 3 (1859): 1039.

63. Storer, "Its Frequency," 278.

64. Storer, "Its Obstacles to Conviction," 850.

65. Storer, "The Duty of the Profession," 1042; 1044.

66. "Minutes of the Twelfth Annual Meeting of the American Medical Association Held in the City of Louisville, May 3, 1859," *Transactions of the American Medical Association XII* (1859): [9]+. *Nineteenth Century Collections Online* (accessed August 30, 2021).

67. "Minutes of the Twelfth Annual Meeting."

68. "Minutes of the Twelfth Annual Meeting."

69. "WANTED—PATIENTS—IMPORTANT SECRET FOR MARRIED LADIES," *Cincinnati Daily Press,* June 1, 1860.

70. "Mrs. E. Burleigh, M.D.," *Daily Missouri Democrat,* December 18, 1860, 2.

71. "Mrs. Burleigh's Lecture," *Daily Missouri Democrat,* December 11, 1860, 2.

6. The Blockade Runner

1. Drew Gilpin Faust, *This Republic of Suffering: Death and the American Civil War* (Alfred A. Knopf, 2008), xi.

2. Margaret Humphreys, *Marrow of Tragedy: The Health Crisis of the American Civil War* (Johns Hopkins University Press, 2013), 48.

3. Judith Giesberg, *Army at Home: Women and the Civil War on the Northern Home Front* (University of North Carolina Press, 2009), 10.

4. Giesberg, *Army at Home*, 10.

5. Libra R. Hilde, *Worth a Dozen Men: Women and Nursing in the Civil War South* (University of Virginia Press, 2012), 1.

6. Daneen Wardrop, *Civil War Nurse Narratives, 1863–1870* (University of Iowa Press, 2015), 7–9.

7. Humphreys, *Marrow of Tragedy*, 13; 49.

8. Humphreys, *Marrow of Tragedy*, 55–59; Louis Fuller, "Biographical Sketch," Mary Edwards Walker Papers (description), Special Collections Research Center, Syracuse University Libraries.

9. Jane E. Schultz, *Women at the Front: Hospital Workers in Civil War America* (University of North Carolina Press, 2004), 12; 47.

10. Schultz, *Women at the Front*, 15; Humphreys, *Marrow of Tragedy*, 65.

11. Schultz, *Women at the Front*, 15; 61–62; 55.

12. Hilde, *Worth a Dozen Men*, 3.

13. Schultz, *Women at the Front*, 49.

14. Humphreys, *Marrow of Tragedy*, 62.

15. "The Great Trial," *Utica Daily Observer*, May 4, 1872, 2.

16. The Brandreth House hotel is an object of intense fascination for me. Located at 294 Canal Street, at the corner of Broadway and Canal, it was constructed in 1857 by Benjamin Brandreth, an English doctor who'd made a fortune in America on laxative pills advertised for a wide range of illnesses ("Purgation is Purification," cried the ads). Brandreth's pills were one of a wide range of patent medicines rumored to be effective abortifacients; one ad from the 1870s claimed that "in cases of suppression, and other female complaints, a judicious use of the Brandreth Pills is generally attended with the most favorable results." But Brandreth's hotel was visited by tragedy more than once. In 1858, just a year after the hotel opened, a guest shot a waiter named Benjamin Graham, "an unusually mild and inoffensive man." The following year, a young woman named Virginia Stewart was gunned down on the steps of the hotel by her ex-lover, Robert MacDonald, who'd chased her all the way from Alabama. In 1927, the hotel was replaced by a branch of the National City Bank of New York (now CitiBank). The building is still there, but it's shuttered and covered in graffiti. Café Cannal, "New York City's First and Only Cannabis Cafe and Lounge," is across the street. "The Great Trial," May 4, 2; Benjamin Brandreth, *Theory and Practice of Purgation, B. Brandreth, M.D. Confirmed by Fifty Years' Experience. Numerous Illustrations of CURE BY BRANDRETH'S PILLS. Truth is established by accumulated facts* (B. Brandreth, M.D., Brandreth House, 1876; "The Brandreth House Tragedy," *Evening Post* (New York, NY), April 28, 1858, 2; "Shocking Tragedy in New York," *Sun* (Baltimore, MD), July 26, 1859, 1.

17. "The Great Trial," May 4, 2.

18. "The Great Trial," *Utica Daily Observer*, May 7, 1872, 1. Barney Donnelly achieved brief notoriety in the New York press in 1859 when he showed a group of politicians a letter written to him by the Virginia governor and vehement secessionist Henry A. Wise in which Wise speculated on the upcoming election and New York's potential to support "a united South." Donnelly's correspondence with Wise marked him as a Confederate sympathizer, but as one newspaper remarked in 1861, after the outrage his actions occasioned in Albany, "he will not be likely to go disunion" ("From Washington," *Commercial Advertiser*, September 24, 1861, 2); "Highly Important from Albany," *New York Herald*, August 4, 1859; "Governor Wise on the New York Democracy—His Last Manifesto, and His Greatest and Best," *New York Herald*, August 5, 1859.

19. "The Great Trial," May 7, 1.

20. "The Great Trial," May 7, 1.

21. Ann Blackman, *Wild Rose: Rose O'Neale Greenhow, Civil War Spy: A True Story* (Random House, 2005).

22. Phyllis F. Field, "Greenhow, Rose O'Neal (1815?–01 October 1864), Confederate spy," *American National Biography*, February 1, 2000; https://www.anb.org/view/10.1093/anb/9780198606697.001.0001/anb-9780198606697-e-0401122.

23. Ishbel Ross, *Rebel Rose: The Life of Rose O'Neale Greenhow, Confederate Spy* (Mockingbird Books, 1973), 3.

24. Edwin C. Fishel, *The Secret War for the Union: The Untold Story of Military Intelligence in the Civil War* (Houghton Mifflin Co., 1996); Sheila Phipps, "Rose O'Neal Greenhow: 'Bearer of Dispatches to the Confederate Government,'" in

Michele Gillespie and Sally G. McMillen, eds., *North Carolina Women: Their Lives and Times, Vol. 1* (University of Georgia Press, 2014), 80.

25. "Treason in Tantrums," *Frank Leslie's Illustrated Newspaper*, February 9, 1862, 179.

26. Rose O'Neal Greenhow, *My Imprisonment and the First Year of Abolition Rule At Washington* (London: R. Bentley, 1863), 258.

27. Greenhow, *My Imprisonment*, 258–59.

28. Greenhow, *My Imprisonment*, 259.

29. "Mrs. Burleigh's Lecture," *Daily Missouri Democrat*, December 11, 1860, 2.

30. Robert's demonstration of the steam gun for Abraham Lincoln himself in 1863 was an unqualified disaster. As a matter of fact, Lincoln laughed in his face. Robert Bruce, *Lincoln and the Tools of War*, (University of Illinois Press, 1989), 131–44.

31. "The Great Trial," May 4, 2; Fishel, *Secret War*, 67.

32. Greenhow, *My Imprisonment*, 259.

33. Thomas F. Curran, *Women Making War: Female Confederate Prisoners and Union Military Justice* (Southern Illinois University Press, 2020); E. Susan Barber and Charles F. Ritter, "'Unlawfully and Against Her Consent': Sexual Violence and the Military During the American Civil War," in *Sexual Violence in Conflict Zones: From the Ancient World to the Era of Human Rights*, ed. Elizabeth D. Heineman (University of Pennsylvania Press, 2011), 202; Crystal N. Feimster, "General Benjamin Butler & the Threat of Sexual Violence during the American Civil War," *Daedalus* 138 (2009), 126.

34. Thomas P. Lowry, *The Story the Soldiers Wouldn't Tell: Sex in the Civil War* (Stackpole Books, 1994), 131.

35. Feimster, "The Threat of Sexual Violence during the American Civil War," 127.

36. Barber and Ritter, "Unlawfully and Against Her Consent," 205.

37. Barber and Ritter, "Unlawfully and Against Her Consent," 210.

38. "Treason in Tantrums," 179.

39. "The Great Trial," May 4, 2.

40. "The Great Trial," May 7, 3.

41. "Fact Sheet: Induced Abortion in the United States," Guttmacher Institute, September 2019. https://www.guttmacher.org/sites/default/files/fact-sheet/fb_induced_abortion.pdf.

42. "The Great Trial," May 4, 2.

43. "New York City directory," Irma and Paul Milstein Division of United States History, Local History and Genealogy, New York Public Library Digital Collections, accessed October 29, 2021. https://digitalcollections.nypl.org/items/c2ab5490-5356-0134-0971-00505686a51c.

44. Alexander J. Wall, *A Sketch of the Life of Horatio Seymour, 1810–1886: With a Detailed Account of His Administration As Governor of the State of New York During the War of 1861–1865* (New York, 1929).

45. A note on Ernest Judson Seymour's name: in historical documents, Josephine and others wrote her son's nickname as both "Juddie" and "Juddy." The former spelling shows up more often, so I use it here, noting otherwise when a source used the alternate spelling.

46. "The Great Trial," May 7, 1.

47. "The Great Trial," May 7, 1; James Bock, "State's Smallest Town Port Tobacco Boasts History, Little Else," *Baltimore Sun*, February 24, 1991.

48. "The Civil War: Fifty Years Ago Today," *New York Press*, August 17, 1912, 4.

49. Alan Alexrod, *The War Between the Spies: A History of Espionage During the American Civil War* (Atlantic Monthly Press, 1992), 66–67.

50. "The Civil War: Fifty Years Ago Today," 4.

51. Axelrod, *War Between the Spies*, 67.

52. "The Oneida Murderess," *Sun* (New York, NY), January 23, 1872, 2

53. "The Oneida Murderess"; "The Great Trial," May 7, 1.

54. "The Oneida Murderess."

55. *Seattle Post-Intelligencer*, October 27, 1897, 4.

56. "The Great Trial," May 7, 1.

57. "The Great Trial," May 4, 2.

58. "The Great Trial," May 7, 2.

59. "The Great Trial," May 4, 2.

7. Mrs. Burleigh, M.D.

1. *The Albany Directory* (Albany: G. Adams, 1865), Albany County Hall of Records. Since she moved there midyear, Josephine is not listed in the 1864 city directory, but it seems likely that the house at Second and Catherine was her first address in the Albany area.

2. Dr. Staats was probably Barent Phillips Staats, a member of the state medical society and a former mayor of Albany.

3. Although her recent affair with the furniture dealer in Pittsfield called the child's paternity into question, Josephine would later insist that Josephine Cleopatra—"Josie"—was Milton Thomson's daughter.

4. "Abortion Case at Troy," *New York Herald*, November 20, 1866.

5. Danielle Thyer, "'The Evil of the Age': The *New York Times* and the Politicisation of Abortion," *Gender & History* 32 (2020): 608.

6. "The Lansingburg Horror: Special Correspondence of the Herald," *New York Herald*, August 31, 1867, 5.

7. "Le Meurtre de Lansingburg," *Courrier de Etats-Unis*, September 2, 1867.

8. "The Lansingburg Horror."

9. "Indictments and Sentences," *Daily Albany Argus*, September 17, 1867.

10. "Close of the Trial of Mrs. P. M. Wager," *Albany Evening Journal*, March 30, 1868.

11. New York State Archives, Ancestry.com, *New York, U.S., State Census, 1875* [database on-line]. Provo, UT, USA: Ancestry.com Operations, Inc., 2013.

12. American Medical Association, *Transactions of the American Medical Association*, 15 (1865): 50.

13. James Mohr, *Abortion in America: The Origins and Evolution of National Policy* (Oxford University Press, 1978), 158; Frederick N. Dyer, *Champion of Women and the Unborn: Horatio Robinson Storer, M.D.* (Science History Publications, 1999), 186–94.

14. Horatio Robinson Storer, *Why Not? a Book for Every Woman: the Prize Essay to Which the American Medical Association Awarded the Gold Medal for MDCCCLXV* (Lee and Shepard, 1867). Further references provided in text.

15. Mohr, *Abortion in America*, 158.

16. Medical Society of the State of New York, *Transactions of the Medical Society of the State of New York for the Year 1867* (Albany: Van Benthuysen & Sons' Steam Printing House, 1867), 50.

17. *Transactions* (1867), 50.

18. Medical Society of the State of New York, *Transactions of the Medical Society of the State of New York for the Year 1868* (Albany: Van Benthuysen & Sons' Steam Printing House, 1868), 4.

19. *Transactions* (1868), 5; 6.

20. Med. Society of New York, *Transactions* (1868), 6.

21. Med. Society of New York, *Transactions* (1868), 6; 47.

22. Mohr, *Abortion in America*, 216.

23. "AN ACT for the suppression of the trade in and circulation of obscene literature, illustrations, advertisements, and articles of indecent or immoral use, and obscene advertisements of patent medicines," *Laws of the State of New York,* Vol. 1, Chapter 430 Section 1, 1868. https://www.google.com/books/edition/Laws_of_the_State_of_New_York/q3A4AAAAIAAJ?hl=en&gbpv=0, accessed June 2, 2023.

24. "Act for the suppression of the trade."

25. Mohr, *Abortion in America*, 217.

26. "AN ACT relating to the procurement of abortions and other life offenses," *Laws of the State of New York*, Chapter 631, Section 1, 1869.

27. "Act relating to the procurement of abortions."

28. Hamilton Child, *Gazetteer and Business Directory of Albany & Schenectady Co., N.Y., for 1870–71* (Syracuse: Printed at the Journal Office, 1870), 448.

29. *Gazetteer and Business Directory of Albany*, 480.

30. Deed to 62 Howard Street, April 7, 1869, Albany City Clerk Records, Albany County Hall of Records.

31. "The Great Trial," *Utica Daily Observer*, May 8, 1872, 1–2.

32. Janet Farrell Brodie, *Contraception and Abortion in Nineteenth-Century America* (Cornell University Press, 1994), 120–24; 91–93.

33. T. D. Crothers, *Mrs. Dr. Emma Burleigh: The Mysterious Death of Margaret Campbell Critically Examined* (Albany, 1872), 4.

34. Crothers, *Mrs. Dr. Burleigh*, 4.

35. Testimony of Mary Cleary, 1871, ACHOR.

36. Testimony of Mary Cleary, 1871, ACHOR.

37. Maggie arrived at Josephine's office around September 2 and died on September 21, suggesting that the abortion probably took place around this time.

38. "The Howard Street Mystery.

8. The Campbell Inquest

1. "Mysterious Affair," *Daily Albany Argus*, September 26, 1871.

2. Paul MacMahon, "The Inquest and the Virtues of Soft Adjudication," *Yale Law and Policy Review* 33 (2015): 279.

3. Jeffrey M. Jentzen, *Death Investigation in America: Coroners, Medical Examiners, and the Pursuit of Medical Certainty* (Harvard University Press, 2009), 11.

4. Jentzen, *Death Investigation in America,* 11; MacMahon, "The Inquest," 276.

5. MacMahon, "The Inquest," 282.

6. Jentzen, *Death Investigation in America,* 20.

7. Jentzen, *Death Investigation in America,* 2–3.

8. MacMahon, "The Inquest," 283.

9. The position of coroner, to which Harrigan was elected in 1868, no doubt allowed him to direct trade to the family business; his father and brothers were also undertakers, with offices on Canal Street in downtown Albany. "Democratic Nominations," *Daily Albany Argus,* October 13, 1868.

10. MacMahon, "The Inquest," 278; 279.

11. Danielle Thyer, "'The Evil of the Age': The *New York Times* and the Politicisation of Abortion, 1871," *Gender and History* 32 (2020): 606; Sahand K. Rahbar, "'The Evil of the Age': The Influence of The *New York Times* on Anti-Abortion Legislation in New York, 1865–1873," *Penn History Review* (2016): 161.

12. Rahbar, "Evil of the Age," 163.

13. Rahbar, "Evil of the Age," 164.

14. "The Least of These Little Ones," *New York Times,* November 3, 1870, 4.

15. "The Least of These Little Ones," 4.

16. "The Evil of the Age," *New York Times,* August 23, 1871, 6.

17. "The Evil of the Age," 6.

18. "The Evil of the Age," 6.

19. "The Evil of the Age," 6.

20. "The Evil of the Age," 6.

21. "The Evil of the Age," 6.

22. *Great Trunk Mystery of New York City. Murder of the Beautiful Miss Alice A. Bowlsby, of Paterson, N.J. Her Body Placed in a Trunk and Labelled for Chicago. Many Strange Incidents Made Public* (Philadelphia: Barclay & Co., 1872), 20.

23. *Great Trunk Mystery,* 20.

24. *Great Trunk Mystery,* 35; 44.

25. *Great Trunk Mystery,* 36.

26. *Great Trunk Mystery,* 41; 42.

27. *Great Trunk Mystery,* 52.

28. *Great Trunk Mystery,* 66.

29. Tanfer Emin Tunç, "Unlocking the Mysterious Trunk: Nineteenth-Century American Criminal Abortion Narratives," in Shannon Stettner, Katrina Ackerman, Kristin Burnett, and Travis Hay, eds., *Transcending Borders: Abortion in the Past and* Present (Palgrave MacMillan, 2017), 52.

30. *Great Trunk Mystery,* 69.

31. "The Howard Street Mystery," *Daily Argus,* September 27, 1871.

32. "The Howard Street Mystery," *Argus,* September 28, 1871.

33. "The Howard Street Mystery," *Argus,* September 28, 1871.

34. "The Howard Street Mystery," *Argus,* September 28, 1871.

35. "The Howard Street Mystery," *Albany Evening Journal,* September 27, 1871.

36. "The Howard Street Mystery." *AEJ*, September 27, 1871.

37. Testimony of Mary Cleary in the inquest of Margaret Campbell, September 1871, Albany City Clerk Records, Albany County Hall of Records (ACHOR).

38. MacMahon, "The Inquest, 276.

39. Testimony of Mary Cleary, 1871, ACHOR.

40. "The Howard Street Mystery," *AEJ*, September 27, 1871.

41. "The Howard Street Mystery," *AEJ*, September 28, 1871.

42. "The Howard Street Mystery," *AEJ*, September 28, 1871.

43. "The Howard Street Mystery," *AEJ*, September 28, 1871.

44. "The Howard Street Mystery," *AEJ*, September 28, 1871.

45. "The Howard Street Mystery," *AEJ*, September 28, 1871.

46. "The Howard Street Mystery," *AEJ*, September 28, 1871.

47. "The Howard Street Mystery," *AEJ*, September 28, 1871.

48. "Evil of the Age."

49. *Great Trunk Mystery*, 33.

50. "The Great Trial," *Utica Daily Observer*, May 8, 1872, 1.

51. "The Great Trial," *Utica Daily Observer*, May 4, 1872, 2.

52. "The Great Trial," May 4, 1872, 2.

53. "The Great Trial," May 4, 1872, 2.

54. "The Great Trial," *Utica Daily Observer*, May 9, 1872, 1.

55. "The Great Trial," May 9, 1872, 2.

56. "The Great Trial," May 4, 1872, 3.

57. "The Great Trial," *Utica Daily Observer*, May 7, 1872, 3.

58. "The Great Trial," *UDO*, May 7, 1872, 3.

59. "The Great Trial," May 4, 1872, 1; May 8, 1872, 2.

60. "The Great Trial," May 4, 1872, 1.

61. "The Great Trial," May 9, 1872, 1.

62. "The Great Trial," May 8, 1872, 2.

63. "The Great Trial," *Utica Daily Observer*, May 14, 1872, 1.

64. "The Great Trial," May 7, 1872, 3.

65. "The Great Trial," May 8, 1872, 3.

66. "The Great Trial," May 8, 1872, 3.

67. "The Great Trial," May 8, 1872, 3.

68. "The Great Trial," May 8, 1872, 3.

69. "The Great Trial," May 8, 1872, 3.

9. The Privilege of Murder

1. "The Great Trial," *Utica Daily Observer*, May 9, 1872.

2. "The Great Trial," *Utica Daily Observer*, May 3, 1872, 3.

3. "The Great Trial," *Utica Daily Observer*, May 7, 1872, 3.

4. "The Tragedy," *Utica Daily Observer*, January 17, 1872, 2.

5. *Utica Daily Observer*, January 19, 1872, 2.

6. "The Tragedy," *Utica Daily Observer*, January 19, 1872, 2.

7. "The Tragedy," January 19, 1872, 2.

8. "The Late Tragedy," *Utica Daily Observer*, January 20, 1872, 3.

9. "Murder and Homicide," *Utica Daily Observer*, January 18, 1872, 2.

10. "The Late Tragedy," 2.

11. "Social Vampires," *Utica Daily Observer*, January 20, 1872, 3.

12. "The Late Tragedy," 2.

13. "The Late Tragedy," 2.

14. "An Editor in Jail," *Utica Daily Observer*, January 29, 1872, 3. That Doolittle was not a regular reader of Payne's work is no surprise; the *Bee* advertised itself in the local city directory as "The only Plain Spoken, Unsubsidized People's Daily Paper in Central New York" and reflected its editor's mistrust of all "Political Rings, Moneyed Monopolists, and other enemies to the public good;" in short, Payne and the *Bee* did not shy away from criticizing authority figures.

15. "THE LATE TRAGEDY—Funeral of the Victim," *Utica Daily Observer*, January 23, 1872, 2.

16. "Jail and Hospital," *Utica Daily Observer*, January 29, 1872, 3.

17. Henry J. Cookinham, *History of Oneida County, New York, From 1700 to the Present Time*, Vol. 1, Part 2 (S. J. Clarke Publishing Company, 1912), 557.

18. Henry J. Cookinham, "Recollections of the Oneida Bar," Year Book No. 10 of the Oneida Historical Society at Utica, N.Y. (1905), 83.

19. Both Stoddard and Babcock were also members of the Utica Central Lodge of a temperance organization known as the International Organization of Good Templars (IOGT). County Chief Templar C. D. Rose wrote in a letter to a fellow member, E. S. Hughes, during the election that "Bro Babcock has repeatedly violated his obligation" to the temperance movement "and been disciplined therefore," though Rose noted that "since his nomination" his behavior had improved with a speed that could be almost called suspicious. Stoddard, by contrast, had "maintained his standing from the first and is known as a consistent and persistent Temperance man." Though the IOGT, like many fraternal organizations, officially discouraged any discussion of politics, Rose warned his correspondent that "good templars should consider these facts and judge accordingly." Given the social power of fraternal organizations and temperance societies in central New York in the 1870s, it's not unreasonable to assume that the rumors of Babcock's intemperance helped to shape the outcome of the 1871 race for district attorney in Oneida County. Letter from C. D. Rose to E. S. Hughes, November 27, 1871. "A Violation of Our Principles: Political Discussion within Walls of the Lodge," March 8, 2016, Scottish Rite Museum and Library, https://nationalheritagemuseum.typepad. com/library_and_archives/2016/03/a-violation-of-our-principles-political-discussion-within-walls-of-the-lodge.html.

20. "The Street Car Tragedy—The McCarty Trial—Before Judge Doolittle," *Utica Daily Observer*, January 31, 1872, 2.

21. "The Street Car Tragedy—The McCarty Trial—Before Judge Doolittle," *Utica Daily Observer*, January 31, 1872, 2.

22. "The Street Car Tragedy—The McCarty Trial—Before Judge Doolittle," *Utica Daily Observer*, January 31, 1872, 2.

23. "The Street Car Tragedy," 2.

24. "The Street Car Tragedy," 2.

25. "The Street Car Tragedy," 2.

26. "Delaying Criminal Prosecutions," *Utica Daily Observer*, February 1, 1872, 2.

27. "The Day Fixed!", *Utica Daily Observer*, February 9, 1872, 2.

28. "Crimes and Casualties," *Troy Weekly Times*, February 10, 1872.

29. Cookinham, "Recollections of the Oneida Bar," 147.

30. "The Albany Murder," *Brooklyn Daily Eagle*, June 5, 1867, 2.

31. Laura-Eve Moss, "'He Has Ravished My Poor, Simple, Innocent Wife!':
Exploring the Meaning of Honor in the Murder Trials of George W. Cole," in
Robert Asher, Lawrence B. Goodheart, and Alan Rogers, eds., *Murder on Trial:
1620–2002* (State University of New York Press, 2005), 222.

32. "An Editor Imprisoned," *Albany Argus*, March 15, 1872.

33. "An Editor Imprisoned."

34. "An Editor Imprisoned."

35. A. Cheree Carlson, *The Crimes of Womanhood: Defending Femininity in a
Court of Law* (University of Illinois Press, 2009), 15.

36. Carlson, *Crimes of Womanhood*, 16.

37. "Why Laura Fair is Not Yet Hung," *Utica Daily Observer*, February 12,
1872, 1.

38. Carole Haber, *The Trials of Laura Fair: Sex, Murder, and Insanity in the Victorian West* (University of North Carolina Press, 2013), 24.

39. Haber, *Trials of Laura Fair*, 129.

40. "Why Laura Fair is Not Yet Hung," 1.

41. "Why Laura Fair is Not Yet Hung," 1.

42. Carlson, *Crimes of Womanhood*, 12.

43. "Why Laura Fair is Not Yet Hung," 1.

10. Mrs. McCarty Takes the Stand

1. "Home Matters," *Utica Daily Observer*, May 1, 1872, 2.

2. "THE UTICA HOMICIDE," *Albany Argus*, March 28, 1872.

3. Home Matters," *Utica Daily Observer*, May 1, 1872, 2.

4. Home Matters," 2.

5. Home Matters," 2.

6. "The Great Trial," *Utica Daily Observer*, May 2, 1872, 2.

7. "The Great Trial," May 2, 2.

8. "The Great Trial," May 2, 3.

9. "The Great Trial," May 2, 3.

10. "The Great Trial," May 2, 3.

11. "The Great Trial," *Utica Daily Observer*, May 3, 1872, 2.

12. "The Great Trial," May 3, 2.

13. "The Great Trial," May 3, 2.

14. "The Great Trial," May 3, 2.

15. "The Great Trial," May 3, 2.

16. "The Great Trial," May 3, 2.

17. "The Great Trial," May 3, 2.

18. "The Great Trial," May 3, 3.

19. "The Great Trial," May 3, 3.

20. "The Great Trial," May 3, 3.

21. "The Great Trial," May 3, 2. John Singleton Mosby [Moseby], also known as the "Gray Ghost," was a Confederate cavalry commander, leader of the 43rd Virginia Cavalry Battalion (Mosby's Raiders), which carried out merciless lightning raids in northern central Virginia. He was briefly imprisoned in the Old Capitol Prison in the summer of 1862, not long after Josephine was released. Unlike Robert E. Lee, Mosby never surrendered. "John Singleton Mosby," American Battlefield Trust, https://www.battlefields.org/learn/biographies/john-singleton-mosby.

22. "The Great Trial," May 3, 3.

23. "The Great Trial," May 3, 3.

24. "The Great Trial," May 3, 3.

25. Carolyn Ramsey, "Intimate Homicide: Gender and Crime Control, 1880-1920," *University of Colorado Law Review* 77, no. 1 (2006): 105; Carolyn B. Ramsey, "The Exit Myth: Family Law, Gender Roles, and Changing Attitudes Toward Female Victims of Domestic Violence," *Michigan Journal of Gender and Law* 20, no. 1 (2013): 1-32; Carolyn B. Ramsey, "Public Responses to Intimate Violence: A Glance at the Past," *Public Health Reports* 121 (2006): 460-63.

26. Ramsey, "Public Responses," 461.

27. Ramsey, "Intimate Homicide," 106.

28. Ramsey, "Public Responses," 461.

29. On the history and use of the battered woman syndrome defense, see Susan D. Appel, "Beyond Self-Defense: The Use of Battered Woman Syndrome in Duress Defenses," *University of Illinois Law Review* 1994 no. 4 (1994): 955-80; Donald Alexander Downs, *More Than Victims: Battered Women, the Syndrome Society, and the Law* (University of Chicago Press, 1996); Patricia Gagné, *Battered Women's Justice: The Movement for Clemency and the Politics of Self-Defense* (Twayne Publishers, 1998); Amy Lou Busch, *Finding Their Voices: Listening to Battered Women Who've Killed* (Kroshka Books, 1999); Jean S. Filetti, "From Lizzie Borden to Lorena Bobbitt: Violent Women and Gendered Justice," *Journal of American Studies* 35, no. 3 (2001): 471-84; and Brenda L. Russell, *Battered Woman Syndrome as a Legal Defense: History, Effectiveness, and Complications* (McFarland and Co., 2010).

30. Ramsey, "Intimate Homicide," 106.

31. Ramsey, "Public Responses," 460.

32. "The Great Trial," May 3, 3. Ramsey's research reveals that this widened evidential scope was typical of nineteenth-century murder trials with female defendants. Ramsey, "Intimate Homicide," 123.

33. Ramsey, "Intimate Homicide," 103; "Public Responses, 461.

34. "The Great Trial," *Utica Daily Observer*, May 4, 1872, 1; 2.

35. "The Great Trial," May 4, 2.

36. "The Great Trial," May 4, 2.

37. "The Great Trial," May 4, 2.

38. "The Great Trial," *Utica Daily Observer*, May 6, 1872, 3.

39. "The Great Trial," May 4, 2.
40. "The Great Trial," May 6, 2.
41. "The Great Trial," May 6, 2.
42. "The Great Trial," May 6, 2.
43. "The Great Trial," May 6, 2.
44. "The Great Trial," May 4, 3.
45. "The Great Trial," May 4, 3.
46. "The Great Trial," May 4, 3.
47. "The Great Trial," May 4, 3.
48. "The Great Trial," May 6, 2.
49. "The Great Trial," May 6, 2.
50. "The Great Trial," May 6, 3.
51. "Some Facts of the Life of the Murderess," *New York Herald*, January 20, 1872.
52. "The Great Trial," May 6, 3.
53. "The Great Trial," May 6, 3.
54. "The Great Trial," *Utica Daily Observer*, May 7, 1872, 1.
55. "The Great Trial," May 7, 2.
56. "The Great Trial," May 7, 2.
57. Ramsey, "Intimate Homicide," 106.

11. The Unwritten Law

1. "The Great Trial," *Utica Daily Observer*, May 8, 1872, 2.
2. "The Great Trial," May 8, 2.
3. "The Great Trial," May 8, 2.
4. "The Great Trial," May 8, 3.
5. "The Great Trial," May 8, 3.
6. "The Great Trial," *Utica Daily Observer*, May 2, 1872, 2.
7. "The Great Trial," May 8, 3.
8. "The Great Trial," May 8, 3.
9. "The Great Trial," *Utica Daily Observer*, May 9, 1872, 1.
10. "The Great Trial," May 8, 3.
11. "The Great Trial," May 9, 1.
12. "The Great Trial," May 9, 1.
13. "The Great Trial," May 9, 1.
14. "The Great Trial," May 9, 2.
15. James Mohr, *Doctors and the Law: Medical Jurisprudence in Nineteenth-Century America* (Oxford University Press, 1993), xiv.
16. Mohr, *Doctors and the Law*, xv.
17. Mohr, *Abortion in America*, 103–4.
18. David Humphreys Storer, "Medical Jurisprudence," May 28, 1851, 136. https://www.massmed.org/About/MMS-Leadership/History/Medical-Jurisprudence-(pdf).
19. Katherine Watson, *Forensic Medicine in Western Society: A History* (Routledge, 2011), 90.

20. Allen D. Spiegel and Peter M. Suskind, "Uncontrollable Frenzy and a Unique Temporary Insanity Plea," *Journal of Community Health* 25 no. 2 (2000): 157–79.

21. Spiegel and Suskind, "Uncontrollable Frenzy," 161.

22. Lawrence M. Friedman, *Crime Without Punishment: Aspects of the History of Homicide* (Cambridge University Press, 2018), 34.

23. *Trial of Aratus F. Pierce, at Lockport, N.Y. for the Murder of Wm. Bullock* (Lockport, NY: M.C. Richardson and co., printers, 1871), 26.

24. *Trial of Aratus F. Pierce,* 28; 52.

25. *Trial of Aratus F. Pierce,* 28.

26. *Trial of Aratus F. Pierce,* 72.

27. *Trial of Aratus F. Pierce,* 101.

28. "Discussion of the unwritten law," Friedman says, "was by, about, and between men." Female defendants could invoke it, but Friedman's research agrees with Carolyn Ramsey's: their trials still revolved around the manhood of the men they'd killed—or, in Josephine's case, tried to kill. Friedman, *Crime Without Punishment,* 29–30.

29. "The Great Trial," May 9, 2.

30. "The Great Trial," May 9, 3.

31. "The Great Trial," May 9, 3.

32. "The Great Trial," May 9, 3.

33. "The Great Trial," May 9, 3.

34. "The Great Trial," May 9, 3.

35. "The Great Trial," *Utica Daily Observer,* May 10, 1872, 1.

36. "The Great Trial," May 10, 1.

37. "The Great Trial," May 10, 1.

38. "The Great Trial," May 10, 1.

39. "The Great Trial," May 10, 1.

40. "The Great Trial," May 10, 1.

41. "The Great Trial," May 10, 2.

42. "The Great Trial," May 10, 2.

43. "The Great Trial," May 10, 2.

44. "The Great Trial," May 10, 2.

45. "The Great Trial," *Utica Daily Observer,* May 11, 1872, 1.

46. "The Great Trial," May 10, 3.

47. "The Great Trial," May 10, 3.

48. "The Great Trial," May 11, 1.

49. "The Great Trial," May 11, 1.

50. "The Great Trial," May 11, 1.

51. "The Great Trial," May 11, 2.

52. "The Great Trial," May 11, 3.

53. "The Great Trial," May 11, 1.

54. "The Great Trial," May 11, 2.

55. "The Great Trial," May 11, 2.

56. "The Great Trial," May 11, 2.

57. "The Great Trial," May 11, 2.

58. "The Great Trial," May 11, 2.

59. "The Great Trial," May 11, 2.

60. "The Great Trial," May 11, 3.

61. "The Great Trial," May 11, 3.

62. "The Great Trial," May 11, 3.

63. "The Great Trial," May 11, 3.

64. "The Great Trial," May 11, 3.

65. "The Great Trial," May 11, 3. Thomson had recently given $500 for the construction of a steeple, a donation which "had procured him an absolution in that quarter.

66. "The Great Trial," May 11, 3.

67. "The Great Trial," May 11, 3.

12. The Smoking Pistol

1. "The Great Trial," *Utica Daily Observer*, May 13, 1872, 1.

2. "The Great Trial," *Utica Daily Observer*, May 14, 1872, 2.

3. "John P. Gray, M.D.," *Diseases of the Mind: Highlights of American Psychiatry through 1900; 19th-Century Psychiatrists of Note*, U.S. National Library of Medicine (NLM), https://www.nlm.nih.gov/hmd/diseases/note.html#gray.

4. Jodie Boyer, "Religion, 'Moral Insanity,' and Psychology in Nineteenth-Century America," *Religion and American Culture: A Journal of Interpretation* 24, no. 1 (2014): 70–99; Allen D. Spiegel and Florence Kavaler, "The Differing Views on Insanity of Two Nineteenth Century Forensic Psychiatrists," *Journal of Community Health* 31, no. 5 (2006): 430–51.

5. Boyer, "Moral Insanity," 85.

6. "John P. Gray, M.D."

7. Spiegel and Kavaler, "Differing Views on Insanity," 433.

8. "The Great Trial," May 13, 1.

9. "The Great Trial," May 13, 2.

10. "The Great Trial," May 13, 2.

11. "The Great Trial," May 13, 2.

12. "The Trial of Mary Harris," *American Journal of Insanity* 22, no. 3 (1866): 341.

13. "The Trial of Mary Harris," 341; 335.

14. Spiegel and Kavaler, "Differing Views on Insanity," 440–45.

15. "The Trial of Mary Harris," 334.

16. "The Trial of Mary Harris," 338. Emphasis mine.

17. "The Trial of Mary Harris," 356; 333; 357.

18. "The Trial of Mary Harris," 358; 360.

19. "The Trial of Mary Harris," 358.

20. "The Great Trial," May 13, 2.

21. "The Great Trial," May 13, 2.

22. "The Great Trial," May 13, 2.

23. Horatio Robinson Storer, "Its Victims," *North American Medico-Chirurgical Review* 3 no. 3 (1859): 455.

24. "The Great Trial," May 13, 3.
25. "The Great Trial," May 14, 1.
26. "The Great Trial," May 14, 1.
27. "The Great Trial," May 14, 1.
28. "The Great Trial," May 14, 1.
29. "The Great Trial," May 14, 2.
30. "The Great Trial," May 14, 2.
31. "The Great Trial," May 14, 2.
32. "The Great Trial," May 14, 2.
33. "The Great Trial," May 14, 3.
34. "The Great Trial," May 14, 3.
35. "The Great Trial," May 14, 3.
36. "The Great Trial," May 14, 3.
37. "The Great Trial," *Utica Daily Observer*, May 15, 1872, 2.
38. "The Great Trial," May 15, 2.
39. "The Great Trial," May 15, 2.
40. "The Great Trial," May 15, 2.
41. "The Great Trial," May 15, 2.
42. "The Great Trial," May 15, 3.
43. "The Great Trial," May 15, 2.
44. "The Great Trial," May 15, 3.
45. "The Great Trial," May 15, 3.
46. "The Great Trial," May 15, 3.
47. "The Great Trial," May 15, 3.
48. "The Great Trial," May 15, 3.
49. "The Great Trial," May 15, 3.
50. "The Great Trial," May 15, 3.
51. "The Great Trial," May 15, 3.
52. "The Great Trial," *Utica Daily Observer*, May 16, 1872, 1.
53. "The Great Trial," May 16, 1.
54. "The Great Trial," May 16, 1.
55. "The Great Trial," May 16, 2.
56. "The Great Trial," May 16, 3.
57. "The Great Trial," May 16, 3.
58. "The Great Trial," *Utica Daily Observer*, May 17, 1872, 1.
59. "The Great Trial," May 17, 1.
60. "The Great Trial," May 17, 1.
61. "The Great Trial," May 17, 1.
62. "The Great Trial," May 17, 2.
63. "The Great Trial," May 17, 1.
64. "The Great Trial," May 17, 2.
65. "The Great Trial," May 17, 2.
66. "The Great Trial," May 17, 2–3.
67. "The Great Trial," May 17, 3.
68. "The Great Trial," May 17, 3.

13. The Representative Bad Woman

1. "The Murder Trial," *Utica Daily Observer*, May 18, 1872, 1.
2. "The Murder Trial," 1.
3. "The Murder Trial," 1.
4. "The Murder Trial," 1.
5. "The Murder Trial," 1.
6. "The Murder Trial," 1.
7. "The Murder Trial," 1.
8. "The Murder Trial," 2.
9. "The Murder Trial," 2.
10. "The Murder Trial," 3.
11. "The Murder Trial," 3.
12. "The Murder Trial," 3.
13. "The Murder Trial," 3.
14. "The Murder Trial," 3.
15. "The Murder Trial," 3.
16. "The Murder Trial," 3.
17. "The Murder Trial," 3.
18. "The Murder Trial," 3.
19. "The Murder Trial," 3.
20. "The Murder Trial," 3.
21. "Rosenzweig: The Malpractice Doctor Indicted for Wilful Murder," *New York Herald*, February 22, 1873; "Rosenzweig, the Abortionist," *Chicago Daily Tribune*, March 1, 1873, 8.
22. "Rosenzweig: A Puzzle for the Lawyers," *Indianapolis Sentinel*, July 11, 1873.
23. "The Criminal Record," *Paterson Daily Press*, March 19, 1873.
24. "Rosenzweig Finally Set at Liberty," *Albany Evening Journal*, November 13, 1873.
25. Clifford Browder, *The Wickedest Woman in New York: Madame Restell, The Abortionist* (Archon Books, 1988), 147.
26. Browder, *Wickedest Woman*, 143; 146.
27. Browder, *Wickedest Woman*, 147; 148. It's worth noting that of the seventeen arrested for abortion in Comstock's April 1873 crackdown, only three saw any appreciable punishment under the new laws. Two escaped outright, three never went to trial, four pled guilty and were let off with fines, and one case ended in a hung jury. Of the remaining seven who did go to prison, four were soon pardoned by the president (151).
28. Browder, *Wickedest Woman*, 150; 152.
29. Leslie J. Reagan, *When Abortion Was a Crime: Women, Medicine, and Law in the United States, 1867–1973* (University of California Press, 1997).
30. Nicola Kay Beisel, *Imperiled Innocents: Anthony Comstock and Family Reproduction in Victorian America* (Princeton University Press, 1997), 45.
31. Rickie Solinger, *Pregnancy and Power: A History of Reproductive Politics in the United States* (New York University Press, 2019), 82.
32. Browder, *Wickedest Woman*, 157.

33. Browder, *Wickedest Woman*, 159; 163.

34. Browder, *Wickedest Woman*, 182–83.

35. Browder, *Wickedest Woman*, 186.

36. Beisel, *Imperiled Innocents*, 46.

37. *Albany Evening Journal*, May 27, 1872.

38. "Mrs. McCarty Alias Burleigh," *Argus*, July 12, 1872.

39. "Our Neighbors," *Schenectady Evening Star*, July 15, 1872.

40. "Brief Mentions," *Schenectady Evening Star*, July 15, 1872.

41. "The Woman's Truth Teller," *Woman's Truth Teller*, July 19, 1872, 3. Special thanks to Marcie ver Ploeg for providing me with a copy of *The Woman's Truth Teller* in 2016.

42. *Woman's Truth Teller*, 5.

43. "The McCarty Jury," *Woman's Truth Teller*, 3.

44. "The Woman's Truth Teller: Woman, Right or Wrong: God's Best," *Woman's Truth Teller*, 4.

45. "Woman, Right or Wrong," *Woman's Truth Teller*, 4.

46. "Woman, Right or Wrong," *Woman's Truth Teller*, 4.

47. "The McCarty-Thomson Case," *Albany Evening Journal*, August 22, 1872; "The Burleigh-Thomson Bastardy Case," *Argus*, August 24, 1872.

48. "Sensation Among the Shakers," *Argus*, October 17, 1872.

49. "State Items," *Trenton State Gazette*, January 11, 1873.

50. Ancestry.com. *New Jersey, U.S., State Census, 1885* [database on-line]. Provo, UT, USA: Ancestry.com Operations Inc, 2007.

51. Ancestry.com. *New Jersey, U.S., State Census, 1895* [database on-line]. Provo, UT, USA: Ancestry.com Operations Inc, 2007.

Epilogue

1. "Milton H. Thomson," *Utica Daily Press*, March 6, 1893.

2. "Lewis H. Babcock," *Woman's Truth Teller*, July 19, 1872, 8.

3. Admission record for Lewis H. Babcock, Oneida County Poor House, New York State Archives Ancestry.com. *New York, U.S., Census of Inmates in Almshouses and Poorhouses, 1830–1920* [database on-line]. Provo, UT, USA: Ancestry.com Operations, Inc., 2011.

4. Ancestry.com. *New York, U.S., Death Index, 1852–1956* [database on-line]. Lehi, UT, USA: Ancestry.com Operations, Inc., 2017.

5. "The Departed Jurist," *Utica Daily Observer*, June 4, 1874, 3–4.

6. Probate record for Charles H. Doolittle, *Wills, Vol 0025–0026, 1873–1876*, Ancestry.com. *New York, U.S., Wills and Probate Records, 1659–1999* [database on-line]. Lehi, UT, USA: Ancestry.com Operations, Inc., 2015; Allen D. Spiegel and Florence Kavaler, "The Differing Views on Insanity of Two Nineteenth Century Forensic Psychiatrists," *Journal of Community Health* 31, no. 5 (2006): 445–49.

7. Spiegel and Kavaler, "Differing Views on Insanity," 449.

8. Frederick N. Dyer, *Champion of Women and the Unborn: Horatio Robinson Storer, M.D.* (Science History Publications, U.S.A., 1999), 391.

9. Dyer, *Champion of Women and the Unborn*, 392.

10. Dyer, *Champion of Women and the Unborn*, 397.

11. Dyer, *Champion of Women and the Unborn*, 463.

12. Quoted in Dyer, *Champion of Women and the Unborn*, 466.

13. Leslie J. Reagan, *When Abortion Was a Crime: Women, Medicine, and the Law in the United States, 1867–1973* (University of California Press, 1997).

14. Dyer, *Champion of Women and the Unborn*, 509; 526.

15. Ancestry.com and The Church of Jesus Christ of Latter-day Saints, *1880 United States Federal Census* [database on-line], Lehi, UT, USA: Ancestry.com Operations Inc, 2010.

16. *The Dental Office and Laboratory*, United States: n.p., 1884, 8; Ancestry. com, *New Jersey, U.S., Marriage Records, 1670–1965* [database on-line], Lehi, UT, USA: Ancestry.com Operations, Inc., 2016.

17. Walter H. Jackson, "The Beginnings and the Rise of the University of Michigan Dental Department," *The Michigan Alumnus*, 1903. http://um2017. org/Beginnings_%26_the_Rise_of_Dental_Dept.html.

18. Scans of Louis's various emergency passport applications from the National Archives can be found on Ancestry.com, *U.S., Passport Applications, 1795–1925* [database on-line], Lehi, UT, USA: Ancestry.com Operations, Inc., 2007. Louis entered his father's name as Robert Seymour on most of his applications.

19. Ancestry.com, *1910 United States Federal Census* [database on-line], Lehi, UT, USA: Ancestry.com Operations Inc, 2006.

20. Wisconsin Historical Society; Madison, Wisconsin; Wi Marriage Records Pre-1907, Ancestry.com. *Wisconsin, U.S., Marriage Records, 1820z-2004* [database on-line]. Lehi, UT, USA: Ancestry.com Operations, Inc., 2022.

21. Ancestry.com, *U.S., Passport Applications, 1795–1925* [database on-line], Lehi, UT, USA: Ancestry.com Operations, Inc., 2007.

22. Ancestry.com, *New York, New York, U.S., Extracted Marriage Index, 1866–1937* [database on-line], Provo, UT, USA: Ancestry.com Operations, Inc., 2014.

23. "THE PEOPLE OF THE STATE OF NEW YORK," *Albany Argus*, September 27, 1870.

24. "Albany Rural Cemetery," home page, https://albanyruralcemetery. org/. Accessed November 8, 2021.

SELECTED BIBLIOGRAPHY

Over the eight years I spent researching Josephine McCarty's life and times, I read countless books, not to mention journal articles and primary sources. All the sources I used in telling her story can be found in the endnotes for this book. In this bibliography, I have collected the books and book chapters that most directly helped me to shape my narrative and arguments and that function best as a "further reading" list for anyone interested in the topics this book has raised.

Alexrod, Alan. *The War Between the Spies: A History of Espionage During the American Civil War.* Atlantic Monthly Press, 1992.

Barber, E. Susan and Charles F. Ritter. " 'Unlawfully and Against Her Consent': Sexual Violence and the Military During the American Civil War." In *Sexual Violence in Conflict Zones: From the Ancient World to the Era of Human Rights,* edited by Elizabeth D. Heineman, 202–14. University of Pennsylvania Press, 2011.

Basch, Norma. *Framing American Divorce: From the Revolutionary Generation to the Victorians.* University of California Press, 1999.

Beisel, Nicola Kay. *Imperiled Innocents: Anthony Comstock and Family Reproduction in Victorian America.* Princeton University Press, 1997.

Blackman, Ann. *Wild Rose: Rose O'Neale Greenhow, Civil War Spy: A True Story.* Random House, 2005.

Bonner, Thomas Neville. *To The Ends of the Earth: Women's Search for Education in Medicine.* Harvard University Press, 1992.

Brodie, Janet Farrell. *Contraception and Abortion in Nineteenth-Century America.* Cornell University Press, 1994.

Browder, Clifford. *The Wickedest Woman in New York: Madame Restell, The Abortionist.* Archon Books, 1988.

Bruce, Robert. *Lincoln and the Tools of War.* University of Illinois Press, 1989.

Busch, Amy Lou. *Finding Their Voices: Listening to Battered Women Who've Killed.* Kroshka Books, 1999.

Carlson, A. Cheree. *The Crimes of Womanhood: Defending Femininity in a Court of Law.* University of Illinois Press, 2009.

Curran, Thomas F. *Women Making War: Female Confederate Prisoners and Union Military Justice.* Southern Illinois University Press, 2020.

Dubow, Sara. *Ourselves Unborn: A History of the Fetus in Modern America.* Oxford University Press, 2011.

Dyer, Frederick N. *Champion of Women and the Unborn: Horatio Robinson Storer, M.D.* Science History Publications/USA, 1999.

Faust, Drew Gilpin. *This Republic of Suffering: Death and the American Civil War*. Alfred A. Knopf, 2008.

Fishel, Edwin C. *The Secret War for the Union: The Untold Story of Military Intelligence in the Civil War*. Houghton Mifflin Co., 1996.

Freedman, Estelle B. *Redefining Rape: Sexual Violence in the Era of Suffrage and Segregation*. Harvard University Press, 2013.

Friedman, Lawrence M. *Crime Without Punishment: Aspects of the History of Homicide*. Cambridge University Press, 2018.

Giesberg, Judith. *Army at Home: Women and the Civil War on the Northern Home Front*. University of North Carolina Press, 2009.

Haber, Carole. *The Trials of Laura Fair: Sex, Murder, and Insanity in the Victorian West*. University of North Carolina Press, 2013.

Haller, John S. *The History of American Homeopathy: From Rational Medicine to Holistic Health Care*. Rutgers University Press, 2009.

Hilde, Libra R. *Worth a Dozen Men: Women and Nursing in the Civil War South*. University of Virginia Press, 2012.

Humphreys, Margaret. *Marrow of Tragedy: The Health Crisis of the American Civil War*. Johns Hopkins University Press, 2013.

Jentzen, Jeffrey M. *Death Investigation in America: Coroners, Medical Examiners, and the Pursuit of Medical Certainty*. Harvard University Press, 2009.

Kelley, Mary. *Learning to Stand and Speak: Women, Education, and Public Life in America's Republic*. Omohundro Institute and University of North Carolina Press, 2008.

Klepp, Susan E. *Revolutionary Conceptions: Women, Fertility, and Family Limitation in America, 1760–1820*. University of North Carolina Press, 2009.

Lewis, Susan Ingalls. *Unexceptional Women: Female Proprietors in Mid-Nineteenth-Century Albany, New York, 1830–1885*. The Ohio State University Press, 2009.

Lowry, Thomas P. *The Story the Soldiers Wouldn't Tell: Sex in the Civil War*. Stackpole Books, 1994.

Mason, Mary Ann. *From Father's Property to Children's Rights: The History of Child Custody in the United States*. Columbia University Press, 1994.

Mohr, James C. *Abortion in America: The Origins and Evolution of National Policy*. Oxford University Press, 1978.

Mohr, James C. *Doctors and the Law: Medical Jurisprudence in Nineteenth-Century America*. Oxford University Press, 1993.

Morantz-Sanchez, Regina. *Sympathy and Science: Women Physicians in American Medicine*, University of North Carolina Press, 2000.

Moss, Laura-Eve. "'He Has Ravished My Poor, Simple, Innocent Wife!': Exploring the Meaning of Honor in the Murder Trials of George W. Cole." In *Murder on Trial: 1620–2002*, edited by Robert Asher, Lawrence B. Goodheart, and Alan Rogers, 207–33. State University of New York Press, 2005.

Peitzman, Steven J. *A New and Untried Course: Woman's Medical College and Medical College of Pennsylvania, 1850–1998*. Alumnae and Alumni Association of MCP Hahnemann School of Medicine, 2000.

Reagan, Leslie J. *When Abortion Was a Crime: Women, Medicine, and Law in the United States, 1867–1973*. University of California Press, 1997.

Riddle, John. *Eve's Herbs: A History of Contraception and Abortion in the West*. Harvard University Press, 1997.

Rosenberg, Charles. *The Care of Strangers: The Rise of America's Hospital System*. Basic Books, 1987.

Rothstein, William G. *American Physicians in the Nineteenth Century: From Sects to Science*. Johns Hopkins University Press, 1972.

Russell, Brenda L. *Battered Woman Syndrome as a Legal Defense: History, Effectiveness, and Complications*. McFarland and Co., 2010.

Schivelbusch, Wolfgang. *The Railway Journey: The Industrialization of Time and Space in the Nineteenth Century*. University of California Press, 1986.

Schultz, Jane E. *Women at the Front: Hospital Workers in Civil War America*. University of North Carolina Press, 2004.

Solinger, Rickie. *The Abortionist: A Woman Against the Law*. The Free Press, 1994.

Solinger, Rickie. *Pregnancy and Power: A History of Reproductive Politics in the United States*. New York University Press, 2019.

Srebnick, Amy Gilman. *The Mysterious Death of Mary Rogers: Sex and Culture in Nineteenth-Century New York*. Oxford University Press, 1995.

Stage, Sarah. *Female Complaints: Lydia Pinkham and the Business of Women's Medicine*. Norton, 1979.

Stansell, Christine. *City of Women: Sex and Class in New York, 1789–1860*. Urbana: University of Illinois Press, 1986.

Starr, Paul. *The Social Transformation of American Medicine: The Rise of a Sovereign Profession and the Making of a Vast Industry*. Basic Books, 1982.

Wardrop, Daneen. *Civil War Nurse Narratives, 1863–1870*. University of Iowa Press, 2015.

Whooley, Owen. *Knowledge in the Time of Cholera: The Struggle over American Medicine in the Nineteenth Century*. University of Chicago Press, 2013.

Williams, Daniel K. *Defenders of the Unborn: The Pro-Life Movement Before* Roe v. Wade. Oxford University Press, 2016.

Young, James Harvey. *The Toadstool Millionaires: A Social History of Patent Medicines in America Before Federal Regulation*. Princeton University Press, 1972.

INDEX

Thomson, Samuel, *see* physicians,
Thomsonianism
transitory mania, 176–178, 180, 187,
192–193

unwritten law, 64, 174–175

Walker, Mary Edwards, 83–84

women
education, 13–15
labor, 13, 17, 35–36, 48, 83–84
medical education, 45–48, 84
reproductive practices, 6–7,
9, 18
sexuality, 13, 17, 54
Wood, William P., 92–94